CU00919227

Extracting Honduras

Extracting Honduras

Resource Exploitation, Displacement, and Forced Migration

James J. Phillips

LEXINGTON BOOKS
Lanham • Boulder • New York • London

Published by Lexington Books
An imprint of The Rowman & Littlefield Publishing Group, Inc.
4501 Forbes Boulevard, Suite 200, Lanham, Maryland 20706
www.rowman.com

86-90 Paul Street, London EC2A 4NE, United Kingdom

Copyright © 2022 by The Rowman & Littlefield Publishing Group, Inc.

All rights reserved. No part of this book may be reproduced in any form or by any electronic or mechanical means, including information storage and retrieval systems, without
written permission from the publisher, except by a reviewer who may quote passages
in a review.

British Library Cataloguing in Publication Information Available

Library of Congress Cataloging-in-Publication Data
Name: Phillips, James J., 1945–, author.
Title: Extracting Honduras : resource exploitation, displacement, and forced migration /
  James J. Phillips.
Description: Lanham : Lexington Books, [2022] | Includes bibliographical references and
  index. | Summary: "This book explores the deeper causes of recent massive emigra-
  tions from Honduras, tracing the roots to the neoliberal extractive development model
  that has created conditions of poverty, corruption, and violence for over a generation
  in the context of the colonial (or imperial) relationship of Honduras to the United
  States"—Provided by publisher.
Identifiers: LCCN 2021054958 (print) | LCCN 2021054959 (ebook) | ISBN
  9781793630339 (cloth) | ISBN 9781793630346 (epub)
Subjects: LCSH: Honduras—Emigration and immigration. | Natural resources. | Forced
  migration—Honduras. | Honduras—Politics and government. | Honduras—Foreign
  relations—United States. | United States—Foreign relations—Honduras.
Classification: LCC JV7419 .P45 2022 (print) | LCC JV7419 (ebook) | DDC
  305.87283—dc23/eng/20211115
LC record available at https://lccn.loc.gov/2021054958
LC ebook record available at https://lccn.loc.gov/2021054959

Contents

Acknowledgments

I am most grateful to Honduran friends and colleagues. Fr. Ismael Moreno Coto, SJ, and the members of his team at Radio Progreso and the Reflection, Investigation, and Communication Team (ERIC) in northern Honduras provided space for me to write and research and a base in Honduras, offered practical support and encouragement, and shared their considerable knowledge about the current state of life in Honduras. They also made available to me the many studies they have completed on topics of importance to the themes of this book. Radio Progreso and ERIC are known in Honduras for fearless investigation of human rights abuses, political corruption, and the experiences of local communities trying to defend themselves against extractive projects.

A dear friend for many years, Rufino Rodriguez, the Honduras and Latin America Director of Kolping Foundation, acquainted me with areas and communities in southern Honduras affected by extractive projects, especially mining, and generously spent many hours in conversation answering my questions and introducing me to Hondurans who felt directly the effects of extractive projects in their communities. He and his family also provided warm and generous hospitality. Kolping Foundation is a European-based Catholic organization that promotes empowering grassroots projects in farming and small community businesses in Latin America, and supports avenues for fair trade in products such as Honduran coffee from small growers—thus providing a model of community development that contradicts the destructive grasp of large scale extractivism.

Bertha Oliva, Director of the Committee of the Families of the Detained/ Disappeared in Honduras (COFADEH), provided important knowledge and analysis of the political and human rights situation in Honduras, and shared her insights from many years of experience defending human rights in the country. I also learned much from members of her COFADEH team who generously allowed me to accompany them on various occasions. Through their work, I was introduced to others who spoke of their experiences as victims of official corruption and repression. COFADEH is known throughout Honduras as a leading human rights organization that has been involved in many emblematic human rights cases, and has been a leading force in preserving the memory of the many disappeared Hondurans, and in showing how the present is rooted in, and tends to repeat, the past unless it is challenged.

I am grateful for the dedicated work of Daniel Langmeier, for his daily and very informative roundups of Honduran news and local Honduran links covering a variety of important topics, most of them directly relevant to the themes of this book. His work provides a great service to researchers and friends of Honduras.

I owe much gratitude to Jenny Atlee, coordinator of the Friendship Office of the Americas and the Honduras Accompaniment Project (PROAH). She and her associates provided me with another analysis of the United States role in Honduras and the work of many U.S. citizens trying to de-colonize the U.S. relationship to Honduras. Her wisdom and insight were always invaluable in interpreting complex situations and in providing me with encouragement when I most seemed to need it.

I must acknowledge the network of scholars who are engaged in research and advocacy around Honduras and issues of immigration and immigration reform in the United States. Many of these colleagues also provide expert witness in cases of asylum seekers from Central America and elsewhere in U.S. immigration courts. Involvement in this work as an expert witness has exposed me, in another and quite personal form, to the fears, concerns, and reasons of Hondurans who decide to leave their country. I especially acknowledge the experiences and courage of these asylum seekers that have been for me a major impetus in writing this book.

I am particularly thankful to my editor, Kasey Beduhn, and her associates at Lexington Books for their encouragement, advice, and counsel in preparing the more technical (and to me daunting) aspects of the manuscript. I am also thankful to the peer reviewer (anonymous to me) who provided various helpful suggestions on the original draft.

Peace House, a regional peace and justice organization in southern Oregon, has been an important part of my life for many years, and has continued to encourage my research and advocacy for Central America. I am especially grateful to the Executive Director, Elizabeth Hallett, who has shared her own dedication and advocacy for the people of Central America over many years.

As always, my wife Lucy has remained my most honest critic and strongest supporter as I shared with her ideas, problems, and concerns about the manuscript. Her own long experience in Honduras has been especially helpful to me.

I remain open to criticism from Hondurans whose experiences I cannot really share, even as I try to understand and describe something of their lives. Please forgive any arrogance or false assumptions that may infect my work. These are my responsibility alone.

Chapter 1

Mapping the Terrain

This book is about the deeper reasons why people leave Honduras seeking survival and a decent life in the United States. Examining these reasons will take us into the realities of daily life in Honduras, but also into the ways in which the United States has shaped Honduras in a relationship that has made that country a colony of the United States. The story of Honduran emigration is also a story about the United States. This is not a pretty story, but it is one that quite literally deals with matters of life and death. This book tries to get beyond the immediate causes to the fundamental ones. The immediate causes of Honduran emigration are repeated often in news media and official pronouncements: poverty, violence, and corruption that make daily life, even survival, difficult for Hondurans. This book tries to show that these immediate causes are really symptoms, consequences, of a deeper project of destruction and death that is rooted in an economy based on the rampant and often illegal extraction of resources from Honduras, a process that radically displaces Hondurans and destroys local and largely self-reliant communities.

The displacement of local communities itself is not the whole story, but in many ways its beginning. Today, we see the results—predicted by many in Honduras—of several decades of extractivism. These results are poverty, violence, and corruption, the immediate causes of emigration. Extractive "development" in Honduras has taken several decades to wreak the full havoc, the perfect storm, that has in some recent years induced as many as 100,000 Hondurans to flee their country. The neoliberal extractive model of development that has caused such destruction was mandated for Honduras by the Reagan Administration and a group of wealthy Hondurans in the early 1980s, and implemented in earnest in 1990.[1] After years of this extractive development, generations of landless people living in poverty with little chance of help from their own government—a government that criminalized their protests and seemed itself corrupt—seek ways to survive. Some people leave Honduras and, if they are lucky, get as far as the deserts of the U.S. Southwest where they might survive from the water and supplies provided by angels of mercy, unless U.S. authorities are efficient in destroying this lifeline by criminalizing the act of leaving water for or helping migrants, or government agents pour out water left for migrants. The extractive model of development that is so vigorously advanced in Honduras in disregard for the most basic human rights contributes mightily to one of the country's major and most lucrative exports—emigrants.

This was not the story of migration told in most of the mainstream international news media. Most mainstream media in the United States, Canada, and Europe did not report how extractive industry has helped to produce the immigration "crisis" at the U.S. southern border. Media explanations of the causes of large Central American migration to the United States cited poverty and gang violence without asking why there is poverty and gang violence in a country like Honduras that is relatively rich in natural resources.[2] But one could reasonably argue, as some scholars have, that resource wealth may also be a curse if it invites exploitation and extraction from outsiders, and that such is the fate of countries like Honduras. The public recognition and exploration of the extractive roots of the "migration crisis" would challenge some of the most important ideological tenets on which the relationship between Honduras and the United States is based—the idea that the relationship is one of "development," that it is mutually beneficial, and that such development is the engine of growth and prosperity for Honduras and its people.

The media story went halfway, mentioning some of the immediate causes of migration—poverty, gangs violence—but not the fundamental contradictions in the model of extractive economic development that sets the conditions for poverty, crime, and violence to thrive. Even less did the media story of migration explore the other set of conditions driving people to flee their country—the collapse or privatization of public institutions amid pervasive state corruption and official impunity. There is an argument to be made that institutional collapse, corruption, and impunity are also largely products of a frantic extraction of resources that represents a massive transfer of wealth from the public weal to a few private hands. How this works in daily life is easily illustrated in two examples: the experience of the people of Guapinol, and the emblematic case of Berta Cáceres.

THE GUAPINOL DEFENDERS

Guapinol is a community in the north of Honduras at the center of an area of communities whose people are mostly small farmers (*campesinos*), who plant corn, beans, and a few other crops and tend cows.[3] Some also work on nearby fruit or palm oil plantations. Their way of life is not easy, but it is dignified and largely self-reliant as long as they have access to their land and rivers. Several rivers in the area provide the water people need and have long used for their crops, their animals, and their domestic needs. Guapinol is in the Bajo Aguán, an area where conflicts over land and resources are frequent, often violent, and sometimes deadly. Large landowners, foreign companies, the police and the military expel small farm communities from the land to make way for the expansion of large-scale extractive industries that are the basis of the government's economic development plan. But Guapinol is adjacent the Carlos Escalante National Park and environmental reserve that is a source of some of the waters on which the communities depend. Because of this, some Hondurans thought the Guapinol communities might just, somehow, be safe from becoming the target of mining companies and hydroelectric projects promoted by the Honduran government. They were wrong.

In 2013, the Honduran Congress passed *Decreto Legislativo* 252–2013, permitting the government to award concessions for mining and logging in the Escalante Park. A mining company owned by one of the richest families in Honduras, obtained the concession to conduct mining operations in the Guapinol area. People in Guapinol said that neither the government nor the company consulted the communities beforehand to provide full information about the proposed mining operations and to obtain the free consent of the people to proceed—the *consulta* that is required by law. This was not the first time that Honduran communities had made such a complaint.

As mining operations moved forward, people in the communities believed that their rivers, their major water supply, would be in jeopardy; some rivers were already showing signs of pollution and dessication. Mining operations can use and contaminate enormous amounts of water, dry up rivers, poison water and soils with toxic metals and chemicals, and destroy the vegetation that prevents erosion. Residents around Guapinol believed that the mining company would destroy the communities' livelihood and their way of life. As usual in such cases, the company offered the promise of jobs and some physical improvements to the community, hoping at least to divide the people, as sometimes happens. There were also threats looming if the people did not accept the mine. Meanwhile, early mining operations in the area had already begun to poison the waters.

Since, in the perspective of many Guapinol residents, the company and the national and local governments did not offer a proper *consulta*, the communities themselves organized and conducted a *cabildo abierto,* a large open community meeting in 2018, after months of fruitless negotiations and arguments with the company and the government. As might have been expected, the more-or-less democratic and participatory community meeting expressed strong rejection of the mining operation, and the people declared their communities to be a mining-free zone. The Honduran government, bent on expanding extractive industry, reacted by detaining dozens of local people.

Rather than being processed as civil cases of disagreement and negotiation between parties, the cases were transferred to the jurisdiction of the national criminal court system, and twelve of the Guapinol community leaders were charged with criminal activity such as illegal association (roughly, conspiracy to commit a crime) and arson (the burning of a truck under mysterious circumstances). While awaiting further court proceedings, the Guapinol defendants were placed in high security prison that is reserved for the worst crimes, and far from their homes. Under strong public and international pressure, the government eventually transferred them to lower security prisons closer to their homes where they remained for over a year without a final adjudication of their case. The message was clear. The Honduran government considered the local defense of water and land to be a crime; but the people of Guapinol succeeded in raising resistance as their case became nationally and internationally known.

Not all communities in Honduras are able to defend their rivers and land as successfully as the people of Guapinol have so far, even though they have not entirely succeeded in that defense. Hundreds of rural communities across the country have been displace by extractive industries that often engage threats and violence against the people and the environment that sustains a way of life. In August of 2019, police violently evicted yet another community near Yorito in northern Honduras to make way for more extractive projects, Soldiers were deployed to the area to put down local resistance.[4] The displaced people of such communities lose their land, the social fabric of their community, their livelihood, and their relative self-reliance. Instead they are likely to become dependent job-seekers in Honduras where work is scarce, and they are often declared criminals.

THE EMBLEMATIC CASE OF BERTA CÁCERES

There have been a few incidents that the international mainstream media and foreign attention could not ignore—incidents that were emblematic of what was happening, if one really wanted to get beyond the simple narratives of gang violence to understand the roots of Honduran emigration and much more. The most (in)famous event was the murder of Berta Cáceres in March 2016. Cáceres was a Lenca, a member of one of the largest Indigenous groups in Honduras, and leader of the Lenca organization, COPINH (Civic Council of Popular and Indigenous Organizations of Honduras).[5] Cáceres led COPINH and the Lenca communities in the area of Rio Blanco in the west of the country, in opposition to the Honduran government's concession to a Honduran-Chinese partnership to build a dam across the Gualquarque River. This was one of dozens of hydroelectric projects promoted by the government to provide electricity for mining and other development projects, almost all of which carried the threat of displacing more communities. Most of these projects proposed damming rivers that were important to the life of Indigenous communities. To the Lenca of Rio Blanco, the Gualcarque River provides both a source of water and a sacred presence. It is where the spirits of ancestors and unborn children might dwell, spirits that help the Lenca in their daily life and struggles, as some Lenca have said.[6]

A turning point for the Lenca came when the company that held the contract to build the dam bulldozed an access road that ran through Lenca lands to the river, and constructed a compound for operations and material staging by the riverside, in preparation for building the contested dam. Some Lenca said that the worst indignity was when company security guards and officials told the Lenca they could no longer use the river that had been so important to their life for generations. Neither the company nor the government had provided the Lenca with full information about the proposed project or asked for their free consent to use Lenca land and the river, as was required by both Honduran and international law and convention.

Lenca people responded by setting up a simple roadblock and keeping a constant presence at the roadblock to prevent company trucks and heavy machinery from passing. They attracted international solidarity as they conducted daily marches or processions along the road down to the company compound, with prayers and incense—a way of reaffirming Lenca possession of their land and perhaps cleansing the land of the project of death that, from their perspective, was unfolding there. Cáceres, COPINH, and the Lenca became internationally known as Indigenous defenders of the environment. In 2015, Cáceres was awarded the international Goldman Prize given to Indigenous environmental activists. But in Honduras, authorities brought criminal charges against Cáceres for inciting violence. They claimed they had found a gun in her vehicle, a charge that many thought was both invented and ludicrous in a country where carrying guns is widespread and open. The police ignored the peaceful nature of the resistance Cáceres was leading. Meanwhile, the Chinese partner withdrew from the dam project, most likely because of the delays caused by these events and the negative international attention the project began to receive. A Honduran company, Desarrollos Energeticos (DESA), assumed the contract to build the dam.

The term "environmental activist" that has become part of the discourse of Western societies may not carry the full implications of struggle, threat, and death that engaged the Lenca people. In Honduras, people tend to use the term "environmental defenders" to highlight the serious costs involved. Cáceres herself received and reported to the police at least thirty-three death threats for her leadership against the dam. The police did not investigate the threats or provide protection for her. The Inter-American Commission for

Human Rights (IACHR) mandated that the Honduran government provide protective measures (*medidas cautelares*) for her, but the Honduran government ignored this mandate and the police took no action.

Cáceres was murdered in her home on March 2, 2016. Her death provoked an international response and a huge outpouring of anger and determination in Honduras. She was known even at the Vatican for her environmental work. Five years after her killing, Hondurans were saying, "Berta didn't die. She multiplied."

Honduras is a country where 95 percent of assassinations of activists receive little or no investigation.[7] It is considered one of the more dangerous countries for environmental defenders.[8] But Cáceres was in the international spotlight, and authorities were forced to conduct an investigation, and they prosecute eight men for the murder, all of them either officials of the dam-building company or the military with connections to the government. Seven of the eight were found guilty after a prolonged legal process that was obstructed at many points by company and government officials. But many Hondurans believed that these men did not act on their own. Three years after Cáceres was murdered, Hondurans were still demanding that the "intellectual authors" of the crime also be brought to justice. At the end of 2019, two investigative journalists outside Honduras obtained documents containing text messages and other communications that seemed to show a close coordination between the actual assassins, who by then had been convicted, and members of the wealthy Honduran family that owned DESA and would lose money if the dam project were stalled or stopped. The documents also seemed to reveal that at least one Cabinet minister in the government was aware of the plan to kill Cáceres.[9] More than a year after this revelation, only one person, an official at DESA, had been brought to trial.

For many in and outside of Honduras, the case of Berta Cáceres, COPINH, and the Lenca became emblematic of the ways that extractive industries and the government that promotes them ignore the fundamental rights of local communities, criminalize any attempt by communities to defend their land and water, and resort to violence, even murder, to ensure the expansion of extractive industries. Here one can find some of the deeper roots of the conditions that encourage or force Hondurans and other Central Americans to flee their homelands. In turn, this form of extractive development is an integral component in the relationship of Honduras to the United States, a nation that enjoys the fruits of the resources extracted from Honduras and deeply influences, even dictates, the political and economic life of the country. It is an essentially imperial relationship. That is the story of this book.

IMPERIAL ADDICTION AND AN
ANTHROPOLOGY OF MIGRATION

This book adopts an anthropological perspective. The primary purpose of anthropology is to chronicle the human spirit in different ways. The imperial addiction is one of the more devastating illnesses to afflict the human spirit. Unfortunately, the sources of the imperial addiction are many and complex. Empires have appeared in human history for a long time, but there is an argument to be made that, like a virus, the imperial addiction has mutated as world conditions have changed, so that modern imperialism is more encompassing, complex, and devious than its ancient predecessors. Despite its long history, the imperial addiction is not simply an inherent characteristic of "human nature," but is rather a complex set of specific characteristics that develops in particular socio-historical contexts. In particular, modern empire was and is fueled by and serves the interests of a modern capitalist global economy that arose out of the early days of modern western imperial expansion (1500–1750), especially Spanish, Portuguese, English, and French colonialism that extracted and accumulated wealth from what is now called the Western Hemisphere, wealth that provided the capital used to finance the so-called Industrial Revolution.[10] Racism was also a useful component of empire and capitalism, maintaining a fictional but crucial line between the colonizers and the colonized. Indigenous and tribal peoples, for the most part and with a few questionable exceptions, did not have empires but, in the modern world at least, are rather more likely to be the victims of empires.[11]

We must study and diagnose this imperial addiction because it afflicts the human spirit, but it is that spirit, not the addiction, that is our primary concern. The imperial addiction drives some humans to violence to satisfy demand and desire, while it can drive others—the objects of violence—to self-violence, or despair. Resistance and migration are also responses of the human spirit. In this book, we explore migration as a response of the human spirit in Honduras to the same imperial addiction. To do so, we must examine and diagnose the ways in which the imperial addiction, as manifest in the "neocolonial" relationship of the United States and the larger global political economy to Honduras, tries to repress and eviscerate the human spirit of the Honduran people, even as it displaces people physically, psychically, and politically. It then becomes clearer how and why emigration is a response of the human spirit that is apt but also limited. It may become clear that the imperial addiction is also a major threat to the human spirit in the centers of empire, in this case the United States, as well as in the "colonies" like Honduras

WHY HONDURAS?

This book centers on the experience of Honduras, one of the countries of Central America's so-called Northern Triangle (Honduras, Guatemala, El Salvador). All three countries share not only some common or similar historical and cultural traits, but also some similar experiences in terms of the impact of extractive industries, poverty, violence, official corruption, and emigration. A large percentage of the migrant population that went north from Latin America in the decade between 2009 and 2019 came from these countries, even as immigration from Mexico to the United States was declining.[12] Of the three Northern Triangle countries, this book concentrates on Honduras. There are several reasons motivating this focus. The simplest reason is that I have more experience in and knowledge of Honduras and more personal connection to that country and some of its courageous people.

But there are other, larger reasons why Honduras. In the years from 2015 through 2019, an average of 300 Hondurans emigrated to the north every day, as many as one hundred thousand in some years, out of a total national population of about 9.5 million.[13] Many were deported back to Honduras. Many of these deportations occurred without benefit of an asylum hearing, and were probably violations of international refugee law and conventions.

Painfully, Honduras is an ideal country in which to explore the themes outlined above, the central ideas of this book—neoliberal extractive development; dislocation of community; rising poverty, crime, and corruption; large-scale emigration; and all of these as integral aspects of the colonial relationship of Honduras to the United States. This exploration will not be an easy journey, both because of the violence involved and because we will have to make several side journeys along the way into the history of Latin American immigration to the United States and the nature of displacement, development, and empire. But perhaps it will yield some understandings and ideas for change.

Another reason for this focus is that scholarship and writing about Honduras, as well as "solidarity" with the Honduran people has lagged behind that accorded to the other Central American countries. There is a history to this neglect, a history in which Honduras is often cast historically and currently as a silent partner in the U.S. system, not like revolutionary Nicaragua, and more so than El Salvador or Guatemala. This passive and subservient image of Honduras that obscures the very active resistance of the Honduran people did not generate the same level of solidarity from the international community that the other countries enjoyed in the turbulent 1980s.

The relative silence about Honduras outside of the country serves the interests of those who prefer to obscure the exploitative nature of its situation in relation to the the United States and the global economy. Little is said in the United States about Honduras, except that the poverty and violence there may contribute to emigration and exacerbate the "crisis" at the U.S. southern border. The crisis in Honduras that sparks this exodus is seldom explored in any detail. That dearth of scholarship and interest has contributed to the popularization of partial, simplified, and seriously deficient explanations of Honduran emigration in ways that obscure the central role of extractive neoliberal economic policies and the role of the United States in shaping this migration "crisis" and the desperation from which it springs. This is a serious problem, not only for the migrants themselves, but also because it leads to simplistic and often counterproductive (or contradictory) proposals for a "solution" to emigration, such as simply sending more development aid or more security aid, or encouraging more foreign investment. This book will argue that this migration is an integral consequence of a system of extraction of resources and transfer of wealth that is nothing less than "imperial" or, if you prefer, colonial in its nature. It will argue also that the current immigration system is a lucrative enterprise in itself, enriching a few at the cost of misery for the many. Far from constituting a critique of this migration, the criminalization of immigrants can be understood as an essential part of this imperial system.

This argument may not be popular with those who prefer to characterize the U.S. relationship to Honduras and the rest of Latin America under the rubric of mutually beneficial "development." The debate over whether the United States is a benevolent promoter of development and democracy or an imperial power extracting wealth from others has been raging for decades in academia and government in the United States and to some extent in Honduras. It may be both vitally important and irrelevant to the people of countries like Honduras. Hondurans live every day with the knowledge that their lives and that of their country have for long been deeply influenced and shaped by the policies and practices of the United States. What the Honduran government does may matter more to Hondurans in direct ways, but they know very well that their government depends heavily on the economic and political support of the United States. "Everyone knows that Honduras is run by the US. Embassy," a former Honduran Congress member once told me. So this book is about the imperial debris through which the rivers of Honduras run. It is also about the problematic meaning of national sovereignty in a globalized world where imperial formations and imperial debris still shape the landscape.

AN IMPERIAL RELATIONSHIP: RESOURCE ACCESS

The saying goes, "In the past, colonies were conquered; now they are bought." In the contemporary re-configuration of empire, the exercise of military conquest is partially replaced by economic and cultural conquest, but the projection of military power, militarization of society, and the threat of force and violence usually underlie these other forms of "soft" power. Together with this re-thinking of the meaning of imperialism, there has been a critique of the discourse and practice of what is termed "international development" that became prominent and then ubiquitous from the 1960s, after the collapse of the modern empires of Europe. According to some of its critics, "development" has become the contemporary vehicle for the projection of imperial systems, the new and more benign face of imperial influence.[14] From this perspective, models of development mandated for countries such as Honduras are vehicles through which modern colonial relationships are maintained with the "developed" world. Examining the consequences and effects of neoliberal extractivism as the official development model of Honduras is therefore a necessary task for understanding how Honduras is a subordinate part of a U.S.-dominated, imperial system.

A consequence of considering Honduras and the United States as poles of the same (imperial) system is that this book must examine some aspects of United States society and history inasmuch as they affect and are affected by a relationship to the people of Honduras and their government. This further implies that the readers of this book might not be simply outside observers or ethnographic tourists, but rather actors also in this system. This imperial relationship is dynamic and highly unstable inasmuch as it depends on several elements that cannot be guaranteed, including a flow of resource commodities from a deteriorating environment in Honduras to the United States, and a docile or acquiescent population in both countries.

The people of Honduras and the United States are closely related in a single system that extracts resources and maintains a wall of separation between the citizens of the empire and the colonial subjects. The mines, large scale commercial agriculture, tourist complexes, and other projects that displace thousands of rural Hondurans provide the kinds of materials, resources, and services that the governments and citizens of countries like the United States, Canada, western Europe, and China use daily—iron ore, antimony (think cell phones), lumber, agricultural products including palm oil (think shampoo, processed foods), and tourist vacations (think Caribbean beaches).

The so-called agrarian problem has been an enduring thread through much of the history of Latin America.[15] It refers to the fact that putting land and labor together is a primary requisite for production, survival, and wealth.

This necessity has created endless agrarian conflict between self-reliant communities who live on the land and produce for their own subsistence, and the political and economic elites who devise systems to force such communities to dedicate or relinquish a part of their production, land, and labor to a political leader, landowner, bureaucracy, ruler, or state. Spanish and Portuguese imperial rule in Latin America established systems for claiming the lands of Indigenous peoples and binding local Indigenous communities to work the land. Sometimes administrators and scholars called these people peasants.[16] If that term seems derogatory, it is because it has acquired and carries the sense of subordination and subservience to more powerful masters. These are issues of "land capture" and "labor capture" that are directly relevant to the question of whether people remain in place or migrate (chapter 4).

In contemporary Central America, land capture and labor capture continue to be essential features of the system, but with new actors. The forcible displacement of self-reliant rural communities from their lands creates a growing pool of landless people seeking work. This may not be simply an unintended consequence of extractivism, but rather an intended outcome that provides a pool of cheap labor for the export agribusiness plantations and growing assembly plant (*maquiladora*) industries of countries like Honduras.[17] Some of the rural people displaced by extractive industries do find work on plantations or in the maquiladoras that dot the outskirts of cities like San Pedro Sula in northern Honduras, where jobs are too few, work is unhealthy, and wages are often too low to support a family. The products assembled in these factories are likely to go to consumers in more wealthy countries like the United States. Many of the companies that operate mines, agricultural plantations, tourist facilities and maquiladoras are owned by U.S., Canadian, European, and East Asian entrepreneurs. None of this provides enough jobs at living wages that allow for survival, much less a dignified existence. In the twenty years from 1999 to 2019, the poverty rate in Honduras tripled to nearly 70 percent, with 45 percent in "extreme poverty," according to Honduran and international sources.[18] Exploitation and extraction of Honduran resources, displacement of communities, increasing poverty and violence provide much of the impetus for Hondurans to emigrate.

But there is more. What happened to the Guapinol defenders and the Lenca of Rio Blanco reveals a much larger and more extensive pattern in which almost any attempt to resist extractive development and to protect local community land, water, and self-reliant ways of life (i.e., to avoid land and labor capture) is met with violence and criminalization. Trying to change the government through fair elections and peaceful protest has also met with violent repression. The use of state sponsored or condoned violence to remove people from the land in order to make way for extractive development projects represents a failure of labor capture in Honduras in the past few decades. Violence does not allow for peaceful change. In Honduras two forms of violence are employed to control the population that is not captured as labor: violence exercised directly by state agents such as the police and the security forces, and violence that is perpetrated by gangs and other "criminal" forces. These two forms of violence are closely related and interpenetrated, and they both serve to induce fear and exercise control.[19]

Living in an unbearable state of precarity with no apparent path to change, Hondurans respond in different ways. The traumas, depression, and despair of life in such a situation produce what social science calls "social pathologies," violent or destructive behaviors turned inward, such as domestic violence and substance abuse to which some turn, encouraged by an official ideology that tells Hondurans that they, not the state or the government, are a violent people who are responsible for all the violence in society.[20] Others turn to popular resistance through organized protest. In recent decades a culture of resistance has been growing in Honduran life. Still others continue to hope against hope that the political system can actually work, and that change can happen through party and electoral politics.[21] Finally, many simply begin to equate survival with emigration.

AN IMPERIAL RELATIONSHIP:
VICTIMS AND CRIMINALS

Maintaining a separation and an inequality between the immigrants who seek to enter and the citizens who already live in the United States is essential to maintaining the relationship of extractive exploitation. Imperial systems operate on a distinction between the colonizer and the colonized, "us" and "them." This wall of separation can be constructed through racism, for example, or through other exclusionary categories, such as "citizenship." Central American immigrants coming to the United States are characterized as both victims and criminals. Both of these characterizations separate them from others. In the popular imaginary, Central American immigrants are at once needy, vulnerable, and dependent victims and illegal aliens and criminals. In the context of massive immigrations of Central Americans to the United States, criminalization takes different forms before, during, and after migration, beginning in Central America, continuing through the journey, and onto U.S. soil. The term "illegal alien" is a form of criminalization. It is also technically incorrect and (probably intentionally) misleading. Despite the common political rhetoric, it is not "illegal" to ask for asylum in another country, even if one enters the country with no documentation. Guaranteeing the safety of such asylum seekers is a fundamental principle of international law to which the United States and other countries are subject.

In relation to migrants from Latin America, U.S. immigration policy was said to be geared to the patterns of labor supply and demand in the United States. When labor was needed, immigration policies were loosened; in times of labor excess, policies were tightened to restrict the flow. For most of the past century, Mexico was an important source of immigration to the United States. This immigration, consisting mostly of single men or married men without their families, was considered an important source of labor. But the "new" immigration from Central America consists of children, youth, women, and whole families. They are seen not as a source of labor but as a potential burden. The rhetoric of politicians in the United States often characterizes these new immigrants as an invading horde or simply as criminals who must be repelled. Sometimes the same end can be achieved by claiming concern for the safety and welfare of the migrants and demanding that they remain in Central America rather than make the perilous journey north. But as migrants themselves point out, this concern for their safety is not shown as long as they remain in their home countries from which they flee precisely because, from their perspective, the dangers there outweigh the problems of the journey.

A PERSONAL JOURNEY

For thirty years I have watched the ebbing and flowing procession of humanity from Central America arriving at the U.S.-Mexican border. For most of that time, I have been skeptical of the tendency in our laws and policies to differentiate between "economic immigrants" who come seeking economic opportunity and security, and "asylum seekers" who are fleeing violence or danger. This dualistic model of motivation—some pulled to the United States as a land of opportunity, others pushed to the United States as a land of freedom and relative security—seemed a little too rigid to accommodate people like Paul (pseudonym), a Haitian who appeared before a Federal court in Miami in 1980 to explain why he should not be deported. He told the judge, "In Haiti, if you are standing on a street corner with others, and you say, 'I am hungry,' the police may interpret that as a criticism of the government, and you will be jailed and probably tortured."[22] I have long wondered how economic poverty and political repression work together to shape the daily lives and miseries of people like Paul and, presumably, so many others. In the early 1980s I was in Nicaragua and Honduras. There were tens of thousands of displaced people and migrants in Central American countries fleeing the violence of conflicts, and thousands more arriving at the U.S. southern border in flight from the same conflicts. But the ideological veneer given the Central American conflicts—the fight against communism—was really a struggle over who would control and benefit from the land and resources of these countries. National elites, foreign corporations waited in the wings. Just as the conflicts formally ended around 1990, the Honduran government adopted the neoliberal resource extraction-based development model pushed on it by Washington, and the corporations and development experts moved in.[23] From the perspective of the Central Americans displaced and seeking asylum in the 1980s, the violence of war may have been the overwhelming cause of their flight; others, however, were aware of the economic stakes involved.

In 1995, I received a call from an immigration lawyer asking me if I would be willing to testify as an expert witness in an immigration asylum hearing in San Antonio, Texas, since I was a social scientist who had a professional and personal knowledge of conditions in Honduras. The asylum seekers were two Honduran peasant farmers who had survived the massacre of other members of their peasant cooperative as they were engaged in cultivating land awarded to them by the Honduran National Agrarian Institute under the 1974 Agrarian Reform Law. But a powerful army colonel had illegally taken de facto possession of the land in question. On the morning of May 3, 1990, the colonel's security guards attacked the peasants who were sleeping on the land. They killed several. The two men who appeared in immigration court in San Antonio five years later were survivors who had fled Honduras. I did not know it then, but the massacre they had survived had become widely and (in)famously known in Honduras as the El Astillero massacre.[24] The judge in Texas granted asylum to the two, explaining that their claim to the land that had cost them and their associates dearly was not only an economic necessity but also an expression of a political opinion opposed to government failure to enact its own laws, and they had been attacked for this. Again, economic need and political persecution were somehow linked in the experience of these refugees.

When large numbers of young people from Central America began arriving at the U.S. border after the coup d'etat in Honduras in 2009, I began receiving, once again, calls from lawyers who were representing Honduran asylum seekers in U.S. immigration courts. In eight years (2012–2020) the frequency of asylum hearings in which I was asked to testify increased, reflecting an increasing flow of emigrants from Honduras and other Central American countries seeking asylum in the United States. Most of the new asylum seekers were either women with children or teenage males, fleeing intensely violent and seemingly impossible situations, as Honduras itself experienced one of the highest murder rates in the world.[25] The land conflicts of the El Astillero sort were still all too frequent in Honduras, but I began to realize that most of the new asylum seekers were not those directly displaced from the land, but rather the children and grandchildren of the displaced peasant communities. The new emigration of women and youth was in large part the secondary consequence of years of peasant community displacements that had created the conditions for the poverty and violence that now seemed to consume Honduran society, as reflected in the stories of these new asylum seekers.[26] Some of them were the children or grandchildren of peasants displaced from their land, who had migrated to Honduran cities and towns in search of work. The government's neoliberal economic development policies, strongly encouraged and supported by successive U.S. Administrations, had turned thousands of self-reliant farm families into landless job-seeking dependents. The 2009 coup put into power post-coup governments that even more fiercely embraced a neoliberal extractive development model, this time accompanied by an increasingly brazen manipulation of law, violation of the country's Constitution, militarization, and widespread corruption. These exacerbated the poverty and violence and provided the context for threatening Hondurans so badly that people began to flee the country in increasingly large numbers.

Ignoring (or perhaps because of) their own complicity in helping create this situation, and in apparent violation of international law, U.S. immigration agencies began deporting Central Americans in large numbers, often without giving them their legal right to an asylum hearing.[27] Economic immigrants and asylum seekers were all one in the political rhetoric and popular imaginary that pervaded the United States, and this fueled the sentiment that all of them deserved to be deported. Increasingly, the image of the Central American immigrant became associated with criminal activity, a fictive association created and promoted by people in the U.S. government and the public out of fear and political opportunism. (Having grown up in a community where we were all immigrants or the second-generation children of immigrants, I understood that this criminalization of the immigrant is an old trope in American racism and xenophobia.) I knew that for most Honduran asylum seekers, deportation meant return to the very real dangers from which they had fled. If so, the United States was legally bound by international and U.S. law not to deport them.[28] This question of safety upon return is critical in most asylum cases in U.S. immigration courts.

On visits to Honduras in 2018 and 2019, I tried to explore what was happening to Honduran deportees. My explorations were informal and very preliminary, consisting largely of extended interviews with Hondurans in human rights leaders, church social services, and social research organizations that track or have direct contact with Honduran emigrants and deportees. I also interviewed deportees, mostly teenage males. It became clear that the migration process is more complex than I had imagined. I also learned something about how the current immigration system between the United States and Central America is a very lucrative economic enterprise that trades in the misery of immigrants, asylum seekers, and deportees and provides a reason why the immigration "crisis" may not be resolved anytime soon; and why criminalizing migrants, or rather turning migrants into both victims and criminals, is a necessary part of this system. I learned why many deportees believe they have little choice but to try repeatedly to enter the United States. Above all, I was struck by the ongoing popular resistance of the Honduran people, their ability to find creative ways to survive and push back the forces threatening their lives. The culture of resistance in Honduras and the flow of emigration out of Honduras were two major forms of survival. In a previous book, I tried to describe the culture of resistance.[29] In this book, I will try to describe the deeper forces that drive emigration from Honduras and its intimate relationship to the United States. Looking deeper at the causes of immigration may help to avoid "solutions" that are either useless or likely to make the situation worse.

I am aware that this is a book about Honduras and its people written by one who is not Honduran. As a U.S. citizen, my concern is with the policies of my government and the understandings of other U.S. citizens. Writing inside the empire runs the risk of seeing things, albeit unconsciously, from an imperial perspective. I have consciously tried to avoid that, and I must ask forgiveness for any failings. I rely heavily on Honduran sources for their analyses and interpretations. These include interviews and conversations I have had in Honduras, as well as published sources, including news and commentary from Honduran media and the websites of organizations, and published books and articles by Honduran scholars and researchers. The narratives (declarations and affidavits) of Honduran asylum seekers that I have read in my capacity as an expert witness in many asylum cases are particularly instructive, although they must remain anonymous. The responsibility for how these and other (mostly U.S. and Latin American) sources are used and how my narrative and interpretation is constructed is mine. I am aware of the ease with which an essentialist picture of Honduran life can be constructed—one that falls into the trap of seeing Hondurans as either victims or criminals. The victim-criminal duality is a piece of imperial mindset that pervades much of the thinking about immigrants from Central America. Reality is so much more complex and nuanced than this simplistic duality. I hope this complexity shows through in these pages.

THEORY AND METHOD

The approach taken in this book combines elements of history and ethnography, but it does not pretend to be a history or an ethnography. The focus that is present here is multi-local. It centers on Honduran society but always in the context of its relationship to the United States and the global political economy. The major theme of migration from Honduras to the United States requires such an approach, as does the larger context of imperial relationships that affect and shape both societies in interactive ways. This approach owes something to the earlier anthropological work of Julian Steward and the proponents of cultural ecology, and even more to that of Eric Wolf and others, including critiques of colonialism, theories of underdevelopment and dependency, global systems, state formation, imperial systems, land-labor capture, development, migration, and more.[30] Many of these highlight the close interrelationship between the "colony" and the "metropolis" as a major force is shaping daily life in both. Related to this theoretical evolution has been an ongoing effort to decolonize anthropology as a discipline and a practice, breaking down the wall, and even complicating the relationship between observer and observed.[31] There is still much to do toward this end, and one cannot adequately interpret or appreciate the imperial/colonial structure of the current world without seeing one's place as an actor in it.

The interrelated, temporary, and dynamic nature of our situation is captured in the more recent theoretical work of anthropologists such as Arjun Appadurai in which the particular "culture" of any particular place at any moment in time is a product of the encounter and interaction of various forces and resources—flows of technology, finance, media, ideology, people and more—that meet or are brought or drawn together for limited periods in different configurations in different places, and then recombine elsewhere in different configurations.[32] From this perspective Honduras and the United States today are both shaped by essentially the same or similar forces and are subject to the instability of these forces as they reshape both societies. Massive emigrations that have become a major characteristic of this relationship are a product and an expression of this inherently interrelated and unstable world of multiple forces and influences, uprooting, destroying, and transforming daily life in ways that seem to make some people superfluous at a particular time and place, the "throw aways" of a changing society.[33] Thus one sees such "superfluous" people in both the emigrants from Honduras and, for example, the newly unemployed workers of the Midwestern United States, the so-called Rust Belt. Why these populations may not immediately understand their affinity to each other is a question that should help to make clearer the nature of the imperial structures in which both try to survive.

Theoretical frameworks both aid and constrain thinking. They can provide clues to the otherwise unseen relationships between forces, people, and conditions. They can also restrict our thinking along certain focused lines that tend to ignore other possibilities or, worse, ignore lived realities. Theory can become too theoretical when it fails to convey or partake of the urgency of daily life. But that is in some sense the purpose of theory: to provide a measured moment of reflection without the need to hurry onward to relief or resolution. Theoretical frameworks should be the servants, not the masters, of daily life and human experience.

Theoretical frameworks are also inherently political, even as their proponents sometimes claim that theory must be "objective." They tend to privilege certain questions and interests and to emphasize the importance of certain aspects of complex and changing life situations, while ignoring or relegating other questions and aspects to secondary importance. Theory can be used as support for or critique of political systems, policies, and practices. Whether this is bad or good depends largely on your purpose, but recognizing that theory has political and real-life implications is important. To understand how and why we humans do what we do, context is crucial. I wrote in an earlier book that

> the example of colleagues in Latin America and the Caribbean has taught me that the social sciences are almost always a matter of urgency. In Central America, the social sciences are critical in at least two ways. They deal with critical issues that deeply affect the lives of people and nations, and they constitute a critical interrogation of what is or seems to be. A sense of both the urgency of daily lives and the analytical interrogation of context are required and mutually complementary in the "dangerous anthropology" of situations in which human lives may be lost or saved daily.[34]

It is difficult, perhaps impossible, to divorce theory from methodology. What we want to know and why we want to know it shape how we go about gathering what we consider relevant information. The information we consciously collect, inadvertently stumble upon, or what is thrust upon us may reshape our concerns and interests, and thus our theoretical framework—or it may simply be seen as support for that framework. When I was doing fieldwork in Jamaica in the 1970s focused on the newly forming sugar workers cooperatives, I adopted a simple theoretical framework based on decision-making and game theory. I asked how individual sugar workers decided to join the new Sugar Workers Cooperative Council and advocate for worker ownership of the traditional corporate-owned sugar plantations. Years later, as I reviewed the materials I had gathered from more than a year of fieldwork, I realized that what I had witnessed could be understood in the framework of post-colonial emergence, globalization, social change theory, and more, that might have allowed me to interrogate the larger context in which the sugar workers were making their decisions, and thus, why they made such decisions. Adopting a new theoretical framework, I wrote an article about how the sugar workers' experience informed us about Jamaica's problematic emergence from British colony to nominally independent nation in a global economy.[35] The information I collected encouraged a re-thinking of its significance as my own experiences in the interim re-shaped my concerns.

Methodology has political and real-life consequences. The United States State Department must periodically certify that the Honduran government is making progress in protecting human rights and democracy. To the consternation and disgust of many Honduran and international human rights groups and popular organizations who experience escalating attacks on human rights and popular expression, the State Department regularly certifies that Honduras is indeed making progress. Analysis of the methods used to gather the information that supports this certification reveals that governments speak only to governments.[36] The official document from the State Department justifying the bases on which the certification is made often contains only statements of Honduran and U.S. government actions, such as forming commissions, initiating policies and laws, and allocating funds to programs. Very little is recorded about the actual results of any of this, and there is seldom any reference to the voices and experiences of Honduran human rights groups and popular and Indigenous organizations or their members. The methodology for collecting the date to justify certification of progress is confined largely to dialogue between the U.S. and the Honduran governments, with little or no apparent attempt to include other voices that might reflect the lived daily experiences of Hondurans. The method dictates the findings to support the desired political purpose—unwavering U.S. support for the Honduran government. The gap between this assertion of "progress" and the lived reality of many Hondurans is always a space where desperation and resistance grow.[37] Methodology has real consequences and can be a political tool. It relates directly to the kinds of sources of information one considers relevant, and how that information is obtained.

STRUCTURE OF THE BOOK

This book is an invitation to look at emigration and its roots in a more holistic way. The focus is on the Central American region, but the approach may be useful elsewhere. The book's title, *Extracting Honduras,* implies both the theft of the country's natural resources and the exile of a significant portion of its people, especially its youth, the social capital of the country.

Chapter 2 outlines aspects of the history of Latin American immigration to the United States within the context of the historic expansionist and imperial pretensions of the United States. The chapter shows how Honduras became first a safe haven for migrants from conflict in the rest of Central America, and then the insecure epicenter of much Central American immigration to the United States. This transformation is traced to the introduction of neoliberal extractivism and in part also to the interventions of the United States in its counterinsurgency operations in Central America during the 1980s and since. Questions arise about the untenable distinction between economic migration and asylum seeking. The chapter concludes with a consideration of the political economy of immigration.

Chapter 3 sets the question of Honduran emigration in the larger context of the imperial relationship between Honduras and the United States, and shows how modern concepts of development became the instrument of U.S. imperial intervention in countries like Honduras. The chapter interrogates the nature of imperial systems, but focuses on the evolution of developmentalism in Latin America after 1950 as the modern face of imperial influence and control. Development theory and practice have gone through several iterations. Concepts of underdevelopment, dependency, and globalization are central to this evolution. Developmentalism is chimeric inasmuch as it holds promise for the poor and marginal but it also creates poverty and marginality and often fails to fulfill its promise. Popular resistance and protest are one result, along with social duress and emigration, as is evident in Honduras.

Chapter 4 explores in greater historical and sociological depth the relationship between development and migration. Its focus is the articulation of systems of land and labor control in Latin America in relation to the dispossession of settled rural communities, and the transformation of such communities into pools of migrant labor, the so-called proletarianization of much of Latin America. While this transformation produced massive internal migrations within Latin America and in specific countries under earlier forms of extractivism and development, the more recent form of development—neoliberal extractivism in a global economy—has encouraged large scale emigration out of Central America where societies were also primed by the violence and corruption introduced during the regional conflicts of the 1980s. The chapter reflects on the moral economy of extractivism and the new migration, and discusses Honduran migration as an example of a lucrative imperial business in which a few profit at the cost of misery for the many.

While chapters 1 through 4 provide a more general discussion of themes and context, chapters 5 through 8 focus more specifically on Honduras. Chapter 5 examines the evolution of the Honduran political economy, and the integration of economic and political power. Here, we encounter neoextractivism and its consequences in the economic life of individuals, communities, and the country; and its consequences in the political life and institutions of the country, including the weakening of democratic citizenship, trust in institutions, gendered violence, and widespread corruption. The two—economic and political consequences—are tied together and mutually reinforcing.

Chapter 6 describes in some detail the functioning and consequences of major extractive industries and projects in Honduras, and how these affect and disrupt the lives of many Hondurans in their local communities and national institutions. The chapter explores mining and logging in detail, with some observations about agroindustry, tourism, and energy generation. Other consequences—including environmental degradation, social inequality, official corruption, and militarization of Honduran society—are briefly discussed. How all of these displace populations and set in motion conditions of duress that may end in emigration is the theme of this chapter.

Chapter 7 focuses on the history and role of the Honduran military and state security forces, and the militarization of Honduran society that has evolved as a crucial force in sustaining the official neoextractive economic model. The Honduran military's role has often entailed systematic violations of human rights, repression of popular protest, and support for governments that are popularly regarded as dictatorial and corrupt. The long and close relationship between the Honduran and the U.S. military is seen as perhaps the most important aspect of the imperial relationship between the two countries. The entire system of immigration of Hondurans to the United States has also become militarized, so that migrants are seen as enemies, or perhaps victims of a war zone.

Chapter 8 is based in the premise that emigration is not only a physical act prompted by physical realities, but also an action of the human spirit, psyche, affect, and mind. The chapter explores some aspects of the moral economy of emigration, its cultural and spiritual roots. It asks: how do people keep body and soul together under the duress of daily life in Honduras? The difficult conditions of life in the current political economy are accompanied by a semi-official ideology, bolstered by certain religious theologies, that place the burden and blame for the condition of the country on the backs of individuals rather than on national policies. People respond to the psychic, moral, and emotional burden in different ways—gang membership and criminal activity as a form of survival and resistance; addictions of various kinds; domestic and family conflict and violence; depression, acceptance, and normalization of the situation; organized popular resistance; and emigration. Some also understand the situation as a "spiritual struggle," and this chapter asks what that might mean.

Chapter 9 summarizes the argument of the book and critically reviews some of the proposed solutions to the "immigration crisis."

Throughout, the reflexive question arises: how is this imperial relationship that forces people to deal with duress and misery, shaped by—and in turn, how does it shape—the people and policies of the center of empire, the United States?

NOTES

1. Margarita Oseguera de Ochoa, *Honduras hoy: Sociedad y crisis política* (Tegucigalpa: Centro de Documentación de Honduras, 1987), 24. Nancy Peckenham and Annie Street, eds., *Honduras: Portrait of a Captive Nation* (New York: Praeger, 1985), 45–49.

2. One example: Jorge Valencia, "Why people are migrating from Honduras—and why many want them to stay," *Arizona Public Media* (September 11, 2019), https://news.azpm.org/p/news-splash/2019/9/11/157941-why-people-are-migrating-from-honduras-and-why-many-want-them-to-stay/.

3. Radio Progreso, "Proyecto minero desplaza familias enteras en Colon," commentary https://wp.radioprogresohn.net/proyecto-minero-desplaza-familias-enteras-en-colon/.

4. Karla Rodas, "Yorito, el pueblo hondureño que expulsó una minería," *Revista Gato Encerrado* (January 9, 2020), https://gatoencerrado.news/2020/01/10/yorito-el-pueblo-hondureno-que-expulso-a-una-minera-de-su-territorio/.

5. There are many reports, articles, and a few books devoted to the case of Berta Cáceres. Two of the more thorough investigations are Danielle Mackey and Chiara Eisner, "Inside the Plot to Murder Honduran Activist Berta Cáceres, *The Intercept* (December 21, 2019), https://theintercept.com/2019/12/21/berta-caceres-murder-plot-honduras/, and Nina Lakhani, *Who Killed Berta Cáceres? Dams, Death Squads, and an Indigenous Defender's Battle for the Planet* (London: Verso, 2020).

6. Interviews with Lenca activists, Rio Blanco, Honduras, August 2013.

7. United Nations Human Rights Council, *Report of the Special Rapporteur on Extrajudicial, Summary, or Arbitrary Executions, on His Mission to Honduras* (April 2017): 5–15, https://www.refworld.org/docid/593a6d944.html.

8. Nina Lakhani, "Indigenous environmental defender killed in latest Honduras attack," *The Guardian* (December 29, 2020), https://www.theguardian.com/environment/2020/dec/29/indigenous-environmental-defender-killed-felix-vasquez. Global Witness, "Honduras: the deadliest country in the world for environmental activism" (January 31, 2017), https://www.globalwitness.org/en/campaigns/environmental-activists/honduras-deadliest-country-world-environmental-activism/.

9. Mackey and Eisner, "Inside the Plot to Kill Berta Cáceres."

10. See, for example, Eric Williams, *Capitalism and Slavery* (Chapel Hill NC: University of North Carolina Press, 1944).

11. For example, John Bodley, *Victims of Progress*, Sixth Edition, (Lanham MD: AltaMira Press, 2015).

12. D'Vera Cohen, Jeffrey Passel, and Ana Gonzalez-Barrera, "Rise in U.S. Immigrants from El Salvador, Guatemala and Honduras Outpaces Growth from Elsewhere," Pew Research Center Hispanic Trends (December 7, 2017), https://www.pewresearch.org/hispanic/wp-content/uploads/sites/5/2017/12/Pew-Research-Center_Central_American-migration-to-U.S._12.7.17.pdf.

13. The number of asylum seekers leaving Honduras in 2009 was 995. By 2019, the number was 122,000, a huge increase. Most of these sought asylum in one of three countries: the United States, Mexico, or Spain. Migration Policy Institute, "Refugee and Asylum Seeker Populations by Country of Origin

and Destination, 2000–2019," https://www.migrationpolicy.org/programs/data-hub/charts/refugee-and-asylum-seeker-populations-country-origin-and-destination.

14. Arturo Escobar, *Encountering Development: The Making and Unmaking of the Third World,* (Princeton NJ: Princeton University Press, 1995). For comparison see Mark Duffield and Vernon Hewitt, *Empire, Development, and Colonialism: The Past in the Present* (Rochester NY: Boydell and Brewer, 2009).

15. Andrés Leon, "Rebellion under the Palm Trees: Memory, Agrarian Reform and Labor in the Aguán, Honduras" (PhD diss., Graduate Center, City University of New York, 2015), 8–9, provides a brief theoretical overview of the land and labor capture concept.

16. For example, Eric R. Wolf, *Peasants* (Englewood Cliffs NJ: Prentice-Hall, 1966); Rodolfo Stavenhagen, ed., *Agrarian Problems and Peasant Movements in Latin America* (Garden City NY: Doubleday Anchor, 1970); Ernest Feder, *The Rape of the Peasantry: Latin America's Landholding System* (Garden City NY: Anchor Books, 1971); and many more.

17. D. Faber, "Imperialism, Revolution, and the Ecological Crisis of Central America," *Latin American Perspectives* 19, no. 1 (1992): 27.

18. World Bank, "Poverty and Equity Brief, Honduras" (April 2020), https://databank.worldbank.org/data/download/poverty/33EF03BB-9722-4AE2-ABC7-AA2972D68AFE/Global_POVEQ_HND.pdf. Independent Honduran sources provide higher indices of poverty, as high as 67 percent in poverty; e.g., the Honduran Social Forum on the External Debt (FOSDEH), "Pobreza sigue en aumento a pesar de milionario gasto estatal: Fosdeh," *Dinero Honduras* (March 8, 2019), http://dinero.hn/pobreza-sigue-en-aumento-a-pesar-de-millonario-gasto-estatal-fosdeh-ine/.

19. Adrienne Pine, *Working Hard, Drinking Hard: On Violence and Survival in Honduras,* (Berkeley: University of California Press, 2008), 26–32.

20. Pine, *Working Hard*, 49–69. Sarah Chayes, *When Corruption Is the Operating System: The Case of Honduras* (Washington DC: Carnegie Endowment for International Peace, 2017), 83.

21. Equipo de Reflexión, Investigación y Comunicación (ERIC) y Universidad Centroamericana José Simeón Cañas, *Sondeo de opinión pública: Percepciones sobre la situación hondureña.* This survey published yearly with an analysis of the data.

22. James Phillips, "Who Is a Refugee?" *Global Justice* 1, no. 2 (Summer, 1995): 10–20; Linda Rabben, *Give Refuge to the Stranger: The Past, Present, and Future of Sanctuary* (Walnut Creek CA: Left Coast Press, 2011); Gary MacEoin and Nivita Riley, *No Promised Land: American Refugee Policies and the Rule of Law* (Boston: Oxfam America, 1982).

23. James Phillips, *Honduras in Dangerous Times: Resistance and Resilience* (Lanham MD: Lexington Books, 2015), 45.

24. Elías Ruiz, *El Astillero: masacre y justicia* (Tegucigalpa: Editorial Guaymuras, 1992).

25. World Bank Data, "International homicides (per 100,000 people)—Honduras," (2021), https://data.worldbank.org/indicator/VC.IHR.PSRC.P5?locations=HN.

26. I draw from the testimonies of Honduran asylum seekers in U.S. immigration proceedings. There is also a variety of other sources, e.g., "With love from

Central America: Four stories of Central American Refugees" (United Nations Refugee Agency (September 11, 2019), https://www.unrefugees.org/news/with-love-from-central-america-four-stories-of-central-american-refugees/ and Sonia Nazario, *Enrique's Journey* (New York: Random House, 2007).

27. For example, Muzaffar Chishti, Sarah Pierce, and Jessica Bolter, "The Obama Record on Deportations: Deporter in Chief or Not?" *Migration Policy Institute* (January 26, 2017), https://www.migrationpolicy.org/article/obama-record-deportations-deporter-chief-or-not.

28. Gary MacEoin and Nivita Riley, *No Promised Land: American Refugee Policies and the Rule of Law* (Boston: Oxfam America, 1982), 12–24 (this entire volume deals with the legal and policy issues of immigration and asylum in the U.S.); Linda Rabben, *Give Refuge to the Stranger: The Past, Present, and Future of Sanctuary* (Walnut Creek CA: Left Coast Press, 2011), 124–126.

29. Phillips, *Honduras in Dangerous Times.*

30. Julian Steward, *Theory of Culture Change: The Methodology of Multilinear Evolution* (Chicago: University of Illinois Press, 1955); Eric R. Wolf, *Europe and the People Without History (Berkeley: University of California Press, 1982).*

31. Faye V. Harrison, ed., *Decolonizing Anthropology: Moving Further Toward an Anthropology of Liberation* (Washington, DC: American Anthropological Association, 1997). An early foray in decolonizing anthropology appears with Dell Hymes (ed.), *Reinventing Anthropology* (New York: Pantheon, 1972).

32. Arjun Appadurai, "Disjuncture and Difference in the Global Cultural Economy," *Theory, Culture, and Society* 7 (June 1990): 295–310.

33. Zigmunt Bauman, *Wasted Lives: Modernity and Its Outcasts* (Cambridge: Polity, 2003).

34. Phillips, *Honduras in Dangerous Times,* 6–7.

35. James Phillips, "Democratic Socialism, the New International Economic Order, and Globalization," *The Global South* 4, no. 2 (Fall, 2010): 178–196.

36. This is revealed by a read through the U.S. State Department's documents of certification for Honduras.

37. James C. Scott, *Weapons of the Weak: Everyday Forms of Peasant Resistance* (New Haven: Yale University Press, 1985), 331–337.

Chapter 2

Latin American Immigration and the United States

During the summer of 2020, large-scale popular protests filled streets for many days and nights in cities across the United States. Initially, their purpose was to protest the death of yet another Black man at the hands of police, and to support the Black Lives Matter movement that had formed out of the outrage about these killings. In Portland, Oregon, protesters were attacked by "law enforcement" agents that wore uniforms without identifiable insignias, and could not be identified by name or agency. These unidentified agents dragged protesters into unmarked cars and whisked them away to some form of detention, usually releasing them the next day. Those detained said that their "law enforcement" captors never revealed their identities or the government agency for which they worked. Such tactics were widely denounced as fascist or as more befitting a police state or a dictatorship than a free, democratic society. It was soon revealed that the agents had been ordered to Portland by the president, and they were drawn specifically from the Department of Homeland Security and those agencies within the Department that dealt specifically with immigration and border control and, to a lesser extent, with anti-terrorism enforcement.[1]

The use of these particular government agents was deliberate. The agents who patrolled the U.S. southern border and dealt daily with immigrants and asylum seekers were trained and accustomed to see their subjects as different, alien, even invaders. These agents were also accustomed to an increasingly militarized mode of operating, as if they were the front lines in a war against an invading horde from the south who were in fact mostly desperate immigrants and asylum seekers from Central America. The use of these militarized agents to enforce "order" in the streets of Portland and other interior U.S. cities showed that the border was less a physical place than a mentality that was based on division—the border moved inland.[2] Now, U.S. citizens who were engaged in mostly peaceful protest, as is normal in a democratic society, were

25

seen in the same light as the invading hordes at the border. Peaceful citizen protesters were like the "illegal" immigrants—they did not belong in the country; they were a security risk. In addition, some of the DHS agencies that deal with immigrants had a history of operating beyond the normal controls or scrutiny of Congress or the courts.

Migrants cross many rivers during their journey on foot from Central America to the United States. These rivers of water are hardly the only obstacles. Physical barriers such as fences and walls, as well as immigration check points hinder their entry, but there are also legal, mental, and ideological barriers in the form of long-standing attitudes, beliefs, and practices in the United States that both embrace and abhor new immigrants.[3] For the people of the United States, immigrants pose perennial and embarrassing questions and unresolved conflicts about the very identity of the United States. From one perspective, the "crisis at the border" is fundamentally a crisis of national identity for the United States itself.

This is not a recent "crisis." It has been this way for a long time, and especially in recent years flows of immigrants from Latin America have been a physical link and a constant reminder that the *crisis at the border* and the *crisis of national identity* in the United States—"what kind of country are we?"—are intimately connected with the *crisis of survival* in Central America that has forced a river of immigrants to flow north. If the United States sees its national identity in terms of promoting democracy, equality, prosperity, and the rule of law everywhere, how could a part of the world—Central America—under the long historical hegemony of the United States become an area where daily survival itself becomes a crisis for many people? What does this reveal about the kind of country the United States is and claims to be? In this chapter, we explore the more apparent aspects of these questions in the flows of migration. In later chapters, we search for the deeper roots of these questions and the very nature of Central American emigration to the United States in the ideology of empire and development; and the political economy and sociocultural roots of the crisis of survival that drives people to leave their home countries in Central America. Honduras is a quintessential example.

IMMIGRANTS, NATIVISTS, AND IMPERIALISTS

It is a truism that the United States is a country of immigrants, a country built over more than three centuries on the talent and labor of millions who have come to its shores seeking a better life or fleeing forms of danger and persecution in their home countries. Immigration is a "hot" issue in the United States in large part because it touches individual and national identity. Most

U.S. citizens can relate in some way to immigration, either as recent natural-ized citizens or as the children or descendants of immigrants. People feel that they know something about immigration because, acknowledged or not, it is in their family history and in some close or distant way, their identity. One would think that they might feel a certain commonality with recent immi-grants and asylum seekers. But for some people, this reality seems too much to accept. Perhaps it touches their identity too closely. They think and act in fear, and reject recent waves of newcomers who are seeking some of the same things that most of our ancestors sought—a better life for their children, to live without constant fear, to be able to survive.

This historical and cultural context provides an opportunity for ambitious politicians and others to see immigration as an "issue" that can be exploited to further their own political ambitions by playing to identity politics, encourag-ing fears about the dissolution of the mythical "cultural purity" of the nation and the supposed stresses that immigrants place on its economic and social institutions, and constructing a concept of nationalism that demands exclu-sion and "security." These fears have been with us since the beginnings of the United States republic. Fear that Chinese immigration in the mid-1800s would overwhelm "American" institutions and culture and steal jobs from citizens and more acceptable immigrant groups led to the Chinese Exclusion Act of 1882, and propelled more than one political career.[4] The nativist "Know-Nothing" movements of the nineteenth century and the white nation-alist and supremacist groups of the early twentieth century railed against those who came to America from societies they deemed too strange and dif-ferent to integrate into the dominant mythic vision of the republic as a white, Anglo-Saxon, and Protestant nation.[5] Such mythical ideas and concerns have shaped and in many ways dominated the institutional, political, cultural, and economic life of the United States for a long time in the face of a real, very different and diverse America.

Nativist sentiments extended also to the treatment of those who were here before the arrival of European colonists—the native peoples of America. Nativist is an oddly ironic term, since the real "natives" were the Native Americans, the American Indians, but they were also seen as posing a threat to the mythic identity of the republic, and therefore had to be removed physi-cally and, if possible, historically from national life. The mindset underlying this irony was on display, for example, in the occupation of the Malheur Wildlife Refuge in eastern Oregon in 2016 by members of a movement promoting private rights to land as against Federal authority. The occupi-ers claimed they were taking back the land that was rightfully theirs.[6] They perhaps conveniently forgot that the first occupants of that particular section of land were Native Americans whose more recent descendants, the Burns Paiute, were still in the area. Historical amnesia is often a characteristic of nativism. Who is the "real" native becomes a strange question in the discourse of settler societies and empires.[7]

Nativism presents itself as exclusionary, but it is a function of expansionism, Manifest Destiny, and nationalism. It is an identity built on differentiating self from others, a necessity only in a context where one faces others in an adversarial, expansionist, mode, or when others arrive whose very presence seems to demand a revision or re-examination of national and personal identity. That America is somehow different from and better than other nations and peoples has long been a rationale for both the exclusion of the "other" and the expansion of American territory by taking the lands of the "other." The United States is "exceptional," unlike any other place.[8] This *exceptionalism,* this differential identity comes with special privileges and a sense of morality in which the well-being of the "native" is more important than that of others. Fear is an important driver—fear that the "other" will undermine the identity or well-being of the "native." This leads to blatantly absurd claims. In the history of the United States, Native Americans whose ancestors have been on the land for thousands of years are now cast as threats or obstacles to the new "natives" of the land. Any new group that comes to the shores of the country from afar may also pose a threat. These groups present the "native' with another contradiction, for the native was also once a newcomer to the shores of the country. This unsettling realization can be dealt with either by acknowledging a certain solidarity with the new groups or, conversely, by reinforcing the sense of difference against the new groups that are seen as threats to the privilege and special status of the "native." Perhaps this is a unique disease that affects settler societies, those based on taking the lands of already settled Indigenous peoples. But it is also a mark of expansionism in general. In part because of the nativist illusion and its inherent contradictions, the immigration history of the United States has been troubled by the image of the immigrant and the asylum seeker as both a victim to be helped and as threat or criminal to be excluded. The discourse of politicians often mirrors this convenient contradiction.

The psychology of this nativist illusion in U.S. history is such that the wealthy and powerful can take advantage of it for their own ends. Politicians in the United States routinely see immigration in relation to labor policy and foreign policy objectives, and can make their own political advantage by manipulating and fostering popular sentiments about immigration. Ironic twists in U.S. politics result, as when a president who represents and preaches unity and inclusion deports more immigrants than any of his predecessors. Unity can mean division, as in "We unite against them." We and they can be redefined to include and exclude other categories of humans, as needed. So Black Americans and "Hispanics" can also be seen as either part of "us" or part of "them." This flexible other-ing has been a major weapon of empire and a major rationale of imperial control.

While imperial powers such as Britain and France held a few smaller areas of Latin American and the Caribbean as colonies, their major colonial expansion was in Africa and south and southeast Asia. Since at least the time of the Monroe Doctrine (1824) Latin America has been the special area of United States influence and imperial reach, albeit sometimes in conflict with Spain or Britain. In this sense, the relationship of the United States to Latin America has been laden with imperial debris. The closest areas geographically to the United States—Mexico, Central America, and the Caribbean—have been those most under imperial influence. These areas drove out Spanish colonial rule, and for some also French and British rule, only to come under U.S. hegemony.

LATIN AMERICAN IMMIGRATION: 1845–1980

Throughout the nineteenth century, immigration from Latin America to the United States was relatively small compared to the flows of immigrants from Europe and East Asia, but it was punctuated several times by events that created large increases in the presence of Latin Americans, primarily Mexicans, in the United States.[9] The so-called Mexican War of 1846 was instigated by the United States and resulted in the annexation of the northern one-third of Mexico. Almost overnight, this made the Mexican citizens and settlers in that vast territory residents of the United States. Irish immigrants in the United States and directly from Ireland formed the San Patricio (Saint Patrick) Brigade that supported the Mexican forces against the United States in this war.[10] The Irish had themselves experienced domination by a colonial power (Britain). In addition, they tended to see the Mexicans as fellow Catholics like themselves who were also fighting Protestant domination.

The Mexican Revolution that started as a movement to overthrow the de facto dictatorship of Porfirio Diaz in 1910—and was aided substantially by leaders of the large German-American community in San Antonio, Texas—became a violent civil war that drove perhaps one million Mexicans to seek asylum in the United States.[11] Many later returned to Mexico, but many also remained permanently in the United States where their descendants live today. The German-American Texans who supported the early call for the Mexican Revolution were themselves exiles from the repression that followed the failed democratic revolutionary movements that swept Germany and central Europe in the mid-1800s (the so-called Liberal Revolutions of 1848).

During this entire period, the border between the United States and Mexico was open, and it was not difficult to move almost unhindered from one country to the other. Mexicans and Mexican culture seeped or flowed into American life especially in the southern regions from Texas to California. In the 1940s and 1950, Hollywood cowboy movies of the old West often portrayed glimpses of this cultural mixing along the border. During the Mexican Revolution, President Wilson sent General Pershing and his troops to chase the Mexican revolutionary leader Francisco (Pancho) Villa along the border and into northern Mexico, but this was considered a response to Villa's raids into New Mexico, not an immigration enforcement action. While the United States had policies that tended to favor western European immigrants over others, there was no U.S. Border Patrol or increased enforcement of immigration law along the U.S. Mexican border until the 1920s. The Emergency Quota Act of 1921 capped the total number of immigrants allowed into the United States from the rest of the world, and set quotas for the numbers of immigrants allowed from each world region, again favoring those from western Europe.[12] The U.S. Border Patrol was initiated in 1924. Since then, the apparatus of immigration law and policy enforcement has grown steadily in the United States to construct physical and legal barriers to immigration from the south, despite periods such as the Lyndon Johnson Administration of the mid-1960s when for a while the law seemed more receptive to immigrants.

Occasional exceptions were made in this enforcement apparatus for some Latin Americans during the mid-twentieth century, most notably in the aftermath of the triumph of the Cuban Revolution in 1959 that resulted in the exodus from that island of thousands of Cubans fleeing the revolutionary government and seeking residence in the United States. The U.S. government suspended its immigration laws (granted an exception) in this event and allowed most of the Cuban exiles immediate residence. From then until the 1980s, there was a sporadic flow of Cubans seeking exile in Florida. During that period, Haitians also began to seek asylum in the United States in significant numbers, fleeing the poverty and brutal repression of the Duvalier dictatorship in their home country. They did not receive the same open welcome that U.S. immigration officials extended to the Cubans who were said to be fleeing political repression. Instead, Haitians caught crossing in boats to Florida were intercepted at sea and deported back to Haiti. Those who managed to arrive in Florida, set foot on U.S. soil, and petition for asylum were either deported or detained pending immigration hearings. In 1980, a U.S. District Court in Miami finally ordered the granting of asylum to many of the Haitians on the grounds that economic insecurity and political repression were two sides of the same reality in Haiti and were inextricably connected.[13] Poverty made people more vulnerable to having their fundamental rights, including life itself, violated.

These events revealed several interesting aspects of United States immigration policy. They showed how immigration policy was shaped by foreign policy considerations. Admitting thousands of Cubans as political refugees gave the message that Cuba under the revolutionary government was an oppressive state. No such consideration applied to the Haitian dictatorship that, for all its brutality toward its own people, was not considered an enemy of the United States. Some critics of this differential treatment also saw racial and class-based biases in U.S. immigration practices. Most of the early Cuban arrivals were white and middle-class or wealthy. Most of the Haitians were black and poor. It was claimed that if the Cubans were deported back to their homeland they would face severe treatment, imprisonment, torture, religious persecution, and worse. Relatively few people asked what would happen to Haitians who were deported back to Haiti to face the Duvalier dictatorship and its police state.

In 1973, the Chilean military deposed the elected government of Salvador Allende in a bloody coup d'etat. Allende had nationalized the huge copper mining industry in Chile. In the aftermath of the coup, the Chilean military carried out a widespread campaign of detention, torture, and killing of thousands of Allende's supporters and those known to be sympathetic with his government.[14] People with no political leanings were also caught in this campaign of terror. Many fled Chile, but could find no secure refuge in neighboring South American countries, most of which were also ruled by military dictatorships. Some found their way to the United States, arriving by plane or, in a few cases, across the Mexican border seeking asylum. Years later, a U.S. Senate committee chaired by Senator Frank Church uncovered the support that U.S. copper companies and agencies of the U.S. government had given to the Chilean military in planning and instigating the coup in which Allende himself died.[15] This coup provides an example of how U.S. corporate interests in resource extraction (copper) combined with conservative anti-communist (anti-socialist) political interests to create a reign of terror that forced people to seek refuge. U.S. support fort the coup was also a move to shut out any intervention or influence from another imperial power—the "Soviet empire"—in the hemisphere. This was one of the more dramatic in a string of similar coups in Latin America staged for the same purposes.

The significant numbers of Chilean asylum seekers presented U.S. officials with an embarrassing fallout from U.S. involvement in the coup, and made U.S. authorities reluctant to admit the Chileans as refugees. The difficulties the Chileans seemed to face in getting the U.S. government to accept their petitions for asylum prompted a small network of U.S. citizens to begin thinking of ways to provide temporary sanctuary for the Chileans, an idea that was put into wider practice in the United States during the 1980s because of events in Central America.[16]

THE CENTRAL AMERICAN REFUGEE
CRISES OF THE 1980S

The Chilean exiles in the 1970s was soon followed by a much larger influx of immigrants and asylum seekers from Central America. In 1979, a popular revolution in Nicaragua led by the Sandinista Front for National Liberation (FSLN), toppled the forty-five-year dictatorship of the Somoza family that had long enjoyed the support of successive United States Administrations from FDR to Jimmy Carter. During the final year of this popular insurrection, Somoza began bombing his own cities and using tanks against his own people. The death toll was estimated at nearly fifty thousand in a country with a population at that time of less than four million. Many Nicaraguans fled the violence by crossing into Honduras where some had relatives, friends, or other acquaintances. Many of them returned to Nicaragua after Somoza was forced into exile in July, 1979.[17]

Within three years, Nicaragua was again plunged into war, this time with some of Somoza's former supporters and officers of his hated National Guard who began receiving financial and logistical support from members of the Reagan Administration. They made common cause to overthrow the revolutionary Nicaraguan government and drive the Sandinistas from power. They were referred to as the counterrevolutionaries or the Contras, although their various factions called themselves the Nicaraguan Democratic Front or other patriotic-sounding names. The Contra War in Nicaragua lasted almost ten years until 1990 when regional peace accords were signed. Thirty thousand or more Nicaraguans died in this war, and thousands more were physically and psychologically injured.[18] Forty to fifty thousand tried to flee the war by seeking refuge in southern Honduras. Many were housed in a large camp administered by international agencies near the southern Honduran town of Jacaleapa. The Nicaraguans' reasons for leaving were often practical and non-ideological. Many were fleeing the violence of the war. Some were young men evading the military draft in Nicaragua. Some were brought to Honduras forcibly by Contra soldiers. The Contras sometimes captured entire rural communities and force-marched them to Honduras as hostages. In addition, almost thirty thousand were young Miskito men from eastern Nicaragua who joined other Miskito communities in Honduras. Some of them wanted to use the Contra war to pressure Nicaragua into granting more autonomy to Miskito communities.[19]

Meanwhile, war in El Salvador between the government and the Farabundo Marti Front for National Liberation (FMLN), together with the government's practice of violently repressing dissent, prompted thousands to flee to Honduras. Whole communities tried to cross the rivers that formed the border between El Salvador and Honduras, only to be attacked by military units of both countries while crossing the rivers, or pursued by Salvadoran military units well into Honduran territory.[20] Salvadoran exiles in Honduras were grouped into two large camps at Mesa Grande and Colomoncagua near the Salvadoran border. Many of the exiles remained in these camps for ten years, until the peace accords of 1990 when most voluntarily returned to El Salvador, even though conditions in that country were still considered dangerous.

As if these two conflicts and the thousands of refugees they produced were not enough, in 1982 the Guatemalan army began what they characterized as a counter-insurgency campaign throughout the mostly Mayan Indigenous communities in western Guatemala. Military units entered four hundred villages over a two-year period, killing all or most residents and looting and burning whatever they could. By some estimates, the soldiers killed as many as two hundred thousand men, women, and children.[21] International organizations and many who knew Guatemala soon characterized these events as genocide. Mayan villagers who managed to escape the killing spent months trying to survive on the run in the hills and forests with little food, health care, or shelter. Some tried to reach Mexico. By 1985, a large camp of Mayan refugees had grown in Mexico not far from the Guatemalan border.[22] A smaller number of Mayans fled to western Honduras.

HONDURAS AS A SAFE HAVEN?

So it happened that for much of the 1980s, Honduras contained three exile populations—at least 40,000 Nicaraguans (the majority Miskito) in the south and southeast, more than 10,000 Salvadorans in the southwest, and hundreds of Guatemalans in the west. Except for the Nicaraguan Miskito Indians, the majority of these exiles were housed in camps administered by the United Nations or the Red Cross, but always under the control of the Honduran government's National Refugee Committee (CONARE) that was headed by an army colonel, a fact that reflected Honduran authorities' tendency to treat refugee populations as potential security threats.[23]

Honduras did not suffer the violence of war or genocide that afflicted its neighbors, but the country and its people were deeply affected by the wars raging around it. The Nicaragua refugee camp near Jacaleapa was not far from training camps and safe havens of the Nicaraguan Contras in Honduras along the Nicaraguan border. UN officials acknowledged that the Contras recruited soldiers from among young Nicaraguans in this refugee camp, a practice that "politicized" the identity of the refugees and complicated the distribution of humanitarian aid intended supposedly for refugees, not for

Contra fighters.[24] The Contra training camps, supplied and supported by the United States, also displaced an estimated ten thousand rural Hondurans from the area, according to workers for the Catholic charity Caritas.[25]

Other events occurred during the 1980s that shaped the future of Honduras to the present. The Reagan Administration began using the country as the major regional base from which to counter the revolutionary movements and insurrections in Nicaragua and El Salvador. The presence of Contra training camps in Honduras with U.S. advisers was part of that policy. The Honduran government also allowed (or was pressured into allowing) the U.S. military to create and expand a significant military presence in the country. The Palmerola (Soto Cano) Honduran military base in the center of the country soon accommodated a sizable U.S. military presence. Since Honduran law forbade the presence of foreign military bases on Honduran soil, Palmerola was "leased" to the United States for temporary use shared with the Honduran military. This "temporary" presence gradually increased over the next decades making it effectively permanent.[26]

Honduran officials agreed to this massive U.S. military presence in part because the apparent success of popular revolution in Nicaragua seemed to pose a threat for the Honduran elite who feared for their own future. Revolutionary Nicaragua was recast as the mortal enemy of both Honduras and the United States. Honduran military leaders, who still exercised control over the civilian government, adopted in full measure the national security doctrine that had characterized the military dictatorships of Argentina, Brazil, and Chile during the 1970s and early 1980s.[27] This doctrine subordinated all individual rights to the survival of the state as the highest good. Almost anything was permissible if it served the survival of the nation. All popular protest and resistance, however peaceful, was regarded as unpatriotic in this "critical" time for Honduras. Military checkpoints appeared throughout the country. Young men were rounded up in public places and forcibly recruited into the Honduran military. Those regarded as potential opponents of the government might expect to be detained and "disappeared" or killed. Labor leaders, peasant leaders, student leaders, human rights advocates, priests, and many others suffered this fate.[28] Military Battalion 316 gained a dubious reputation as a death squad.[29]

In the Honduran national security state of the 1980s, peasant group take-overs of unused land (*tomas de tierra*) were declared illegal and labeled ter-rorism.[30] Because of the government's inability or unwillingness to enforce the 1974 Agrarian Reform Law, such land takeovers had become the major weapon of Honduran peasants who had long been involved in a struggle with powerful landlords and foreign corporations claiming the land of peasant communities. For peasant groups trying to regain their right to access land, agrarian conflict became illegal and dangerous, and it often resulted in death or imprisonment. Honduras is a country where much of the population lives by cultivating the land and where many factors have steadily reduced the area available to peasants and small farmers. Thousands without access to land sought employment on corporate plantations, in the cities, or in other countries. Many who were labeled criminals for engaging in land takeovers or had been the victims of violence from powerful landowners had an incentive to leave Honduras. This situation abated somewhat but did not end with the regional peace accords of 1990 and the consequent winding down of national security measures.[31]

Throughout the 1980s, Honduran authorities and the military kept a wary eye on the thousands of Salvadoran, Guatemalan, and Nicaraguan refugees inside Honduras. The initial kindness and hospitality that many Hondurans showed toward these refugees from neighboring countries was complicated by the increasing problems Hondurans themselves faced. The perception grew in neighboring countries that even Honduras, under an oppressive national security regime, might not be a safe haven. These were some of the turbulent developments that encouraged a massive exodus of Central Americans who began seeking asylum in the United States in the early and mid-1980s.

CENTRAL AMERICAN ASYLUM SEEKERS IN THE 1980S

By 1984, significant numbers of Central Americans were seeking asylum in the United States. U.S. and international law required that the government allow asylum seekers to remain on U.S. soil until they received a hearing before an immigration judge to determine the legitimacy of their claims to asylum.[32] In public perception, Central American asylum seekers were often equated with undocumented immigrants arriving from Mexico, many of whom were not seeking political asylum, and presumably did not have the same right to a hearing as most of the Central Americans. The Reagan Administration was not disposed to declare many of the Central Americans refugees, a designation that probably would have allowed them legally to remain in the United States without fear of deportation. Acknowledging large numbers of refugees fleeing Central America would raise embarrassing questions about what conditions were precipitating such an exodus from a region in which the United States had an admittedly dominant influence and a long history of investment. The Reagan Administration placed the blame for the refugee influx on the turmoil and conflict allegedly caused by Nicaraguan revolutionaries, and by communist influenced insurgency in El Salvador. Apparently, Central Americans could not make revolutions and insurgencies for themselves on their own terms, but they needed the Soviets and others to direct them—a classic assumption of imperial racism by U.S. officials.

As the numbers of asylum seekers grew, their impact was felt in border towns and rural areas in the United States, raising concern that these undocumented arrivals might overwhelm local public facilities and services and put longer-term stress on health, education, law enforcement, and safety. Old historic stereotypes of the dirty, disease-ridden, and criminal immigrant surfaced once again in some areas. The Federal immigration system seemed strained to provide proper legal process for the growing numbers. These concerns gave the Reagan Administration a measure of popular support and a practical rationale for a policy of rapid deportation of many, and large-scale confinement of many others in detention centers located in places such as Port Isabel, Texas, and El Centro, California, where the majority of detainees were Central Americans awaiting asylum hearings. Conditions were often prison-like. Detainees wore orange prison jumpsuits, were not permitted to receive visitors, and were often ignorant of their right to a lawyer and legal representation. Most did not understand English, and so were uncertain of their status and the legal process that would determine their future.[33]

The vulnerable situation of so many Central American arrivals and the inability or unwillingness of authorities to provide decent conditions and proper legal process for them prompted small groups of U.S. citizens to seek ways to offer a more humane response, even if that meant ignoring or violating U.S. immigration laws. Their disposition was reflected by a group of citizens in Vermont (far from the Mexican border) who in 1984 were arrested and charged with trespass for occupying their U.S. Senator's office in order to encourage him to address the foreign policies that were feeding war and violence in Central America. Their argument was a variation of the so-called "necessary defense" doctrine: a minor law (trespassing) yields to a major imperative (prevention of war crimes, saving innocent lives). This defense prevailed, and the jury acquitted them.[34]

During these years, Federal law made knowingly transporting and housing undocumented arrivals a Federal offense. The government gradually increased the penalties for violation as it became clear that increasing numbers of U.S. citizens were willing to break the law in order to offer humanitarian aid and protection to Central American asylum seekers. Groups of citizens and religious congregations in areas along the Mexican border began offering food, clothing, and other services to newly arrived asylum seekers, and they set up safe houses and transported new arrivals to these in private vehicles. Some of these actions violated Federal law, and some citizens were prosecuted and jailed for their involvement in these acts of mercy and solidarity.[35]

THE SANCTUARY MOVEMENT

During the 1980s religious groups and congregations across the United States began to return to the concept of *sanctuary* as a short-term way of assisting Central American asylum seekers. The Sanctuary Movement consisted of a network of religious facilities, institutions, and individuals working together to protect at least some undocumented Central American asylum seekers from deportation, and to humanize the asylum seekers—to promote awareness of who they were and why they fled their countries.

Sanctuary is a practice with very long historical roots.[36] In the ancient Mediterranean world, certain groves of trees, temples, and other places were considered sacred precincts. With a few exceptions, almost anyone—including convicts, debtors, runaway slaves, political opponents of the ruler—who managed to reach such sacred areas could claim and be afforded divine protection against prosecution. The Hebrew Bible contains examples of cities within the kingdom of Israel that performed a similar function. Indigenous and tribal communities in many parts of the world also have practices similar to these examples of sanctuary. In Medieval western Europe, certain churches, abbeys, and shrines became sanctuaries for those pursued by the king or other civil authorities. Entering these places to remove or execute someone was considered blasphemy and an affront to God. In the charged political context of medieval Europe, sanctuary also became a sign of ecclesiastical authority that challenged and sought to limit secular and especially royal political authority.[37]

Examples of citizens providing something resembling sanctuary or asylum occurred in Europe and the United States, in parts of Latin America, and elsewhere throughout the nineteenth and twentieth centuries. In the United States the best known was the underground railroad that, before the Civil War, brought slaves from the South to northern states or to Canada. In Europe during the 1940s especially, individuals, communities, and religious groups harbored Jews and others in danger from Nazi authorities. Examples from Latin America in the 1970s included efforts by groups within military dictatorships in Chile, Argentina, and elsewhere to hide those targeted by the military or to assist their safe exodus abroad. This is how many Chileans managed to escape the Pinochet dictatorship to seek asylum in the United States or Europe in the 1970s. Most of these historical situations involved people weighing the risks to themselves and their families against the moral or religious imperative to assist those in danger or need by providing a safe place.

While the prominence of *sanctuary* waned in the increasingly secularized European world, the idea of *asylum* became gradually more pronounced.[38] Asylum in a modern sense came to designate broadly the practice of accepting

into one's territory and protection individuals or communities who were fleeing from other political (usually national) jurisdictions where their safety was
somehow threatened. In this sense, asylum was a legal, political, and secular
practice that did not always invoke religious sanctions for its justification.
Almost anyone fleeing danger by coming to another country and asking for
protection could be said to be seeking asylum. Gradually in the nineteenth
and especially the twentieth century, the practice of asylum was given a basis
in international laws and agreements and was related to the emerging concept
of the refugee, the one who flees a home country to seek safety and protection
of sorts in another country. International law and a series of covenants, treaties, and conventions began to define what receiving governments could and
could not do to these refugees and asylum seekers. This process was greatly
accelerated in the aftermath of the Second World War that produced millions
of displaced persons and the determination to find instruments of international protection for those persecuted by their own governments and those
fleeing state sponsored terror, as in Nazi Germany. In particular, international
law mandated that governments were legally bound to grant asylum or at
least temporary protection to anyone who asked for it and could demonstrate
a "well-founded fear" of persecution in their home country because of their
race, ethnicity, religion, political views, or membership in a targeted social
group. There are some further requirements, but this became the general rule.
The legal term for this injunction is the French expression, *non refoullement*
(roughly translated as "no return").[39]

During the conflicts of the 1980s, the United States directed unusually large
sums of military aid to El Salvador to assist in defeating the popular insurgency there. U.S. military presence in and aid to the military of Honduras was
also significant. Aid to the Contra fighters trying to topple the Sandinista-led
revolutionary government in Nicaragua was illegal under U.S. law but was
provided through clandestine means, notably the so-called Iran-Contra
Affair.[40] Later, Congress did authorize several allocations to the Contras. As
we shall see (next section) criminal enterprises were also employed to supply
the Contra forces, a practice that had devastating consequences for Central
America long after the end of the Contra war.

The 1990s brought regional peace accords to Central America, an easing
of wartime conditions such as the Honduran security state, and a reduction
in the numbers of Central Americans seeking asylum in the United States.
Yet, with the possible exception of post-revolutionary Nicaragua, the fundamental power structures and political cultures of Central American societies remained almost unchanged. Many of the Salvadorans who had fled to
Honduras during the 1980s returned to El Salvador despite the sense that the
situation there remained unsafe. Small and powerful elites still controlled

the institutions of the state, the judiciary, the security forces. The wide gulf between the elites and the majority urban and rural poor remained. But stable conditions for more foreign investment seemed to improve. The United States maintained its regional military presence in Honduras and began to promote development programs for the region. The purposes of "development" were to facilitate recovery from the wars of the 1980s, stimulate U.S. and other foreign investment in Central America, prevent another Nicaraguan/Sandinista-style popular revolution elsewhere in the region, and transform the image of U.S. hegemony over the region from exploiter of banana republics to senior partner in the "development" of the region. But today, many older Hondurans who experienced the draconian measures of the national security state and U.S. military presence of the 1980s say that conditions in Honduras since the 2009 coup have become as bad as or worse than those of the 1980s.[41]

IMPERIAL CRIMES, COLONIAL PUNISHMENT, 1980–2006

During the 1990s as Honduras was experiencing a neoliberal transformation of its economy and society, the United States was deporting young people from cities such as Los Angeles who had arrived in the United States from Central America as infants or children with their undocumented parents. They grew up in the difficult conditions in which their families were often forced to live, in a culture with urban youth gangs.[42] Deported to El Salvador or Honduras, countries they did not know, some of these young deportees found a means of survival, identity, and protection by recreating the gang culture they had experienced in the United States. By deporting these young people, U.S. authorities were also exporting a version of U.S. gang culture to countries such as Honduras where, in the difficult economic "transitions" of the 1990s, gang culture found the conditions for its expansion. What had been a small and mostly contained gang population earlier now expanded into a major powerful source of violence and concern for Central American youth and their families.

At the same time, two criminal practices that had roots in the regional wars of the 1980s were transformed into major components of the perfect storm of violence that was gathering in Honduras during the 1990s. When the regional peace accords of the 1990s mandated disarming of the Contras and other armed groups, Central American countries found themselves awash in "decommissioned" weapons that were quickly obtained by arms dealers, many of them Honduran military officers who made money selling the weapons. The rise in gun trafficking and availability in Central America fueled the further growth of gangs and contributed to the deadliness of their activities.[43] The narcotics trafficking networks organized to support the Contras in the 1980s began to attract members of drug cartels from both Mexico and Colombia who saw a lucrative opportunity in Central America during the 1990s.[44] The conjunction of large amounts of arms now for sale and a growing narcotics network exacerbated the conditions for violence and corruption in countries like Honduras. Police and official corruption, already widespread in the 1980s, began to grow as security forces and government officials themselves became implicated in criminal enterprises and collusion with drug networks and gangs.

Thus, during the 1990s, policies and practices of the United States contributed directly to creating a more dangerous situation for people in Central America, and especially in the so-called northern triangle countries of Honduras, El Salvador, and Guatemala. The other Central American countries—Nicaragua, Costa Rica, and Panama—also felt the effects, but their economic and political structures and policies helped to lessen the negative impact within their countries, at least keeping violence at lower levels than in the northern triangle. Costa Rica and Panama had not experienced most of the direct impact of the regional wars of the 1980s. Nicaragua had undergone a major revolution that introduced a new power structure, institutions, and an ethos that seemed to protect its people from the worst of these criminal enterprises, even after the Sandinista Front lost power in elections in 1990.

To address the rising level of violence in Honduras, the government of Ricardo Maduro (2001–2005) resorted to a *mano dura* (hard hand) policy against those identified as perpetrators of criminal violence. Mano dura is a zero tolerance for crime policy that allows security forces to arrest and detain individuals for minor crimes and infractions, or even for suspicion that the individual might be connected to one of the major gangs. This policy did little to stop the violence because it did not touch the underlying causes. Rather, it exacerbated them, making clear that force was more important than dealing with the economic and social dislocations of society. Maduro's government could not touch the fundamental causes of the violence because these were the direct outcome of the model of economic development to which Honduras was tied. When the next Honduran president, Manual Zelaya (2005–2009), tried to alter this situation, he was pushed aside by an even greater show of force and an apparent disregard for the law, perpetrated by the country's Congress and its Supreme Court.

HONDURAS: FROM SAFE HAVEN TO
SOURCE OF EMIGRATION

In 2005, Manuel Zelaya was elected president of Honduras.[45] Although he was a member of the economic and political elite, some of Zelaya's policies began to worry the traditional elite that controlled the Honduran state. Washington also became concerned. Zelaya's government imposed a moratorium on mining concessions until their impact on the environment and on rural communities could be assessed, thus directly challenging the extractive economic development model by introducing a concern for its potential victims. He opened relations with the Alianza Bolivariana (ALBA) that had been formed by Venezuelan president Hugo Chavez as an alternative to the U.S.-sponsored Central American Free Trade Agreement, Plan Puebla-Panama, and other U.S. dominated regional economic pacts. Zelaya showed interest in hearing and including the voices of ordinary Hondurans, rural communities, and others as public policy was formed, and opening the political process beyond the traditional control of the elites.[46] He told peasant communities in the Aguán region that he would redress the land conflicts between their peasant cooperatives and three of the most powerful landowning families in the country that had been expanding their lands at the expense of the cooperatives. He proposed a public referendum on the question of whether a process should be initiated to reform the 1982 Constitution in order to permit broader public participation in the political process. For some, this move threatened the monopoly of power and political office held by the country's two major traditional parties, National and Liberal. Some began to consider Zelaya a traitor to his elite social class. The word was spread to ordinary Hondurans that Zelaya was introducing Venezuelan-style socialism into Honduras.[47]

All of these moves raised opposition from vested interests in Honduras and in Washington. On June 28, 2009, the day scheduled for the referendum, units of the military, on orders from the Congress and the Supreme Court, detained Zelaya and sent sent him into exile. The president of Congress, Roberto Micheletti, became de-facto president of the country until regularly scheduled elections were held in November. Micheletti was replaced as head of the Congress by Juan Orlando Hernandez. In November, 2009, Porfirio (Pepe) Lobo became president of Honduras. All three of these prominent politicians—Micheletti, Hernandez, and Lobo—were among the small group of politicians, military generals, and wealthy business leaders that engineered the coup, *golpistas* as many Hondurans called them. At the least, the coup was a statement of power and reassertion of control by the elites to repress any public aspirations for major change in economic development policies and wider democratic participation. It also signaled that Honduras would remain a loyal colony of the United States. After a short period of hesitation (useful to create the fiction of distance, neutrality, or mild disapproval) the U.S. government officially recognized the post-coup government.[48]

The coup ignited immediate and massive popular protests, and many accusations that the removal of Zelaya was unconstitutional—an accusation supported by legal scholars in Honduras and internationally—and that the *golpistas* (those directing the coup) had acted illegally, even criminally.[49] Massive demonstrations continued for months, and the November election that put Porfirio Lobo in the presidency was held in a context of violent repression of the protests. Many Hondurans considered the post-coup governments illegitimate, and began to doubt the possibility of major change. For many, frustration gradually turned to desperation as the growing evils of gangs, narcotics trafficking, official corruption, and displacement of communities due to extractive industries all flourished under the aegis of post-coup governments during the following decade. In the years after the 2009 coup, the country's murder rate reached a peak of 90 per hundred thousand, the highest in the world. Since then, under post-coup governments led by *golpistas,* the official rate declined to about 45 per hundred thousand by 2018. In contrast, the rate in neighboring Nicaragua throughout this period hovered around 7 per hundred thousand.[50]

In the presidential campaign of 2013, National Party candidate (and coup leader) Juan Orlando Hernandez promised to curb crime and violence by increasing military presence in the cities. The government portrayed itself as taking effective measures to combat violence and terrorism and to provide a safe and stable context for foreign and internal business investment. Terrorism became a term to describe different types of peaceful protest and peasant land takeovers, and led to passage of laws that criminalized many of these activities, even as official corruption flourished, gang and drug violence continued almost untouched, and police and military repression increased.

Government officials, members of the country's powerful elite, drug traffickers, gangs, and the security forces seemed increasingly inter-related in what some characterized as a national criminal enterprise protected by a culture of official impunity.[51] Victims of violent crime and those threatened by powerful interests could not depend on police, government, or courts to protect them or to prosecute the perpetrators. But if people engaged in peaceful protest or resistance against this situation, they were criminalized and might suffer violent repression—beatings and tear gas attacks in the streets, police and military police invasions of homes, arrest and torture, disappearance, or even death as security forces fired live bullets into popular demonstrations or individuals were killed by hired assassins.

In 2017, Hernandez announced that he wanted to seek a second term. The Honduran constitution contained a one-term limit, but the Supreme

Constitutional Court decided that the president's rights would be violated if he were not permitted to run again. In effect, the Court declared that the Constitution was unconstitutional—a creative use of the discourse of individual rights.[52] This capped months of massive demonstrations led by the Convergencia Contra el Continuismo (Convergence against Continuance) a grouping of human rights and popular organizations strongly opposed to a second term. Opposition groups and political parties united around candidate Salvador Nasralla to oppose Hernandez in the 2017 election. Major irregularities marred the election process. When the vote count was half completed, Nasralla held what election officials admitted was an unsurmountable lead. But the vote count was suspended and two days later Hernandez was declared winner by a slim margin. For some Hondurans, this seemed to signal the end of any hopes for peaceful change.[53]

THE STORY OF MANOLO

The hundreds of thousands of youth who lived in poor neighborhoods were victims of the turmoil. Many saw emigration as their only option for survival. The number of young people from Honduras seeking asylum at the U.S.-Mexican border increased dramatically during the first and second presidential terms of Hernandez (2013–2021). The stories of those young asylum seekers who managed to gain hearings in U.S. immigration courts mirrored their desperate situation. Manolo (pseudonym) was one such youth.[54] He was from a poor, gang-controlled neighborhood in Tegucigalpa. Manolo fled Honduras when he was nineteen, after running afoul of two gangs, a narcotics syndicate, and the police. When he was twelve, the gang that controlled his neighborhood tried to recruit him to sell drugs. According to his testimony, Manolo tried to resist gang pressure until he was fifteen when the gang began to threaten to harm his grandmother if he did not join them. As a way to save both his grandmother and himself, Manolo agreed to participate in some gang activities such as drug selling, as ordered by the gang leaders. During this time he was often stopped and harassed by the police for his gang affiliation and because, as he said, the police routinely detain teenage males. Manolo knew that many police were themselves corrupt and working in collaboration or in competition with gangs and drug traffickers, and that some police were also gang members for rival gangs. His own gang leaders did not entirely trust him because of his initial resistance. They wondered if he might be a double agent for a rival gang or the police.

Manolo fled to Mexico and lived there for several months, but he returned to Honduras because he was worried about his grandmother. He knew that Honduran gangs frequently took "revenge" on family members of those who seem to challenge or elude their control. Upon return, Manolo was detected and caught by his former gang. They beat him and said they would kill him, but the gang leader offered him one more chance if he would rob the home of the leader of a drug trafficking ring. He agreed, but the robbery failed. The police caught him and beat him savagely. Manolo thought it was because the police were protecting the drug ring or because they were sending a signal to Manolo's gang. To make things worse, Manolo realized that the drug traffickers would now know that it was he who had tried to rob their leader's house. And he knew that as a member of his gang he was a target for a powerful rival gang. With two gangs, a narcotics ring, and the police all threatening him with torture or death, he fled Honduras, reached the U.S. border, and asked for asylum.

After months in an immigration detention center and a prolonged hearing, Manolo was finally granted not outright asylum but rather withholding of removal, based on the likelihood that he would be tortured or killed if he were deported back to Honduras. This allowed him a few years in the United States, after which his case would again be reviewed. Like so many Honduran teens who seek asylum in the United States, he had to admit to having worked with a gang in Honduras. This was a major problem for his asylum application. Like so many others, his defense was that he did so because the alternative was being killed or seeing a family member killed. His work with the gang did not seem to include killing others, but there was concern that he might be recruited by Central American gangs in the United States. Withholding of removal seemed to give him and the court a trial period to prove his good intent.

CARAVANS: MASS EMIGRATION

Manolo's story is similar to that of many other young people in Honduras but also in El Salvador and Guatemala. In the summer of 2014 thousands of young people from these countries arrived at the U.S. southern border. There are many descriptive accounts of the harrowing journeys of Central American migrant children and youth, and the high number of casualties along the way.[55] The dangers of the journey are well-documented. Sonia Nazario's prize-winning book, *Enrique's Journey*, details one young Honduran's path to the U.S. border. In interviews I conducted in Honduras in August 2019, Honduran teens described how their journey to the U.S. border was interrupted when they were detained by Mexican authorities near Veracruz and deported back to Honduras. All had witnessed brutality, some had seen accidental deaths, some had been robbed.

In parts of Mexico, the journey to the United States in search of work or separated family members has long been a part of tradition and local culture. Many folk songs (*corridos*) have been composed, depicting the journey as an epic, sometimes a rite of passage for manhood, often ending on a cynical or melancholy note of failure—the emigrant did not make it to the border or did not thrive in the United States, or was apprehended and treated like a criminal—no streets paved with gold. The context of this narrative was a United States that saw Mexican (and to a lesser extent Central American) immigration as primarily a form of short term or seasonal labor. U.S. immigration policy was an instrument for regulating the flow of this south-of-the-border labor supply.[56] The normal image of immigration during these times was that of single men (occasionally women), coming to the United States to find work. This was formally recognized several times, most of all with the Bracero Program that brought thousands of Mexican men to work in the agricultural fields of the United States during and after the Second World War.[57] This immigration was often intended to be temporary, geared to the ebb and flow of labor needs in the United States. Regulating its flow could be managed in part by tightening or loosening restrictions on immigration and border monitoring. Keeping much of this labor pool in an "illegal" status made for a more docile workforce that knew it would risk deportation if it called attention to itself by protesting labor conditions. Most U.S. labor unions publicly denounced this practice because undocumented workers could be used by employers to undermine attempts at unionization.

This "normal" immigration flow has been disrupted several times in the history of Latin American migration, primarily due to political upheavals such as revolutions (Mexico, Cuba, Nicaragua), repressive military dictatorships (Chile), or civil wars and conflicts (Central America in the 1980s). At these disruptive times, the flow of immigrants to the United States changed in composition and intent. Women, young children, and entire families emigrated, most of them seeking asylum from political oppression or violence in their home countries. Another major change emerged in the nature of Central American migration in particular from at least 1980 onward. Differentiating economic immigration from political asylum seekers became increasingly difficult as land evictions displaced rural communities and violence from gangs, drug trafficking, and political corruption spread throughout the country, preying on a population that was rapidly becoming poorer. These immigrants were no longer simply single men seeking work and able to become part of the ebb and flow of the U.S. workforce. Instead, they were women and children asylum seekers—not considered economic assets to the job pool, but rather economic dependents and liabilities. Restricting this flow became a priority, and draconian measures were instituted, including large numbers of deportations, increasing militarization of the U.S. border, and later, separation of families and an intense campaign of criminalization. There was talk of the "crisis" at the border. Relatively few people seemed to realize that this crisis was only a symptom of the real crisis in the countries to the south. It was a harbinger of what was to come.

Between January and August of 2014, the U.S. Department of Homeland Security reported the arrival of 66,000 children and teenagers from Honduras, Guatemala, and El Salvador at the U.S. southern border seeking asylum. U.S. officials, news media, and many people in the United States seemed surprised by this surge of young immigrants, and had little idea why they had come, why then, and what to do with them.[58] By 2016, almost three hundred people each day—nearly one hundred thousand in a year—were emigrating from Honduras, most of them traveling alone or in small groups of family or close friends.[59]

In March 2018, a group of more than fifteen hundred people—80 percent of them from Honduras but also Guatemala and El Salvador—set out to walk to the U.S. border in what some called a *viacrucis migratorio* (migrant way of the cross).[60] This term carried a wealth of meaning for many Central Americans. Its core meaning referred to the Catholic religious observance of the journey of Jesus carrying the cross to his execution. It was an embedded part of the traditional culture of much of Latin America. As such, it carried a moral weight and immediacy and was also used to characterize, highlight, or call attention to intolerable situations, and it was appropriated as a symbol of popular political protest that invoked divine support. Applying this spiritually and politically charged term to a mass emigration in 2018 highlighted its character as not only one of the suffering of innocent victims and of protest but also as seeking a kind of resurrection.[61] Mass emigrations could increasingly be seen not only as a collective cry for liberation but also as a form of resistance against current conditions. Individual migrants could be ignored. Collectively, people were speaking loudly with their feet. Those who controlled an imperial relationship with Central America could not afford to ignore this.

On October 13, 2018, people began gathering at the bus terminal in San Pedro Sula, second largest city in Honduras; people from the city and surrounding areas, a few dozen, then a few hundred. They set out to travel together to the United States. As word spread through social media and word of mouth, other Hondurans traveled from different areas of the country to join the growing caravan. By the time the group reached the Guatemalan border, it included perhaps three thousand and was still growing. These were young families with children, teenage males, single men and women, elderly people, and some with physical infirmities. Within a few days, a second group was forming around Choluteca and San Lorenzo in the south of Honduras, including hundreds of people who began heading to the Guatemalan border near

Ocotepeque in the southwest. When they heard that President Hernandez had ordered deployment of police and military at that border to stop the migrants from leaving Honduras, the group began to move toward El Salvador on their way to Mexico. But it seemed that El Salvador would also close its borders and refuse the Hondurans passage through that country. Since Honduras, El Salvador, and Guatemala, together with Nicaragua have a mutual agreement to allow free passage of citizens holding only an identity card (the so-called CA-4), these border stoppages were probably violations of that agreement.[62] Within a day, reports came of yet another caravan forming in the northern Honduran Caribbean coastal city of La Ceiba. So quickly did these groups form in different regions of Honduras that keeping track of them and the numbers involved in this mass exodus was difficult. The total number of people who were on the move in these migrating groups in the autumn of 2018 was estimated at upwards of seven thousand.[63]

Local residents along the route of the caravans offered the migrants food, water, shoes, and rides in pickup trucks and vans. Local government officials in towns along the migrants' route allowed them to camp in parks and public spaces. The night before the first group set out from San Pedro Sula, a young Honduran doctor came to their staging place and provided free medical exams for the children in the caravan. These supporters seemed to know quite well why the migrants were fleeing. The young doctor must have been aware that the public medical system in Honduras had virtually collapsed, leaving only private care that was too expensive for the large majority.

The mass migration of thousands, and the likelihood of more behind them, was especially troubling because of its rapidly growing size, its origins in different parts of Honduras, and the desperation and determination of the migrants who steadfastly walked on to confront and move past the deployed police and soldiers of three countries (Honduras, Guatemala, Mexico), around mountains and across rivers to reach a land where they could find survival. In response, U.S. and Honduran authorities issued a barrage of claims to undermine the significance of the caravans. They were full of criminals, human traffickers, even terrorists and ISIS militants. They were an "invasion" that was attacking the United States. They were the pawns of criminal enterprises or of partisan political opponents of Trump and Hernandez. The Democrats and George Soros or the Honduran political opposition had masterminded the caravans. Without a shred of evidence, authorities in both the United States and Honduras proposed all of these fictive explanations.[64] Even to many people with little real knowledge of the situation of the migrants, these suggestions must have seemed ludicrous, such as the image of a crowd of poor, tired, ragged, and desperate people posing a real threat to the sovereignty and safety of the United States—never mind the inscription on the base of the

Statue of Liberty. There seemed to be no recognition that the people of the "banana republics" did not need outsiders to show them what to do.

The caravan people largely ignored the admonitions of U.S. Vice-President Mike Pence and Honduran President Juan Orlando Hernandez that the prudent and safe course for these desperate people would be to remain in Central America instead of exposing themselves and their families to the dangers of the trek northward. In what must have seemed like an expression of wishful thinking rather than a statement of reality, the Chargé d'Affaires at the U.S. Embassy in Tegucigalpa tweeted the fleeing migrants, "The situation in Honduras has improved notably but this will continue only if its citizens stay and invest their extraordinary potential here."[65] Honduran and foreign observers familiar with the situation began to imagine that these political authorities were either thoroughly ignorant or naive, or that their admonitions were a cynical political cover for a situation that the growing caravans threatened to expose: the stark reality of the worsening conditions that forced people to leave Central America. Claims that the authorities were really concerned about the safety of the migrants rang hollow, since such concern seemed sorely lacking while the migrants were still exposed to the violent conditions in their home country.

Several features made these "caravans" different from previous patterns of Central American migration. They were public acts rather than private journeys. They formed with the help of social media and diffuse networks of communication. Participants in caravans have expressed various reasons for traveling in such mass groupings. The large numbers provide protection against the dangers en route, allowing emigrants to avoid paying for guides (coyotes). Large groups could command more attention to the international legal norms and protections for emigrants, such as rights of protection by authorities, asylum processes, and free movement across international borders, especially important in a context in which emigrants have been subjected to torture, kidnapping, disappearance, and execution with little protection from authorities in various countries. Whether the caravans represent expressions of an emerging category of transnational citizenship is also contemplated by some observers.[66] This history raises questions about the dual or chimeric character of Central American immigration and the "unbearable ambiguity of the border."[67] The border is a movable thing. It is at once a physical barrier, a legal prohibition, and a social status. It can run through central or southern Mexico as that country agrees to deport back to Central America immigrants transiting Mexico to reach the United States. The institution of a "third country" policy agreement in 2019 meant that Central American immigrants and asylum seekers could be deported from the United States back to a Central American country that was "safe."[68] Thus, Guatemalans could find themselves deported to Honduras, a country that is arguably more violent and "unsafe" than Guatemala itself—from frying pan into fire. The creativity of those desperate to find ways to keep out immigrants is impressive. It is a perfect cover for economic and political opportunism. But historically it has proven no match for the desperation of people who brave many rivers, political obstacles, and dangers coming to the U.S. border to find survival and a measure of security.

THE POLITICAL ECONOMY OF MIGRATION

The classic analysis of migration used a "push-pull" model. People migrate because they are pushed out of their homeland by violence, political oppression, war, famine; or they are attracted to another land because of a perceived better life there. Both of these forces can be at play at the same time. The perceived "better life" can be simply freedom from violence or the other conditions that push people to leave. Law and custom also differentiate between "economic immigrants" and "asylum seekers." But the actual reasons why people leave their homeland are seldom simple. Central American migrants often say they have left their homeland to find work or to flee domestic violence or a particular gang in Central America that has been threatening them. But these specific reasons are usually products of a much broader and deeper context of forces that have shaped the migrant's life. Honduran migrants today often say they left Honduras to escape the poverty and to find work. But in a country like Honduras, poverty almost always equals vulnerability to violence. When people say they are fleeing poverty, it is almost always a way of saying that they are fleeing the insecurity and vulnerability of poverty and violence. The classic legal, political, and social distinction between economic immigrants and political asylum seekers breaks down. People are seeking basic security and freedom from constant fear and anxiety about survival. There are other reasons why people migrate, and family reunion is often first among these other reasons. Reuniting with family members in another country is a powerful inducement to migrate that may have personal affective and group identity as well as economic implications. In a context of severe poverty and violence (the precarity of life), family reunion may be a powerful symbol or promise of greater security.

This review of Latin American migration to the United States seems to have emphasized political forces such as war, violence, and political oppression. In this sense, the narrative has been describing symptoms or consequences rather than underlying causes. In Central America, violence, war, and political repression are themselves symptoms or consequences of economic forces and policies that are accompanied by political forms, policies, and practices. This political economy is imperial in nature, involving the relationship of

Central America to the United States in particular and, more broadly, to other areas of the "developed" world. It is a relationship that provokes migration and profits economically from it, but also must criminalize it. Criminalization of migrants does not imply rejection of migration but rather its usefulness in an imperial enterprise.

NOTES

1. For example, Deborah Bloom, "In Portland, some Black activists frustrated with white protesters," *Reuters* online (July 31, 2020) https://www.reuters.com/article/us-global-race-protests-portland-activis/in-portland-some-black-activists-frustrated-with-white-protesters-idUSKCN24W2QD.

2. José Luis Rocha, *Expulsados de la globalización"Políticas migratorias y deportados centroamericanos (Managua: Instituto de Historia de Nicaragua y Centroamérica de la Universidad Centroamericana, 2010), 95–96.*

3. Alejandro Portes and Rubén Rumbaut, *Immigrant America: A Portrait*, Fourth Edition (Oakland CA: University of California Press, 2014), 1–2, 46–47; David W Haines, *Immigration Structures and Immigrant Lives: An Introduction to the U.S. Experience* (Lanham MD: Rowman & Littlefield, 2017), 51–54.

4. United States Department of State, Office of the Historian, "Chinese Immigration and the Chinese Exclusion Acts" (n.d.), https://history.state.gov/milestones/1866-1898/chinese-immigration; Portes and Rumbaut, *Immigrant America,* 12, 179; Rocha, *Expulsados,* 63–69.

5. "This is a white, Protestant, and Gentile man's country, and they are going to run it," Ku Klux Klan speaker Charles Mathis speaking in Myrtle Creek, Oregon, 1924, quoted in Lawrence J. Saalfeld, *Forces of Prejudice in Oregon, 1920–1925* (Portland: University of Portland Press, 1984).

6. Tay Wiles, "Malheur occupation, explained," *High Country News,* Jan 4, 2016, https://www.hcn.org/articles/oregon-occupation-at-wildlife-refuge.

7. For a discussion of important aspects of settler societies, see Patrick Wolfe, *Settler Colonialism and the Transformation of Anthropology: The Politics and Poetics of an Ethnographic Event* (London and New York: Cassell, 1999).

8. Stephen M. Walt, "The Myth of American Exceptionalism," *Foreign Policy* online (October 11, 2011), https://foreignpolicy.com/2011/10/11/the-myth-of-american-exceptionalism/; Eric Levitz, "American Exceptionalism Is a Dangerous Myth," *New York Magazine* online (January 2, 2019), https://nymag.com/intelligencer/2019/01/american-exceptionalism-is-a-dangerous-myth.html.

9. Portes and Rumbaut, *Immigrant America*; Haines, *Immigration Structures*; Rocha, *Expulsados.*

10. Francine Uenuma, "During the Mexican-American War, Irish-Americans Fought for Mexico in the 'Saint Patrick's Battalion,'" *Smithsonian Magazine*, March 15, 2019, https://www.smithsonianmag.com/history/mexican-american-war-irish-immigrants-deserted-us-army-fight-against-america-180971713/.

11. Lawrence A. Cardoso, *Mexican Emigration to the United States, 1897–1931* (Tucson: University of Arizona Press, 1980); Juan Gonzalez, *Harvest of Empire: A History of Latinos in America* (New York: Penguin Books, 2011).

12. Haines, *Immigration Structures*, 32.

13. *Haitian Refugee Center v. Civilletti,* 503 E. Supp. 442 (1980).

14. *Washington Post* archives, "Pinochet's Chile," online https://www.washingtonpost.com/wp-srv/inatl/longterm/pinochet/overview.htm; Orlando Letelier, "Chile: Economic 'Freedom' and Political Repression," Transnational Institute Pamphlet Series 1 (Washington DC: TNI, 1976), https://www.tni.org/es/node/5972.

15. Senate Select Committee on Intelligence Activities Staff Report, *Covert Action in Chile, 1963–1973,* declassified ISCAP 2010-09, document 17, "photocopy from Gerald R. Ford Library," https://www.archives.gov/files/declassification/iscap/pdf/2010-009-doc17.pdf.

16. Margaret Power, "The U.S. Movement in Solidarity with Chile in the 1970s," *Latin American Perspectives* 36, no. 6 (November 2009): 46–66; My interviews with Sanctuary Movement co-founder Gary MacEoin, 1990s.

17. Interviews with returnees from Honduras in Esteli and Condega, Nicaragua, 1985.

18. "The Contra War, 1981–1990," *New York Times,* June 29, 1990, 24, online archive, https://www.nytimes.com/1990/06/29/opinion/the-contra-war-1981-1990.html; J. D. Gannon, "Living with the Contra War's Legacy," *Christian Science Monitor,* July 19, 1989, online archives, https://www.csmonitor.com/1989/0719/ocont.html.

19. My field notes, northern Nicaragua, 1986.

20. Patrick Mcdonnell, "Return to Morazan: Despite the Still-Raging Civil War, a Brave Band of Salvadoran Refugees Goes Home," *Los Angeles Times,* July 29, 1990, online archives, https://www.latimes.com/archives/la-xpm-1990-07-29-tm-1517-story.html.

21. There are many accounts of the Mayan genocide in Guatemala. Two of the more authoritative are Ricardo Falla, *Masacres de la selva: Ixcán (1975–1982)* (Guatemala: Editorial Universitaria, 2007) and Shelton Davis and Julie Hodson, *Witnesses to Political Violence in Guatemala* (Boston: Oxfam America, 1982).

22. Faith Warner, "Refuge Repatriation, and Ethnic Revitalization: Q'eqchi' in Maya Tecun, Mexico," in *Selected Papers on Refugee Issues 4*, ed. Ann Rynearson and James Phillips (Washington DC: American Anthropological Association, 1996), 45–72.

23. Alan Riding, "In Honduras Refugee Tangle, UN Takes Charge," *New York Times*, April 27, 1982, https://www.nytimes.com/1982/04/27/world/in-honduras-refugee-tangle-un-takes-charge.html; Yvonne Dilling, *In Search of Refuge* (Scottsdale PA: Herald Press, 1984).

24. Elizabeth Ferris, *The Central American Refugee* (New York: Praeger, 1987), 34. Ferris quoted a U.S. government report of 1987 that reported regarding Nicaraguans in Honduran refugee camps: "The designation of these individuals is controversial and the politicization of refugees is very clear."

25. My interviews and field notes along the Honduran-Nicaraguan border, 1988.

26. Alex Sanchez, "Honduras Becomes U.S. Military Foothold for Central America," *NACLA* (September 4, 2007), https://nacla.org/news/honduras-becomes-us-military-foothold-central-america.

27. José Comblin, *The Church and the National Security State* (Maryknoll NY: Orbis Books, 1979); Genaro Arriagada, "National Security Doctrine in Latin America," *Peace and Change* (January 1980), https://onlinelibrary.wiley.com/doi/abs/10.1111/j.1468-0130.1980.tb00404.x. A note written by translator Howard Richards appears with this article by Arriagada: "One of the most interesting studies of [national security] took the form of a book, published as a private edition not for sale under the protection of the Catholic Church, that being the only way to avoid censorship [by the Pinochet military dictatorship]. Part of that book was also published in the Jesuit magazine *Mensaje,* the only independent monthly that survived the government's rigid control of the press. It is that part which is made available in English here."

28. My field notes, Honduras, 1988.

29. Americas Watch, *Honduras: Without the Will* (Washington DC: Americas Watch, 1989), 8–22; Terri Shaw and Herbert H, Denton, "Honduran Death Squad Alleged," *New York Times*, May 2, 1987, https://www.washingtonpost.com/archive/politics/1987/05/02/honduran-death-squad-alleged/b5ed4183-626d-4183-8b78-592631b2b330/; Gary Cohn and Ginger Thompson, "When a wave of torture and murder staggered a small U.S. ally, truth was a casualty," *Baltimore Sun*, June 11, 1995, https://www.baltimoresun.com/maryland/bal-negroponte1a-story.html.

30. Alison Acker, *Honduras: The Making of a Banana Republic* (Boston: South End Press, 1988), 94.

31. Elías Ruíz, *El Astillero: masacre y justicia* (Tegucigalpa: Editorial Guaymuras, 1992).

32. Gary MacEoin and Nivita Riley, *No Promised Land: American Refugee Policies and the Rule of Law* (Boston: Oxfam America, 1982); Linda Rabben, *Give Refuge to the Stranger: The Past, Present, and Future of Sanctuary* (Walnut Creek CA: Left Coast Press, 2011), 123–126.

33. My visits and interviews at Port Isabel Detention Center in south Texas, and interviews with visitors to El Centro Detention Center in southern California. Gary MacEoin, "The Constitutional and Legal Aspects of the Refugee Crisis," in *Sanctuary: A Resource Guide*, ed. Gary MacEoin (San Francisco: Harper and Row, 1985), 124–125.

34. Gary MacEoin, "A Brief History of the Sanctuary Movement," in *Sanctuary: A Resource Guide*, ed. Gary MacEoin (San Francisco: Harper and Row, 1985), 14; S. B. Coutin, *The Culture of Protest: Religious Activism and the U.S. Sanctuary Movement* (Boulder CO: Westview Press, 2000).

35. MacEoin, "A Brief History of the Sanctuary Movement," 14–29.

36. Rabben, *Give Refuge to the Stranger*.

37. Francis X Murphy, "A Historical View of Sanctuary," in *Sanctuary: A Resource Guide,* 75–84; Rabben, *Give Refuge to the Stranger.*

38. Rabben, *Give Refuge*, 71–98.

39. Rabben's *Give Refuge* is a detailed global history of asylum and asylum law. The Zolberg Institute on Migration and Mobility (New School, New York) maintains a library of studies on asylum issues and law, https://zolberginstitute.org/.

40. Lawrence E. Walsh et al., *Final Report of the independent Counsel for Iran/Contra Matters,* Volume 1 (Washington DC: United States Court of Appeals for the District of Columbia, 1993), https://fas.org/irp/offdocs/walsh/index.html. Congressional hearings on the Iran-Contra dealings were extensively covered on television and in the print media.

41. My interviews in Honduras with human rights activists, September 2013.

42. Marlon Bishop, "Central American Gangs, Made in LA," *Latino USA*, January 22, 2016, https://www.latinousa.org/2016/01/22/central-american-gangs-made-in-la/; Tim Johnson, "U.S. Export: Central American gangs began in Los Angeles," *McClatchy News*, August 5, 2014, https://www.mcclatchydc.com/news/nation-world/world/article24771469.html.

43. Julieta Castellanos, *Honduras: Armamentismo y violencia* (Tegucigalpa: Fundación Arias para la Paz y el Progreso Humano, 2000); Lora Lumpe, "The US Arms Central America—Past and Present," Norwegian Initiative on Small Arms Trade, May, 1999, http://nisat.prio.org/Publications/The-US-Arms-Central-AmericaPast-and-Present/.

44. National Security Archive, *The Contras, Cocaine, and Covert Operations*, National Security Archive Electronic Briefing Book 2 (Washington DC: George Washington University, n.d.), https://nsarchive2.gwu.edu//NSAEBB/NSAEBB2/index.html; Gary Webb, *Dark Alliance: The CIA, the Contras, and the Crack Cocaine Explosion* (New York: Seven Stories Press, 1998).

45. There are many narratives of Zelaya's policies and the 2009 coup. The report of the Inter-American Commission on Human Rights, *Honduras: Human Rights and the Coup D'etat* (Washington DC: Inter-American Commission on Human Rights, 2009: 13–22), provides one of the more detailed accounts. For a more personal narrative, see Dana Frank, *The Long Honduran Night: Resistance, Terror, and the United States in the Aftermath of the Coup* (Chicago IL: Haymarket Books, 2018).

46. Andres Leon, "Rebellion under the Palm Trees: Memory, Agrarian Reform, and Labor in the Aguán, Honduras" (PhD diss., Graduate Center, City University of New York, 2015), 5–8.

47. News media focused on the connection between Zelaya and Hugo Chavez of Venezuela, for example, Gustavo Palencia and Anahi Rama, "Left behind by the U.S., Honduras turns to Chavez," Reuters, August 26, 2008. I must credit fieldwork by Jordan Levy in Honduras during the 2009 coup; Levy discovered widespread popular belief that the coup against Zelaya was justified because Zelaya wanted to impose Venezuelan-style socialism in Honduras.

48. Nina Lakhani, "Did Hilary Clinton stand by as Honduras coup ushered in an era of violence?" *The Guardian*, August 31, 2016, https://www.theguardian.com/world/2016/aug/31/hillary-clinton-honduras-violence-manuel-zelaya-berta-caceres.

49. Doug Cassel, "Coup d'Etat in Constitutional Clothing?— Revision," *American Society of International Law* 13, no. 9

(October 15, 2009), https://www.asil.org/insights/volume/13/issue/9/honduras-coup-d%E2%80%99etat-constitutional-clothing-revision.

50. U.S. Department of State Overseas Security Advisory Council, "Honduras 2020: Crime and Safety Report," March 31, 2020, https://www.osac.gov/Country/Honduras/Content/Detail/Report/14441101-11fd-487c-9d15-18553e50609c. The Violence Observatory of the National Autonomous University of Honduras (UNAH) keeps ongoing records of rates and incidents of violence in the country. InSight Crime also reports regularly on violent crime in Honduras, https://insightcrime.org/.

51. Sarah Chayes, *When Corruption Is the Operating System: The Case of Honduras* (Washington DC: Carnegie Endowment for International Peace, 2017).

52. Sarah Kinosian, "Call for Fresh Honduras Election after President Juan Orlando Hernandez Wins," *The Guardian,* December 18, 2017; "Honduran President Declared Winner, but O.A.S. Calls for New Election," *New York Times,* December 17, 2017, https://www.nytimes.com/2017/12/17/world/americas/honduran-presidential-election.html.

53. "Honduran President Declared Winner, but O.A.S. Calls for New Election," *New York Times,* December 17, 2017, https://www.nytimes.com/2017/12/17/world/americas/honduran-presidential-election.html.

54. Adapted from the declaration of an asylum seeker in the United States.

55. Amnesty International, "Key facts about the migrant and refugee caravans making their way to the USA," November 16, 2018, https://www.amnesty.org/en/latest/news/2018/11/key-facts-about-the-migrant-and-refugee-caravans-making-their-way-to-the-usa/; Priscilla Alvarez, "What happened to the migrant caravans?" *CNN,* March 4, 2019, https://www.cnn.com/2019/03/04/politics/migrant-caravans-trump-immigration/index.html. For a different perspective see, José Luis Rocha, "La exitosa desobediencia civil de ligrantes indocumentados, informales, y cuentapropistas," *Envío Honduras*, 17, no. 59 (September, 2019): 42–51. There was considerable coverage of the caravans in the news media.

56. Portes and Rumbaut's *Immigrant America* offers extended discussions of the historical relationship between immigration and U.S. labor supply.

57. Portes and Rumbaut, *Immigrant America*, 21–23 and elsewhere.

58. Diana Villers Negroponte, "The Surge in Unaccompanied Children from Central America: A Humanitarian Crisis at Our Border," Brookings Institution, July 2, 2014, https://www.brookings.edu/blog/up-front/2014/07/02/the-surge-in-unaccompanied-children-from-central-america-a-humanitarian-crisis-at-our-border/; Joseph E. Langlois, "The 2104 Humanitarian Crisis at the Border: A Review of the Government's Response to Unaccompanied Minors One Year Later, before the Senate Committee on Homeland Security," U.S. Citizenship and Immigration Service, July 16, 2015, https://www.uscis.gov/archive/the-2014-humanitarian-crisis-at-our-border-a-review-of-the-governments-response-to-unaccompanied.

59. *La Prensa*, "Iniciativa de gestion de la información en el Triángulo Norte," August 20, 2018, 4.

60. For example, *El Pais* (Mexico): "Viacrucis migrante llama a las puertas de Estados Unidos," April 3, 2018, https://elpais.com/elpais/2018/04/03/album/1522754657_996005.html.

61. During the Contra War of the 1980s, Nicaraguans organized a march or walk (*caminata*) from the Honduran border to the Nicaraguan capital, Managua—a distance of more than 200 kilometers—during the Christian season of Lent, the time of repentance, change, and preparation for observing the death and resurrection of Jesus at Easter. This *viacrucis* was seen as a way of giving meaning to the suffering of Nicaraguans during the Contra War, but also of demanding peace and an end to the war and the intervention of the United States.

62. International Organization for Migration (IOM), "Northern Triangle of Central America Regional Integration," n.d., https://triangulonorteca.iom.int/regional-integration.

63. For Example, *BBC News*, "Migrant Caravan: What Is It and Why Does It Matter?" November 26, 2018, https://www.pewresearch.org/hispanic/wp-content/uploads/sites/5/2017/12/Pew-Research-Center_Central_American-migration-to-U.S._12.7.17.pdf.

64. Julia Ainsley and Daniella Silva, "Five Myths about the Honduran Caravan Debunked," *NBC News*, October 22, 2018, https://www.nbcnews.com/news/latino/five-myths-about-honduran-caravan-debunked-n922806.

65. Patrick Goodenough, "US Diplomat in Honduras Tells 'Caravan' Migrants to Return Home, But Still They Come," *CNS News,* October 18, 2018, https://www.cnsnews.com/news/article/patrick-goodenough/us-diplomat-honduras-tells-caravan-migrants-return-home-still-they.

66. Raúl Diego Rivera Hernández, "Making Absence Visible: The Caravan of Central American Mothers in Search of Disappeared Migrants," trans. Mariana Ortega Breña, *Latin American Perspectives* 44, no. 5 (September, 2017): 108–126.

67. Victor M. Ortiz, "The Unbearable Ambiguity of the Border," *Social Justice* 28, no. 2 (Summer, 2001): 96–112.

68. For the text of the agreement see, American Immigration Lawyers Association, "U.S. and Guatemala Enter into Agreement Designating Guatemala as a 'Safe Third Country,'" July 26, 2019, https://www.aila.org/infonet/us-guatemala-agreement-safe-third-country.

Chapter 3

Imperialism, Development, and Honduras

In a mountainous village in Honduras in 2016, the people, mostly small farmers, had been trying for months to keep an international corporation from beginning a mining operation in the area. They feared it would contaminate their land and water, making farming impossible, and cause health issues. They knew what had happened in other communities in Honduras when mining operations invaded the land. Elders in the community said that the people had farmed the land for generations and that the land was what gave them life and identity. One elderly farmer pointed to a large mango tree on a ridge above the village. "That tree is our symbol of hope. It is rooted there above us guarding our land. As long as it is there, we are here." One morning, the community awoke to find mining company bulldozers plowing up the land. The mango tree was gone.[1] The bulldozers uprooted the livelihood, identity, pride, and spirit of the community without regard for any of it.

In 1967, Pope Paul VI published his long letter, *Populorum Progressio* (roughly, The Progress/Advancement of Peoples), in which he said that "development is the new name for peace." But for many people, development became the new name for empire. Development still portrays itself as the opposite of empire, a benevolent effort by the wealthier to help the poorer countries. In many cases, this is true. But development discourse is also the discourse of empire deniers who direct the exploitation of resources and environments in the lands of other people and call this foreign investment, foreign aid, or progress.[2] The words *empire* and *imperial* are shunned in polite company or are pronounced by scholarly critics, usually far from the halls of power.

This chapter describes how development became the new name for empire. It explores the close, integral relationship between empire and development. The primary purpose of modern European empires and imperial projects was to accumulate wealth that became the basis of the capital that financed the expansion of industrial development in Europe. The primary purpose of modern development—at least as it is always advertised and sold—is also to generate capital wealth for both the investor country and the country that is the site of investment and "development." This relationship is crucial to our understanding of Honduras today and much of Latin America, because Honduras exists in a colonial relationship to the United States. This relationship is expressed primarily in terms of economic development, investment, and the stated purpose of making capital for both the United States and Honduras. It is accompanied by the militarization of Honduran society.

Development is promoted as a way to generate money for Honduras through profits from the sale of the country's natural resources and the economic improvement of local communities. Both of these purposes are sources of conflict in Honduran society. The sale of the country's natural resources is done in a way that only a small elite benefit in Honduras while many accuse the few of selling out the country (*vendepatria*). The improvement of local community is understood in two diverse ways: (1) bringing or forcing local communities into dependency upon the government and the international capitalist economy or (2) helping local communities to maintain a relatively self-reliant way of life. The first is the extension of dependency and control over local communities; it provides the basis for further resource extraction from local people, and sometimes for capturing their labor, as well. The second—strengthening self-reliance—is a challenge to this control because it allows people alternatives to complete dependency upon global capitalism and those who control it. The ways in which these two understandings of development are argued, re-defined, mingled, imposed, and resisted generates much conflict in Honduras and other Latin American societies.

At times, it is easy to lose sight of the imperial nature of development as it is practiced in Honduras, precisely because it assumes the guise of benevolent development supposedly for the good of the country. Modern imperial formations want us to forget that they are imperial and exploitative, and to believe instead that they are developmental and helpful. But our forgetfulness can be deadly for so many people and communities. Remembering requires watchfulness, questioning, and critique. To understand how development became a major instrument of U.S. imperial reach in Honduras, it is useful to examine briefly how development became the new name for empire.

(UNDER)DEVELOPMENT AND THE
WHITE MAN'S BURDEN

The Doctrine of Discovery promulgated by Pope Alexander V in 1493 declared that a Christian monarchy (in that case, Spanish) that planted its flag and the cross in a non-Christian place could claim it and its people as subject, since the highest good was to Christianize the "pagans" of the world.[3] This provided the theological rationale for the "conquest" of Latin America. The doctrine was then secularized and appeared as the idea that white, "civilized" Christian nations could declare their dominion over non-white, less "civilized" peoples. The "white man's burden" that rationalized or even demanded European colonization of Africa was a later version. The Monroe Doctrine also reflects the mentality of the Doctrine of Discovery. This Christian nationalism became an integral component of American "exceptionalism," racism, nativism, and imperial aspirations. Its legacy also infused some of the white nationalist and white supremacist movements in the United States in the past and into the present.[4]

The United States started its national life as a settler society, pushing Indigenous people aside or eliminating them in order to occupy the land. The new nation soon entered a long phase of expansionism, spreading its control over areas and peoples across the continent, an expansionism that gradually transformed it from a settler society into an imperial power intervening in and assuming hegemony over foreign countries in Central America and elsewhere.[5] This intervention and hegemony have created many waves of immigration.[6] We must examine imperialism inasmuch as the imperial nature of the U.S. relationship to Honduras and other Central American countries—based on the one-sided extraction of wealth and resources with studied disregard of the consequences for the people of those countries—creates the conditions that impel people to leave Central America. Imperial relationships also shape the ways in which colonized people come to regard the centers of empire as better places to be, or as bearing some responsibility to the victims of empire, and thus as preferred destinations of emigration.

Imperial reach was extolled for the wealth and national pride that holding colonies could impart, even after the cost of maintaining an empire began to outweigh the profit. Internal debates arose between those who were determined to continue to maintain imperial influence and those who pointed out the mounting negative effects on the imperial power itself. Such a debate in the British parliament and society contributed to the abolition of slavery in the British empire in the early 1800s, and finally to the independence of former British colonies in the mid-twentieth century.[7] In the United States, President Eisenhower, leader of a growing imperial power, pointed out starkly how militarism undermined social programs and human development in the United States itself. At the same time, he presided over U.S. interventions in Guatemala, Guyana, and elsewhere in the hemisphere. But the cost of militarism was not simply economic. Too much use of military violence also damaged the image of benevolence toward colonized peoples that the colonizing power wanted to maintain for its own citizens and world opinion.

The other major argument for empire was that it was good for the subjects, the colonized peoples. In Latin America, the presence and influence of the United States was said to be lifting countries and people out of poverty and helping them by investing in and controlling their development. This was a U.S.-Latin American version of the "white man's burden," the ideology that European countries had used to rationalize European colonial regimes in Africa and parts of Asia.[8] This benevolent face became more useful as the open embrace of imperial aspirations became more difficult to defend with the collapse of the classic European empires after World War II. The era of decolonization and formal political independence that followed the war in much of Africa, Asia, and the Caribbean further encouraged a rising critique of old style colonialism and its evils. The Cold War encouraged the portrayal of the Soviet Union as an imperial power bent on controlling the world, and the West, led by the United States, as the free and democratic alternative and counterforce to such imperial aspirations. The realization of Western imperialism would have been embarrassing and undermining in this context. Instead, new forms of discourse were proposed that maintained the need to intervene in, direct, and extract the wealth of countries, but under the benevolent rubric of "development." By the early 1960s, planners, politicians, some academics, and others in the "developed" countries of Western Europe and the United States described much of the rest of the world as poor, underdeveloped and in need of "modernization."[9]

Caribbean and African critics of the old colonialism also employed the description of their countries as underdeveloped to emphasize the damage done by many years of Western imperial intervention, but many of these critics were also skeptical of the new agenda of Western development as the cure, seeing it as colonialism in disguise, or neocolonialism.[10] After India became independent of British imperial rule in 1947, a serious debate about the future of the country ensued between modernizers (such as Prime Minister Nehru) who embraced much of the developmental discourse of Western and Soviet economists, and traditionalists (such as Mohandas Gandhi) who preferred a more inward and culturally rooted future based in local village life—sometimes called villageism.[11] In Tanzania—the newly formed union of two former European colonies in East Africa—President Julius Nyerere proposed a similar path of villageism based on the area's tribal culture of local cooperation.[12] He warned that this path would not lead to rapid increases in the country's gross national product but it would keep Tanzania freer from dependency on foreign "development" and exploitation, and would promote national identity and well-being rooted in long traditional ways of life now free from imperial control. Nyerere called his path to the future *ujamaa*—a concept hard to translate adequately in English, with elements of extended family, cooperative economics, local community self-reliance, identity, and citizenship based on participation in local community. These ideas of villageism and *ujamaa* represented a challenge to a concept of development that seemed to mean a dependent role in the global economy. Some elements of this thinking were also incorporated into so-called third way models of post-colonial national development, such as the democratic socialism of Michael Manley's government in Jamaica in the 1970s.[13] The double dilemma for third way models was how to preserve a measure of local control while functioning in a global economy dominated by imperial forms of dependency; and how to keep a population satisfied without the temptations of rapid economic growth.

In the new discourse of development, most of the "underdeveloped world" was considered different because of its poverty, lack of social capital, and need. The people were cast as different and wanting in many ways that it was the duty of the developed world to address, but never to the point of equalizing the situation. The myth of "racial differences" could be employed as an often unspoken assumption of inherent inferiority for the peoples of Central America. The underdeveloped world had to be seen as different in its backward neediness, for had it been like the wealthier "developed" world there would have been no need for intervention in the form of development. Crucially, these characterizations and definitions of reality did not arise from the people but from the planners and politicians of the "developed" world.[14] Global financial institutions such as the International Monetary Fund and the World Bank that had been initiated and were controlled by the United States and its allies and a rapidly growing network of foreign aid and non-governmental organizations (NGOs) that emerged in the 1950s and 1960s formed the structures through which development programs were to be implemented in Africa, Asia, and Latin America.

Even in its conception, the discourse of development was largely the result not of a consultative process but rather of an externally imposed version of reality. The problem was to make the people who were the objects of development believe that they needed it and only it.

"Hegemony is, after all, fundamentally about the misrepresentation of objective interests."[15] In practice, development achieved this through projects that re-made the institutions of society in ways that would present and highlight the advantages of development and dependency upon the state and upon foreign assistance, or would eliminate self-reliance in ways that made clear that there was no alternative to dependency. The apparent prosperity and consumerism of the developed countries were presented to people and governments of the world as the goal to be achieved, an elementary fetish. The cure for people's poverty would be development that would build schools, infrastructure, modern institutions of governance, and the requisites for foreign investment. The "underdeveloped" world needed saving from the imperial debris left by centuries of imperial domination, so more imperial reach in the form of development was confidently prescribed for its salvation.

Development was about power and subjective identity tied to economic forces that were beyond the control of most local people and communities, and even of national governments, and were therefore forces for producing dependency. This very political purpose, however, had to be hidden so as to obscure the loss of political power it entailed for the people and governments of the colonized. As one critic of development put it, "the purpose of development strategies is not so much to develop but to produce the 'anti-politics' illusion."[16] Development was depicted as humanitarian and economic, not political. As it evolved over decades, developmentalism contained contradictions that provoked resistance and alternative visions, especially among marginalized peoples. Despite these, it proved quite difficult to preserve or construct alternative ways of living that escaped the dominant paradigm and power of developmentalism.

The worldview imposed by development admitted no legitimate alternatives or challengers. It was used to shape the aspirations of national leaders and peasant farmers alike, imposing a univision of a reality to be desired. In this reality, the alternative and subaltern voices of the world's Indigenous and marginal peoples provided no viable wisdom for human development. As James Scott wrote, "the function of a system of domination is to accomplish precisely this: to define what is realistic and what is not realistic and to drive certain goals and aspirations into the realm of the impossible. . .the realm of idle dreams and wishful thinking."[17] If nothing else worked, however, the religion of development could be spread with the aid of the sword.

U.S. IMPERIAL REACH: NICARAGUA AND HONDURAS

The Central American countries gained independence from Spain in the early 1820s. In the 1850s, as the slavery question divided the United States, expansionists and pro-slavery interests turned their gaze to Nicaragua and Honduras. Pro-slavery groups and emerging capitalist interests in the United States saw control of these countries, along with Cuba, as areas for extending slavery and expanding resource extraction. In the 1850s, a U.S. citizen named William Walker gathered a band of Californians and intervened in Nicaragua's perennial political conflict, gaining brief control over areas of the country. By decree, English replaced Spanish as the official language, Protestantism replaced Catholicism as the accepted religion, and slavery became legal—all contrary to Nicaraguan history and cultural values. A popular uprising evicted Walker from Nicaragua, but he was persistent. In 1860, he and his men landed on the Caribbean coast of Honduras, intent on imposing their control over that country. British soldiers (representatives of another global empire contending for influence in Central America) met them and handed them over to Honduran authorities who promptly shot them.[18] The more level-headed business and political leaders in the United States saw the "Walker Affair" as a threat to their own plans for economic investment and extractive industry in countries like Honduras and Nicaragua. Southern Nicaragua was an ideal location for a canal connecting Atlantic and Pacific. These business leaders and investors, along with the U.S. government, provided no effective support for Walker's actions. There were right and wrong ways to expand control over other countries. Done too brazenly, it was worse than useless.

This affair revealed differences of thinking in the methods but not the ultimate vision. Crudely put, military force or economic control were the methods of expansionism, but the exact mix of the two in any given country or context was always an important consideration in United States relations to Latin America. In the early 1900s, as U.S.-based banana companies were expanding their plantations and their economic and political influence over Central America, these influences were backed by the threat or promise of military might or "gunboat diplomacy." From 1900 to 1954, the United States staged several dozen military interventions in Central America and the Caribbean, always to protect or expand economic investment and influence.[19] In the 1920s, these interventions or "foreign occupations" incited a popular resistance in Nicaragua, led by Augusto Cesar Sandino and his "army of free men." They engaged in a guerrilla-style warfare with U.S. Marines in the northern Segovia mountains from 1927 until the Marines withdrew from Nicaragua in 1934, as a result of the Good Neighbor policy of the new Franklin Roosevelt Administration.

Being a "good neighbor" meant supporting economic development and refraining from direct military intervention in Latin American affairs. Instead, the dirty work of keeping control was relegated to local proxies with the support of the United States. By the 1940s, these proxies were mostly brutal dictators and their armies or *guardias*. The most brutal and long lasting were Jorge Ubico in Guatemala, Tiburcio Carías Andino in Honduras, Rafael Trujillo in the Dominican Republic, and the most long lasting of all, the Somoza family in Nicaragua that was finally overthrown by a popular revolution in 1979. But where pliant dictators were unavailable or national leaders were the problem, internal opposition could be fomented and supported to act as a proxy force against the problem leader or government. This was tested in the 1954 overthrow of the Guatemalan government of Jacobo Arbenz in which the CIA trained dissident Guatemalans to stage a revolt.[20] It was tested again in the 1964 ouster of Prime Minister Cheddi Jagan in Guyana, where racial division between the country's Black and East Indian populations was fomented into political violence, aided by the deceptively named American Institute of Free Labor Development (AIFLD) and U.S. labor leaders who accused Jagan of intending to impose a marxist regime over Guyana.[21] These strategies for control—economic influence, violence by proxy (foreign militaries), fomenting internal popular unrest, and the use of front groups (like AIFLD) funded and directed by U.S. agencies—were all used successfully in the 1973 Chilean military overthrow of the Allende government.[22] In the 1980s, they became the core of the policy and practice for the Reagan Administration's active support for the Nicaraguan Contras in attempting to overthrow the revolutionary Sandinista-led Nicaraguan government. Proxy warfare and promoting internal conflict along with, and in defense of extractive development became a staple of United States expansionism in Latin America. It has included some creative twists, such as the use of criminal gangs and drug trafficking rings to provide some of the violence and the money to support these operations.[23]

Honduras became a pliant colony of the United States through the application of U.S. military and economic influence starting more than a century ago. In Honduras, one could see the components of a triple strategy that included: (1) rapacious extractive development policies; (2) the use of the Honduran military (tied to foreign "security aid") and criminal and drug gangs to provide the necessary violence and its useful by-products, fear and precarity to control the population; and (3) the creation of dependency. Honduras depended upon the United States for security aid, investment, and especially for its political and diplomatic seal of approval. The United States depended upon the Honduran government and military to maintain and protect extractive development and the control of internal popular opposition. This chain of dependency rested ultimately upon a pliant or acquiescent population in both countries.[24] In Honduras, extractive development, proxy militarized and criminal violence, and relations of dependency became the trifecta of U.S. imperial control. All of this created the very big problem of mass emigration that became both a necessary part of and a threat to the imperial relationship of Honduras to the United States.

ITERATIONS OF DEVELOPMENT IN HONDURAS

Since the 1950s, the theory and practice of development has evolved through several iterations to respond to changing global conditions. The most important of these iterations included modernization, trilateralism, neoliberalism, and neoextractivism. Honduras was subjected to all of these in turn.

Stages of Growth and Modernization (1955–1970)

One of the earlier forms of development theory preached that countries go through stages of economic growth from producers of raw materials—agricultural products, metals and minerals, and forms of energy—to industrialization, and that this should be the desired end for all countries.[25] To achieve this, countries must modernize their infrastructures and transform or eliminate traditional economic, political, and social patterns that reduced a country's ability to industrialize and compete in the world market. This would require foreign aid and investment. In the early 1960s, the Kennedy Administration introduced the Alliance for Progress, precisely to provide aid and investment that was aimed at building the infrastructure and services that could support private investment in development projects in Latin American countries. Honduras received a small portion of this aid. Along with receiving large loans to undertake infrastructure projects, Latin American governments were pressured to introduce policies that would effectively convert their large peasant and Indigenous populations from self-reliant small farmers to landless workers—a process that some critics and analysts called proletarianization.[26] Such policies were accompanied by an ideology that characterized peasant and Indigenous communities as backward hindrances to progress and modernization. Latin Americans that had accepted modernization ideology often referred to the "Indian problem," what to do with the Indigenous population.[27] This classist and racialized mentality outlived the modernization phase of development and remained very much in play throughout the entire evolution of development to the present.

In Honduras before the early 1900s, a limited mining industry mostly in the south and the beginnings of a banana/fruit exporting industry in the north relied on a rudimentary infrastructure that barely connected south to north. Haciendas were a characteristic of rural life in many places, producing very little on large areas of land. Indigenous and other local communities often lived relatively isolated from most larger national, much less international, control. By the 1950s, the foreign owned banana empire in northern Honduras had transformed a significant portion of the country's land and labor into a modernizing export industry. Foreign fruit companies built limited rail lines for the sole purpose of carting the fruit from their plantations to their own seaside docks for shipping. Honduran governments—controlled by an expanding national elite that now included those who had made their fortunes not on the land but in commerce and international trade—began to embrace the concept of "development" and modernization. Advancing national development and transforming older patterns involved a certain degree of force, in large part because modernization and the export fruit industry generated a large pool of workers whose vision moved beyond local farming life and began to demand rights and a voice in national affairs. A strong Honduran labor movement arose and gained a voice by the 1950s.

A modernizing civilian government (1957–1963) was followed by military rule that tried to balance the advancement of modernization and reform with the demands of those who saw reform as a threat. Military repression of labor and peasant activism was followed by a brief period of "reform" highlighted by passage of the Agrarian Reform Law of 1974 under a military government. By 1975, military repression of labor, peasant, Indigenous, student, and other popular activism had returned. Modernization had brought Honduras to a first "stage of growth" by expanding the power and control of foreign investment and the idea that the export economy was a path to progress and capital accumulation for the nation. It can be argued that Honduras has never advanced beyond that stage as a supplier of raw materials, in large part because those who controlled much of the global economy and polity decided that it would be better for them if countries like Honduras remained suppliers of raw materials. Honduras and other countries incurred debts trying to modernize, and their indebtedness to the financial institutions controlled by capitalist developed countries could not be erased as long as the money they gained through sale of their raw materials never equaled the prices they had to pay for the loans and finished products they had to buy from the "developed" countries. Development theory and practice was reshaped to ensure this dependency. The new face of development was called trilateralism.

Trilateralism (1970–1980)

In the late 1960s and throughout the 1970s, trilateralism preached as doctrine that the road to national prosperity for countries like Honduras did not really lie in trying to reach a stage of industrialization, but rather in digging down more deeply into the role of supplier of raw materials. Each country should concentrate on increasing the export of the materials they had in abundance, their "niche" in the global market. For Honduras, this clearly meant minerals and metals, lumber, and agricultural products, especially tropical fruits and coffee. Some also dreamed of making Honduras a tourist destination. Trilaterialism was the product of development gurus, academics, business leaders, and government politicians in "developed" countries, some of whom formed an international Trilateral Commission to shape policy and oversee management of the global economy. It was trilateral because it posited that the United States, Western Europe, and Japan formed the three partners that would manage the global economy and polity. The premise was not much different from that of classic imperialism. It was the right and duty of these countries to manage, control, and direct the economies and polities of the "developing" world, countries like Honduras:

To put it simply, trilateralism was saying: (1) the people, governments, and economies of all nations must serve the needs of multinational banks and corporations; (2) control over economic resources spells power in modern politics (good citizens are supposed to believe that political equality exists in western democracies, whatever the degree of economic inequality; and (3) the leaders of capitalist democracies—systems where economic control and profit, and thus political power, rest with the few—must resist movement toward a truly popular democracy. In short, trilateralism [was] the attempt by ruling elites to manage both dependence and democracy, at home and abroad.

Honduras in the 1970s was a country where popular demands for reform were met with increasing repression under the military governments that ruled throughout the decade. The military grew into its role in suppressing "movement toward truly popular democracy" in Honduras on behalf of the "leaders of capitalist democracies." The military also realized that "control over economic resources spells power in modern politics." The 1970s was the pivotal decade in which workers and peasants organized and attained a political voice, and the Honduran military emerged as a major economic and political player in Honduras, able to make and break civilian governments. Despite the rising voice and power of labor and peasant movements, military governments and the elites they served ensured that Honduras remained firmly a servant of foreign investment and a "developmentalist state" (*estado desarrollista*).[28]

The trilateral partners controlled the international financial institutions, including the International Monetary Fund, the World Bank, and other institutions. They were also the primary importers of materials from countries like Honduras. In this position, with the aid of repressive militaries, the trilateralists could set the prices of raw materials on the world market, keeping them lower than what the proponents of a New International Economic Order were demanding in the 1970s. By the early 1980s, Honduras was experiencing a climbing foreign debt, an economic crisis, and a weak internal economy, thanks in part to the world that trilateralism had shaped.

Neoliberalism (1980–2009)

In the last decades of the twentieth century, the centers of economic power and capital accumulation that financed and promoted developmentalism abroad experienced a "crisis" of over-accumulation of capital, stagnation of markets, and declining profitability. The economic problem included the inability of development per se to expand purchasing power among the poor fast enough (if at all) to keep up with the accumulation of capital that needed to find sources for investment. The result was both a trade deficit—poor countries and their poor people could not buy the products of the "advanced countries"—and a loss of jobs and manufacturing in the wealthy countries that sold finished products. Stagnation of markets and profits were consequences. Critics of development also described development's human "crisis."[29] The problem affected life in the United States as an imperial center, as well as its ability to justify development in areas like Central America. Critics of U.S. imperial reach pointed out the far-reaching effects of this within the United States itself: "The true cost [of empire] to the United States should be measured in terms of crime statistics, ruined inner-cities, and drug addiction, as well as trade deficits."[30]

To meet this "crisis of capitalism," political and financial leaders of the wealthy countries produced a set of economic policy recommendations for managing the economic development of the "developing" countries. This agreement became known as the Washington Consensus.[31] It produced a revised form of development theory that returned in some ways to the economic liberalism of earlier centuries. The new development theory became known as neoliberalism. It has been interpreted and characterized in different ways by its proponents and its critics.[32] One example:

> Neoliberalism is in the first instance a theory of political economic practices [i.e., a political economy] that proposes that human well-being is best advanced by liberating individual entrepreneurial freedoms and skills within an institutional framework characterized by strong private property rights, free markets, and free trade.[33]

Neoliberalism re-defines the role of government in relation to individuals and private enterprise in the development of a country. In this model, the primary role of the government is to promote freedom for investment and private development initiatives in various ways, primarily by removing any restrictions to this freedom. Governments must reduce or eliminate taxes and regulations on private enterprise, protect enterprise from legal challenges, eliminate or restrict popular or local resistance, reduce or eliminate government ownership and expenditure for public social services, and transfer public services, utilities, banks, toll highways, public health and education to private companies—privatization.

Neoliberalism valued social, cultural, and environmental life and resources in terms of their market value in the global economy; the transformation of human and environmental capital into economic-finance capital. The mango tree that symbolized the resilience of a rural community was simply an obstacle to a new mining project. Land lost its value as a place of identity where generations toiled and thrived, and became simply a commodity to be bought and sold, freed up for investment and exploitation by those who could afford to buy it. Neoliberalism promoted the freedom of (some) individuals and corporations to engage in economic enterprise at almost any human cost. It also "freed" the land and its resources from communitarian social and cultural values that had defined its use and importance for generations. It displaced whole communities, and "freed" the land from the people that had lived these traditional values. Thus, neoliberal thought continued the strains of racism, ethnocentrism, classism, and blaming that labeled Indigenous and peasant communities, their ways of life, and their values as obstacles to progress.

Even as it was introduced to countries in the early 1980s, neoliberal development had its critics. "The misery financing the model of development" was how the Honduran daily *El Tiempo* headlined its interview with central bank economist Edmundo Valladares in January, 1980. Valladares was not the only Honduran to have concerns about the human cost of the emerging model of national development, nor was he the last.[34] To the political and economic elite in countries like Honduras, neoliberalism promised new opportunities for individual wealth under the guise of streamlining and making more efficient the "development" of the country. Those who insisted on the communitarian and social nature of land and resources were branded as obstacles to development and prosperity by the more enthusiastic promoters of neoliberalism. Those who resisted could be branded as selfish and unpatriotic, while in reality these brands were better suited to the elites and foreign interests that promoted the new model of development. In Honduras, people had a name for this brand of unpatriotic selfishness—*vendepatria* (selling the country).

In the neoliberal model of development, "inequality becomes naturalized."[35] In the past, development was presented as the road to prosperity for all as a desirable end result. In neoliberalism, development achieves prosperity for some by the necessary sacrifice of others. In Honduras, those who were sacrificed were, first of all, the people of rural communities—peasant and Indigenous—whose land and the resources were defined as desired market commodities in the neoliberal regime. Such regimes and their results generate forms of popular resistance, so that neoliberal development inevitably requires a more or less militarized security state, not to curb crime but to operate, often with organized crime, as control over a potentially restive population.[36] Although the Honduran military returned government to a civilian president in the early 1980s, the military had by then made itself into a primary economic and political power in the country, and it was reinforced in this with the buildup of a U.S. military presence and support during that decade and since (see chapter 7). The United States had a major stake in mandating and enforcing the neoliberal "development" of Honduras, and a crucial partner in this was the Honduran military.

Neoliberal development is far more than a simple theory of economic development. Its ability to reduce everything in human life to a monetary value has led to explorations of how neoliberalism co-opts areas of daily life. This has generated discussions of "military neoliberalism," how neoliberalism's inequalities and destruction of much that people value in life provokes popular resistance and protest that must be repressed, even as militarization of society is rationalized and presented as a guarantee of security for the people.[37]

"Green neoliberalism," references how development pretends to be environmentally friendly even as it devastates ecosystems.[38] In Honduras, for example, hydroelectric dam projects that confiscate sacred rivers from indigenous communities are presented as providing "clean, sustainable energy" for the country, even as the projects displace and destroy Indigenous communities, and the energy generated is used to fuel the most unsustainable and environmentally destructive forms of mining. Along the Caribbean coast of Honduras, Garifuna communities were restricted from entering areas along the coast and the islands where they had made a living for generations. Wide sections were designated environmentally protected zones, in what anthropologist Keri Brondo labeled and example of green neoliberalism. Tellingly, the areas closed to Garifuna fishermen were often open to tourist and game fishing excursions.

"Spiritual neoliberalism," highlights how religion is used to promote neoliberal development, and how neoliberal values replace or distort traditional spiritual perspectives on human life.[39] Spiritual neoliberalism via organized religion is especially useful in discouraging popular protest and collective resistance to neoliberal policies. Religious leaders and institutions are relied upon to promote a civic and moral identity in which individuals are encouraged to take responsibility for their own behavior and welfare rather than protesting violations of their human rights—an encouragement that conveniently ignores or portrays as natural and necessary the widespread differences in power and resources within society, and absolves the state and its development policies of responsibility for the evils plaguing countries like Honduras. According to anthropologist Adrienne Pine, this is indeed the case in Honduras. Preachers encourage personal discipline, individual responsibility, and piety, and warn against turning to anger or cynicism, a slightly coded reference to popular protest and collective resistance. But religious leaders and institutions sometimes became opponents of neoliberal misery, preaching a gospel of justice and human rights. The conflicts over development in civil society are mirrored by disagreements and conflicts within major religious institutions in Central America. Older divisions along denominational lines—Catholic, Protestant—have become instead divisions over the human cost of development and the very meaning of development in which denominational differences become secondary or meaningless.[40]

By way of summary and reflection on neoliberalism, three final points deserve mention. First, critical studies of Latin American neoliberalism often point out that it is a form of development that both enables and disciplines, where development is characterized by limit points that "limit the possibilities for social change by satiating desires and channeling energies toward what is practical and obtainable."[41] It is presented as the freeing of human economic, entrepreneurial potential and the liberating of resources for productive ends, but it also necessitates the repression of criticism, alternatives, and resistance. It destroys self-reliant ways of life and introduces or deepens forms of dependency that condition the survival of many on the largess of the few. Second, neoliberalism's reliance on militarization and its co-optation of religion harken back to the national security doctrine of the Latin American military dictatorships of the 1970s and 1980s.[42] The doctrine of national security was imposed on Honduras in the early 1980s, complete with death squads, military checkpoints, arbitrary arrests and disappearances, and more, so that many Hondurans who lived that period remember it as a nightmare. Third, green neoliberalism, military neoliberalism, and spiritual neoliberalism all reveal the contradiction at the heart of this model of development: the contrast between the positive image of it presented to society and the reality of daily life under it—that is, "the misrepresentation of objective interests."[43] Neoliberalism became a most efficient form of capitalist expansion and imperial reach.

Neoextractivism

The history of Honduras as a provider of raw materials, reinforced under trilateralism, and the unbridled freedom from restrictions for investment and extraction that neoliberalism provided made Honduras an easy victim of neoextractivism.

Extraction of raw metals, minerals, ores, and agricultural products or commodities has been a major feature of Latin American and Caribbean societies for five centuries. At the end of the twentieth century, this extractive activity greatly increased in both intensity of exploitation and geographic expansion. The new extractivism (neoextractivism) built on the long history of the old, but it was also different in important ways that altered the mode and relations of production and the role of the government, and replaced older norms and values of how society should function. Neoextractivism seemed to contradict some of the basic tenets of development. The extraction of raw materials became a primary feature, and in some cases the core, of neoliberal development at the start of the twenty-first century. The "freeing" of land and resources for commercial commodification under neoliberalism paved the way for a frenzied grab for land and resources via extractive projects in the

twenty-first century, a grab that pushed aside the idea of national development for the good of the country and its people.

By the 1990s, an increasing demand for raw materials and commodities
and an increasing sense that many of these raw materials and resources were
in dwindling supply led to what some called a "commodities consensus," a
greatly increased determination (frenzy?) to intensify the ways in which raw
materials and commodities were produced, and to expand the areas in which
they were produced. Individuals and corporations that had the wealth and
power hurried to acquire land and resources.[44] In Latin America, governments
seemed to buy into this new rush for resources, supported by what was often
referred to as the "*eldoradista* illusion," the belief that Latin America was
a place of abundant natural resources that could be turned into great wealth
for countries—a modern version of the colonial belief in El Dorado, the
fabled city of gold that Spanish and later colonial explorers sought.[45] In this
vision there is a curious mixture of hopeful opportunism and a skepticism
or resigned acceptance of a subordinate place in the global order. Honduras
was a prime example of this elusive vision. The country was rich in natural
resources still there and not yet fully exploited.

This new form of "development" has many critics. In Honduras, studies
by independent economists reveal that neoextractivism does not produce
significant wealth for the country, and may even be a drain on the national
economy.[46] Concessions granted to Honduran and foreign companies for
rights to mine areas of the country increased greatly in the first decades of
the twenty-first century—amounting by 2015 to nearly 30 percent of the
country's land area—but the concessions often allowed companies to avoid
taxation, ignore environmental concerns, and employ labor that was not
local.[47] The government also allowed and often supported the displacement
of self-reliant and productive local communities. It was estimated that the
longer-term costs of environmental destruction, rising unemployment and
dependency cancelled or exceeded the income the state received from extractive industries, an income that was further offset by the liberal concessions
to companies and the pocketing of profits by private and government functionaries rather than the state treasury. As a result, neoextractivism increased
poverty and extreme economic inequality as it failed to enrich the country.[48]
It became an instrument of personal wealth rather than national development.
It also reshaped the composition and orientation of economic elites that
became increasingly divorced from any relationship to or concern about the
large populations of people seeking work.[49] In this sense, "by the early 1990s,
the capitalist classes had undergone a major transformation and Honduras no
longer looked like the 'banana republic' of old."[50]

NGOS

Developmentalism as a set of beliefs, policies, and practices depends on many different actors—governments, international financial institutions, and private non-governmental organizations (NGOs)—to effect development. The manipulation of images is fundamental to the promotion of development and to shaping how people think about the nature and purpose of development. Images are powerful shapers of affect, and affect is a powerful shaper of action. Non-governmental organizations are especially good at the manipulation of images and the creation of imaginaries of development. They can depict the people of a foreign land as needy, hungry, dependent victims waiting for a handout from donors; and create a relationship that allows the donor to feel an odd combination of nearness and distance, charity, and superiority. Other NGOs prefer to depict the potential recipients of aid as hard-working people who want to preserve and develop their self-reliance, and who might even have something to teach. Here, the imaginary shapes a different relationship, somewhat more mutual, but not entirely without a colonial otherness. Non-governmental organizations have the flexibility to appeal to and communicate directly with populations (such as donors and recipients of charity or aid) that governments and large international agencies often lack.

In the first decades of the twenty-first century, there were an estimated one million NGOs in the world, although the number may fluctuate since the definition of NGO admits of some ambiguity and may include or exclude different types of organizations.[51] NGOs as developmental partners are of many kinds. Some provide immediate material aid in disasters, so that the definition of "disaster" becomes another part of the imaginary. Even when material development projects are for longer-term development rather than disaster relief, when they are formulated and carried out with the active guidance and participation of local people as partners, and when attempts are made to overcome the othering or alterity that characterizes colonial/imperial relationships, a fundamental problem remains for NGOs that are dependent on donors and the permission of governments. The problem was summed up in a statement attributed to Brazilian Catholic bishop Pedro Casaldaglia in the 1980s. "When I feed the hungry, they call me a saint. When I ask why the hungry have no food or are poor, they call me a communist." Asking the most fundamental questions is dangerous in a system that exists by enforcing dependency. NGOs can give food to the poor or even try to address poverty but they can seldom afford to ask why people are poor in the first place. Some NGOs might try to work in ways that support indirectly the empowerment of people, using material aid or development projects in ways that encourage communities to make their own community decisions and gain a sense of their ability to direct their own development. But this is seldom easy.

Some NGOs do not engage in humanitarian aid or material development but in political and ideological development. Many of these are funded by governments such as the United States to be used as instruments for gaining, extending, or maintaining influence in other countries. This practice is notable in Latin America. Some of these ideologically oriented NGOs claim that their purpose is to promote democracy and the institutions of democracy in "underdeveloped" and "developing" countries. Through the instrumentality of such NGOs, democracy becomes another word-image in the imaginary of development and imperial reach. It is dependent democracy or guided democracy—*democracia tutelada*.[52] Governments with imperial intent can be particularly creative in forming and funding NGOs with high-sounding names that are fronts for promoting internal political opposition and regime change, or conversely, for supporting an unpopular government, protecting U.S. and other foreign investment in extractive development projects. The U.S. government has created or funded a variety of such organizations since at least the 1960s, such as the American Institute of Free Labor Development that was instrumental in toppling the government of Cheddi Jagan in Guyana in the 1960s, and the National Endowment for Democracy that has been accused of supporting opposition groups and "regime change" in Nicaragua.[53] Such NGOs belie the term "non-governmental" since they may be seen as instruments of foreign intervention.

In Honduras, a wide spectrum of foreign and Honduran NGOs operate with differing agendas. Some support the government and (intentionally or not) further the neoliberal agenda by relieving the government of providing needed services, fostering privatization, or repairing some of the damage caused by neoextractivism. Others exist to promote human rights that are violated by neoextractivism, the greed of capitalist elites, or official corruption, to denounce these crimes, or to offer some defense for the victims. These NGOs are regarded as threats to the accumulation of capital, and if they are Honduran they are the object of intimidation, threat, defamation, and violence by the government and the elite that controls the country. If they are foreign-based, they are treated more cautiously in ways that undermine or negate their effect while allowing their presence.

A CONTEXT OF GLOBALIZATION

Since the 1970s, development theory and practice have evolved within a world that is increasingly globalized. In some ways globalization has reinforced the decline of development for the good of the nation and its people, and obfuscated the role of elites and private players in development, making popular resistance perhaps more difficult.

> By categorizing people and countries as "undeveloped," "underdeveloped," "developing," or "developed," international development promised that today's poor would be tomorrow's not-so-poor. . . . The categories informed people's definitions of progress, their expectations for the future. Because the categories were linked to activist states and an international aid industry, people generally knew what development was supposed to look like and who was supposed to deliver on it. Globalization, in contrast, does not promise (however falsely) that everyone will benefit from its program. Nobody is "unglobalized," such that they can be set upon a path to progress. To the contrary, globalization has "winners and losers" and "people left behind."[54]

People who are directly experiencing the negative effects of extractive development in countries such as Honduras are aware that the immediate agents of their misery are their own political and economic elites and the foreign companies these elites engage. But in a globalized context, the larger forces that shape these elites are often unknown and diffuse, so that protest and resistance remain focused on the actors but do not change the script. The very awareness that the fruits of development accrue to a few while the burdens are thrust upon the many is itself a cause for response ranging from despair to resistance to emigration. But in a globalized world, even emigration is at best a partial solution. What does emigration mean in a globalized world where international boundaries mean so much and yet so little?[55]

CRITIQUE OF IMPERIAL DEVELOPMENT

In the 1960s and 1970s, a group of intellectuals raised concerns about the apparent lack of a moral or ethical core in the economic models of development. They believed that development needed to be informed by a moral philosophy and by the voices and decisions of the recipients of development.

> Indeed, the development problem resurrects, in a new mode, the most ancient ethical questions: what is the good life, what is a just society, what stance should societies take vis-a-vis the forces of nature and of technology or artificial nature? . . . More than anything else, however, it is the very bankruptcy of conventional wisdom on development which summons moral philosophy to a rebirth.[56]

One of the more salient critics of development, Colombian sociologist Orlando Fals-Borda refused the invitation to join a group of international scholars acting as advisers to development initiatives for the United Nations. Fals-Borda considered the group elitist, leaving no space for the voices of the recipients of development. In 1969, he wrote, "I cannot identify myself with any institution of the United States that would uphold or sustain the present economic and social policies pursued toward the nations of the Third World."[57] Unlike the majority of the development specialists of his time, Fals-Borda engaged in the kind of ethnographic field research routinely familiar to anthropologist. He spent several years living in peasant villages in his native Colombia, wrote the ethnographically based, *Peasant Society in the Colombian Andes*, and became increasingly involved in the struggles of peasant communities.[58] These experiences seem to have shaped his sense of the necessity of a kind of development that began with, was controlled by, and was intended for the marginalized communities of Latin America and much of the world.

By the 1970s, some scholars in the "Third World," began to formulate sharp critiques of the ways in which newly independent former colonies were still forced to deal with the ongoing effects of colonialism, its imperial debris—racially stratified societies, poverty, loss of sovereignty over economic resources, archaic or foreign political institutions, paternalistic cultural attitudes and institutions, pervasive psychologies of inferiority, and much more. Formal political independence and formal claims of national sovereignty were undermined by de facto economic dependency and loss of control over national resources. Consequently, the hoped for prosperity that was supposed to lift people to a better life failed to materialize or was painfully slow in coming.

By the 1980s, the discourse of human rights was increasingly employed to critique the human cost of development policies. In Honduras, new organizations specifically dedicated to defending human rights began to cast the murder and repression of peasant, Indigenous, and environmentalist leaders and communities specifically as human rights matters.[59]

By the 1990s, criticism of modern imperial expansion also came from those who warned of the consequences of empire building for the United States itself. These critics—many of them U.S., Latin American, or European academics—were not shy about applying the label of imperialism to the foreign policies of the United States at a time when that characterization was still widely considered extreme or unpatriotic. The term "blowback" became shorthand for referencing a long list of negative and unintended consequences that would result from U.S. policies. Scholars like Chalmers Johnson and others used the terms "imperial" and "empire" to characterize United States involvement in Latin America and Asia via forms of "development" and "security aid."[60] The consequences of this expansive agenda, they said, could be seen in the rising levels of popular resistance movements in many countries; the resort to military buildup, militarization, and outright war; the support for local dictators and oppressive regimes that contradicted and undermined basic values of democracy and human rights; the financial costs for the United States of maintaining a worldwide military presence; the misery inflicted on other peoples; and the ways in which these imperial policies shaped racial conflict, poverty, erosion of democracy, and many more evils in the United States itself. Imperial formations reshaped life in the centers of power as surely as in the "colonies. Belief in the benevolence of empire had not died."[61] But critics warned that the United States was losing its most cherished values because of its pursuit of imperial relationships abroad.[62]

In the first decades of the twenty-first century, a generation of scholars of "imperial studies" was proposing a different and more dynamic analysis of imperial systems. Imperialism was a collection of many characteristic and flexible policies and practices that were combined, reshaped, and applied in new ways to new historical situations; these "imperial durabilities" were apparent today in much of the world.[63] These formations or characteristics employed by modern imperial powers like the United States today would be found both in the colonies and in the centers of empire—for example, both Honduras and the United States. These included:

- the widespread use of categories of division such as race, religion, ethnicity, and gender
- the attempt to control human bodies through racial and sexual mandates and prohibitions promoted by medicine, religion, and law
- patriarchy and hierarchy as "normal," even necessary and accepted social and cultural values
- the multiplication of forms of detention and physical separation such as detention centers, concentration camps, prisons, military installations, work farms, ghettos that segregated certain sets of people
- barriers and walls—physical, legal, and sociocultural—prohibiting the free movement of people such as migrants
- promotion of a sense of privileged and non-privileged populations through legal fictions such as citizenship
- the need to collect and record huge amounts of data and information, including forms of surveillance of populations
- use of defamation and criminalization against resisters, opponents, cultural rebels, and potential threats to control
- the manufacturing of false threats, foreign and domestic, and the use of scapegoating or stereotyping of groups as threats
- the use of fear to control and shape popular sentiment

- forms of policing, militarism, and the use of force and violence as direct forms of control or, preferably, as indirect threats in order to assure control
- a tendency to externalize the solution to internal national problems and conflicts, such as fighting the "war on drugs" not by treating the social roots of demand in the United States, but by deploying military eradication campaigns in Central America and Colombia, or demanding that Mexico and Central American countries detain emigrants before they reach the U.S. border

These imperial characteristics are often presented under the rubrics of *social order* (read racism, classism, sexism, patriarchy), *citizenship (read nationalism, hyper-nationalism, and exclusion), and security* (read surveillance, militarization, and creation of enemies). Some of these items are present in non-imperial states, and not every item on this list is evident in every imperial situation. Rather these constitute the "tool kit" of imperial rule. But in this list, one can easily recognize practices that directly shape immigration policies and the treatment of immigrants such as those from Central America seeking asylum in the United States. The list also invites comparison between practices in "colonized" societies like Honduras and practices in the United States and perhaps other centers of imperial systems. Governments in imperial relationships may be forced to regard the list above as a set of problems to be confronted, but also as somehow necessary conditions for their survival as imperial powers. This contradiction is central to creating the conditions that both provoke and criminalize migration.

CONCLUSION: CREATING AND NEGATING THE IMMIGRANT

Critics of development as the modern face of imperial reach point out that the portrayal of countries and their peoples as inferior, needy, or different—the so-called colonial difference—is a necessary aspect of imperial systems, and is also crucial for the project of foreign "development" in Central American countries like Honduras.[64] No physical wall keeps out immigration. The more effective ideological wall is the sense that "they" are not like us, and are in fact inferior or wanting in some way. From this perspective, U.S. citizens who treat immigrants as fellow humans might themselves be considered as threats who must be criminalized for subverting or blurring the differences. The criminalization of the Sanctuary Movement activists in the 1980s and the water angels in the Arizona desert in 2018 are examples of this guilt by association.

The truly insidious and tragic aspect of this situation is that the "othering" implied or stated in much development discourse can also be used to construct the "othering" of the immigrant. Development in practice is often a disruptive force in a country like Honduras, and thus is a creator of conditions that encourage emigration. Development in theory and discourse too often promotes the mentality of the colonial difference, a subtle or not-so-subtle support for anti-immigrant thinking, even criminalization of the immigrant who reaches the U.S. border. In this sense, imperial reach in the guise of development both creates and negates the immigrant.

NOTES

1. Equipo de Reflexión, Investigación, y Comunicación (ERIC), *Impacto Socioambiental de la minería en la region noroccidental de Honduras a la luz de tres estudios de casos* (El Progreso: ERIC-Radio Progreso, 2016), 86.

2. Arturo Escobar, *Encountering Development: The Making and Unmaking of the Third World* (Princeton NJ: Princeton University Press, 1995); John Narayan and Leon Sealy-Huggins, "What Has Become of Imperialism?" *Third World Quarterly* 38, no. 11 (2017): 2376–2395.

3. Gilder Lehrman Institute of American History, "The Doctrine of Discovery, 1493," n.d., https://www.gilderlehrman.org/history-resources/spotlight-primary-source/doctrine-discovery-1493; Roxanne Dunbar-Ortiz, *An Indigenous Peoples' History of the United States* (Boston: Beacon Press, 2014): 197–201; Steven T. Newcomb, "The Evidence of Christian Nationalism in Federal Indian Law: The Doctrine of Discovery, Johnson v. McIntosh, and Plenary Power," *New York University Review of Law and Social Change* (1993): 303–343, https://socialchangenyu.com/wp-content/uploads/2017/12/Steven-Newcomb_RLSC_20.2.pdf.

4. For example, in 1924, a speaker at a public event in Oregon declared that "this is a white, Protestant, and Gentile man's country, and they are going to run it." Lawrence J. Saalfeld, *Forces of Prejudice in Oregon, 1920–1925* (Portland OR: Archdiocesan Historical Commission, 1984).

5. For a detailed history and analysis of the development of U.S. imperial expansion in Latin America, see, e.g., Greg Grandin, *Empire's Workshop: Latin America, the United States, and the Rise of the New Imperialism* (New York: Henry Holt, 2006). For a historical review of U.S. imperial intervention in Central America, see Aviva Chomsky, *Central America's Forgotten History: Revolution, Violence, and the Roots of Migration* (Boston: Beacon Press, 2021).

6. See, for example., Juan Gonzalez, *Harvest of Empire*, revised ed. (New York: Penguin Books, 2011).

7. Eric Williams, *Capitalism and Slavery* (Chapel Hill NC: University of North Carolina Press, 1944); Eric Williams, *From Columbus to Castro: The History of the Caribbean 1492–1969* (London: Andre Deutsch, 1970), 280–327.

8. For the text of Rudyard Kipling's poem "The White Man's Burden" (1899), see https://www.americanyawp.com/reader/19-american-empire/rudyard-kipling-the-white-mans-burden-1899/. For an analysis, see Lit Charts, "The White Man's Burden Summary and Analysis," at https://www.litcharts.com/poetry/rudyard-kipling/the-white-man-s-burden.

9. Escobar, *Encountering Development*.

10. Some classic examples of the imperial/colonial critique: George L. Beckford, *Persistent Poverty: Underdevelopment in Plantation Economies of the Third World* (New York: Oxford University Press, 1972); Walter Rodney, *How Europe Underdeveloped Africa* (London: Bogle-L'Ouverture Publications, 1972); James D. Cockcroft, André Gunder Frank, and Dale L. Johnson, eds., *Dependence and Underdevelopment: Latin America's Political Economy* (New York: Anchor Books, 1972).

11. Bharatan Kumarappa, *Capitalism, Socialism, or Villagism?* (Madras: Shakti Karalayam, 1946).

12. Julius Nyerere, *Ujamaa: Essays on Socialism* (New York: Oxford University Press, 1971).

13. Michael Manley, *A Voice at the Workplace: Reflections on Colonialism and the Jamaican Worker* (Washington DC: Howard University Press, 1991).

14. Walter D. Mignolo, *Local Histories/Global Designs: Coloniality, Subaltern Knowledges, and Border Thinking* (Princeton NJ: Princeton University Press, 2000); Escobar, *Encountering Development*.

15. James C. Scott, *Weapons of the Weak: Everyday Forms of Peasant Resistance* (New Haven: Yale University Press, 1985), 335.

16. Escobar, *Encountering Development*, 143, citing James Ferguson, *The Anti-Politics Machine: Development, Depoliticization, and Bureaucratic Power in Lesotho* (Cambridge: Cambridge University Press, 1990).

17. Scott, *Weapons of the Weak*, 236.

18. For a review of six books on the William Walker "affair," see Ralph Lee Woodward Jr., "Review: William Walker and the History of Nicaragua in the Nineteenth Century," *Latin American Research Review* 15 no. 1 (1980): 237–270.

19. For a list of U.S. military interventions in Latin America, see Marc Becker, https://www.yachana.org/teaching/resources/interventions.html.

20. Stephen Schlesinger and Stephen Kinzer, *Bitter Fruit: The Untold Story of the American Coup in Guatemala* (Garden City NY: Anchor Books, 1983).

21. Cheddi Jagan, *The West on Trial: The Fight for Guyana's Freedom* (London: Michael Joseph Ltd., 1966).

22. TelesurHD, "Chile Marks Anniversary of Coup Against President Allende, September 11, 2019," https://www.telesurenglish.net/news/Chile-The-Coup-Against-President-Allende-Was-The-First-911--20190911-0002.html; Oscar Guardiola-Rivera, *Story of a Death Foretold: The Coup Against Salvador Allende, September 11, 1973* (London: Bloomsbury Publishing, 2013).

23. William Blum, "The CIA, Contras, and Crack," Institute for Policy Studies, November 1, 1996, https://ips-dc.org/the_cia_contras_gangs_and_crack/; Gary

Webb, *Dark Alliance: The CIA, the Contras, and the Crack Cocaine Explosion* (New York: Seven Stories Press, 1998).

24. James Phillips, "The Misery Financing Development: Subsidized Neoliberalism and Privatized Dependency in Honduras," *Urban Anthropology and Studies of Cultural Systems and World Economic Development 46*, nos. 1 and 2 (Spring–Summer, 2017): 1–59.

25. W. W. Rostow, *The Stages of Economic Growth: A Non-Communist Manifesto* (Cambridge: Cambridge University Press, 1960).

26. Sidney Mintz, "The rural proletariat and the problem of rural proletarian consciousness," *Journal of Peasant Studies* 1, no. 3 (1974): 291–325. For a later use and comparison, see Jan Breman, "Work and Life of the Rural Proletariat in Java's Coastal Plain," *Modern Asian Studies* 29, no. 1 (1995): 1–44.

27. Paul Doughty, "Ending Serfdom in Peru: The Struggle for Land and Freedom in Vicos," in *Contemporary Cultures and Societies of Latin America*, Third Edition, ed. Dwight B. Heath (Prospect Heights IL: Waveland Press, 2002), 225–243.

28. Marvin Barahona, *Honduras en el siglo XX: Una síntesis histórica* (Tegucigalpa: Editorial Guaymuras, 2005).

29. Wasudha Bhatt, "The Crisis of Development: A Historical Critique from the Focal Point of Human Wellbeing," *The Indian Journal of Political Science* 68, no. 1 (January–March, 2007): 41–55.

30. Chalmers Johnson, *Blowback: The Cost and Consequences of American Empire* (New York: Henry Holt, 2000).

31. John Williamson, *Latin American Adjustment: How Much Has Happened* (Washington DC: Institute for International Economics, 1990).

32. For example, Alcides Hernandez, *El Neoliberalismo en Honduras* (Tegucigalpa: Guaymuras, 1987).

33. Mark Goodale and Nancy Postero, "Revolution and Retrenchment: Illuminating the Present in Latin America," in *Neoliberalism Interrupted: Social Change and Contested Governance in Contemporary Latin America*, eds. Mark Goodale and Nancy Postero (Palo Alto: Stanford University Press, 2013), 7–8.

34. Hernandez, *El Neoliberalismo*.

35. Analiese Richard, "Taken into Account: Democratic Change and Contradiction in Mexico's Third Sector," in *Neoliberalism Interrupted*, 139.

36. Aaron Ettinger, "Neoliberalism and the Rise of the Private Military Industry," *International Journal* 66, no. 3 (2011): 731–752.

37. Elana Zilberg, "Yes We Did! Si se podo! Regime Change and the Transnational Politics of Hope Between the United States and El Salvador," in *Neoliberalism Interrupted*, 230–246; Aaron Ettinger, "Neoliberalism," 731–752.

38. For example, Keri Vacanti Brondo, *Land Grab: Green Neoliberalism, Gender, and Garifuna Resistance in Honduras* (Tucson: University of Arizona Press, 2013).

39. Miguel Angel Contreras Natera, "Insurgent Imaginaries and Postneoliberalism in Latin America," in Goodale and Postero, eds., *Neoliberalism Interrupted,* 250–258.

40. James Phillips, "Body and Soul: Faith, Development, Community, and Social Science in Nicaragua," *NAPA* (National Association of Practicing Anthropologists), Bulletin 33 (2010): 12–30.

41. Brondo, *Land Grab*, 129–152, 168–188.

42. José Comblin, *The Church and the National Security State* (Maryknoll NY: Orbos Books, 1979).

43. Scott, *Weapons of the Weak*, 335.

44. Maristella Svampa, "Commodities Consensus: Neoextractivism and Enclosure of the Commons in Latin America," *South Atlantic Quarterly* 114, no. 1 (2015): 65–82, https://read.dukepress.edu/south-atlantic-quarterly/article-abstract/114/1/65/3719/Commodities-Consensus-Neoextractivism-and?redirectedFrom=fulltext.

45. Maristella Svampa, *Las fronteras del nuevoextractivismo en América Latina: Conflictos socioambientales, giro ecoterritorial y nuevas dependencias* (Guadalajara: Universidad de Guadalajara, 2019), 24–25.

46. Thomas M. Power, *Metals Mining and Sustainable Development in Central America* (Boston: Oxfam America, 2008), https://s3.amazonaws.com/oxfam-us/www/static/media/files/metals-mining-and-sustainable-development-in-central-america.pdf; Extractive Industries Transparency Initiative (EITI), "Honduras" (February 4, 2021), https://eiti.org/honduras.

47. Mario Sorto, Wilfredo Serrano, and Bladimir López, *Coyuntura desde los territorios: Los bienes comunes naturales: La actual disputa socio-política en las comunidades de Honduras* (Tegucigalpa: Centro de Estudio para la Democracia, 2019), 4, which cites figures from the Honduras Institute of Geology and Mines.

48. Joel Alemán, "Fiscalidad y Desarrollo: Los Privilegios Fiscales no son Desarrollo," Honduran Social Forum on the External Debt and Development (FOSDEH), October 10, 2019, https://fosdeh.com/editoriales/fiscalidad-y-desarrollo-los-privilegios-fiscales-no-son-desarrollo/.

49. James Phillips, *Honduras in Dangerous Times: Resistance and Resilience* (Lanham MD: Lexington Books, 2015), 22–24.

50. Tyler Shipley, *Ottawa and Empire: Canada and the Military Coup in Honduras* (Toronto: Between the Lines Press, 2015), 24.

51. International Business Standards Organization, "Facts and Stats about NGOs Worldwide," (October 6, 2015), https://www.standardizations.org/bulletin/?p=841. For a more conservative estimate and discussion, see Sally Leverty, "NGOs the UN and APA," *American Psychological Association* (2008), https://www.apa.org/international/united-nations/publications.

52. Barahona, *Honduras en el siglo XX*, 233–275.

53. Benjamin Waddell, "Laying the groundwork for insurrection: A closer look at the U.S. role in Nicaragua's social unrest," *Global Americans*, May 1, 2018, https://theglobalamericans.org/2018/05/laying-groundwork-insurrection-closer-look-u-s-role-nicaraguas-social-unrest/; Tom Ricker, "Manufacturing Dissent: The N.E.D., Opposition Media, and the Political Crisis in Nicaragua," *Quixote Center News from Nicaragua,* May 11, 2018, https://www.quixote.org/manufacturing-dissent-the-n-e-d-opposition-media-and-the-political-crisis-in-nicaragua/.

54. Nora Haenn et al., "Trump's First World Revivalism Pits Globalization against Development," *Anthropology News* (March 20, 2020), https://www.anthropology-news.org/index.php/2020/03/20/trumps-first-world-revivalism-pits-globalization-against-development/.

55. Victor M. Ortiz, "The Unbearable Ambiguity of the Border," *Social Justice* 28, no. 2 (Summer 2001): 96–112, https://www.jstor.org/stable/29768078?seq=1.

56. Denis Goulet, *A New Moral Order: Development Ethics and Liberation Theology* (Maryknoll NY: Orbis Books, 1974): 4–5.

57. Goulet, *A New Moral Order,* 51.

58. Orlando Fals-Borda, *Peasant Society in the Colombian Andes* (Gainesville: University of Florida Press, 1955).

59. Some of the independent Honduran human rights organizations that began in the early 1980s were CODEH (Committee for the Defense of Human Rights in Honduras); COFADEH (Committee of the Families of the Detained/Disappeared in Honduras); ERIC-SJ (The Jesuit Reflection, Investigation, and Communication Team); and CODEH (Honduran Documentation Center).

60. For example, Johnson, *Blowback.* Greg Grandin, *Empire's Workshop: Latin America, the United States, and the Rise of the New Imperialism* (New York: Holt Paperbacks, 2007).

61. For example, Robert D. Kaplan, "In Defense of Empire," *The Atlantic,* April 2014, https://www.theatlantic.com/magazine/archive/2014/04/in-defense-of-empire/358645/.

62. Johnson, *Blowback*; Grandin, *Empire's Workshop*; Narayan and Sealy-Huggins, "What Has Become of Imperialism?"

63. Ann Laura Stoler, *Duress: Imperial Durabilities in Our Times* (Durham, NC: Duke University Press, 2016).

64. Mignolo, *Local Histories*; Escobar, *Encountering Development.*

Chapter 4

Migration, Development, and Honduras

Empire has much to do with the control of resources, both natural and human. An obvious and critical place where this occurs is in the regimes deployed to capture and control both land and people to work the land—land and labor capture—and to eliminate alternative systems or choices for the people whose bodies supply labor. In the colonial history of Latin America, different systems have been introduced to ensure this. The great threats to these regimes have been subversion or open rebellion among the laborers, and the availability of alternatives that can tempt workers away from the control of the landowners. Migrating labor seems to have choices. Historically, there have been three primary ways to control a population of workers on the land and to keep them there: (1) make other land unavailable, (2) impose rigid and hierarchical (usually patriarchal) cultural symbols, rituals, and practices to bind workers legally and affectively to the land and its owners, and (3) physical violence to drive workers to work and to restrict them from leaving. Slavery, serfdom, and forms of indentured servitude are classic forms of labor capture.

Control over land and labor has historically also been a primary pillar of political power. In some places and times, millions of scattered small peasant farmers cultivating their own plots of land in far-flung communities were controlled through the state's or the monarch's imposition of taxes and land restrictions, backed by military force. In recent times, relatively independent peasant production is sometimes controlled by encouraging or demanding that peasants form production cooperatives that, by law, had to be registered and monitored by state authorities who could control the levels of production and channel it in ways the state and its managers saw fit. States as centralized political powers also rely on enterprises that bring together large numbers of workers in patterns easily monitored and controlled. Humans seem to show a persistent desire for autonomy and relative independence, even—and maybe especially—when the issue is basic subsistence. Having a bit of land to feed oneself and one's family has been a rallying cry in many times and places.[1] The independent peasant farmer has been a powerful symbol of freedom and the bane of elites and governments wanting a controllable and regimented use of land and labor. In some times and places, peasants were forced into serfdom and dependency so as to be controllable, and were also policed by the rulers, as in czarist Russia.[2] This control could be exercised also through local elites or landowners supported by a central authority and a set of cultural and legal obligations and social ties, such as the myth and patriarchal ritual of the hacienda as a family, as in colonial and post-colonial Latin America.[3] Sometimes these controls failed and peasants rebelled, usually for short-term gains, but sometimes as part of a larger revolutionary vision that they may or may not see with relative clarity.[4]

In the modern world, slavery, debt peonage, and other forms of servitude are still extant, but the rise of capitalism and the more recent introduction of "development" as a new form of imperialism have also brought new ways of ensuring more control over land, labor, and the production of wealth. Basing national development on specific extractive industries such as mining and plantation export agriculture and agribusiness provides specific structures and forms of production that arrange the land and channel labor that can be more easily observed, monitored, and controlled.

> How did the state gradually get a handle on its subjects and their environment? . . . whatever their other purposes, the designs of scientific forestry and agriculture and the layout of plantations, collective farms . . . all seemed calculated to make the terrain, its products, and its workforce more legible—and hence manipulable—from above and from the center.[5]

Citing Vandana Shiva, Andres León writes that Shiva, "is right when she argues that monocultures have more to do with social control and political domination than with agriculture."[6] One could specify this political domination further as imperial domination. The sugar plantations of the colonial Caribbean and the banana plantations of the "banana republics" of Central America attest to the connection between plantation monocrop and imperial power.

This regimented labor pool has historically reflected the racial and patriarchal strains of imperial enterprises. Indigenous and black people worked the plantations and the mines of the Americas, a pattern that largely remains today as if the imperial enterprise had not ended but merely changed hands.

CAUTIONARY TALES

Jamaica

The island of Jamaica was a British colony for slightly more than three hundred years (1655–1962). For much of that history, sugar was its major product, with plantations (locally known as estates) that used slaves imported from Africa as the work force. This system of bondage and misery made a few British plantation owners quite rich. But the handful of white plantation owners, managers, and colonial officials who oversaw this system in Jamaica lived in constant fear that the much larger population of slaves would one day revolt.[7] Such revolts occurred with some regularity in different parts of the Caribbean, most dramatically in Jamaica's closest neighbor, Haiti, in 1790, where slaves drove out French colonial rulers in a bloody insurrection, and established the second independent country in the Western Hemisphere. In Jamaica, a garrison of soldiers was always needed to forestall such an event. The cost of maintaining such military forces was part of the cost of maintaining an empire. Slave labor turned out to be rather expensive to maintain— financially and morally—and by 1800 it was clear to members of Britain's parliament that Jamaican sugar was too costly, especially since Britain could purchase sugar from Brazil or elsewhere for less than it could be produced in Jamaica.[8]

Britain ended the slave trade in 1808, ended the favored position of Jamaican sugar in British markets, and emancipated the slaves in British colonies in 1834, a process that was completed by 1838. In place of forced slavery, plantation owners and the local authorities now had to rely on offering wages to entice former slaves to work for them. To many of the newly freed, wages were paltry compared to the deeply felt historical and physical scars of slavery and the desire for freedom. Former slaves abandoned the plantations and went into the mountainous interior of the island where there was plenty of unused but rugged land. Free former slaves carved out plots of land for cultivation and established small local communities of free people living by their own food production. They also established small local markets where they sold their produce to each other and to the few white colonial functionaries and their families that lived on the island.[9]

Jamaica underwent a major transformation, its population transformed from slaves to self-reliant small farmers. This transformation seemed to place the population beyond the control of the plantation owners and the colonial authorities. Plantation owners (who also controlled the colonial government of the island) demanded that colonial authorities find ways to force these self-reliant communities back under their control. Heavy land taxes were laid on the free farming communities since the unused land on which these famers were "squatting' was legally considered government (Crown) land. Plantation owners refused to sell their land to former slaves, and colonial authorities passed laws to restrict the availability of land. Without land, people would be forced to work for others. Indentured labor was imported from other British colonies, especially India—passage to Jamaica in exchange for five to seven years of labor on Jamaican plantations.

All of this provoked protests from peasant farmers, the former slaves, and their children. In the autumn of 1865, as the Civil War that ended slavery in the United States was winding down, a group of peasant farmers (mostly former slaves) staged a protest demonstration at the courthouse in the town of Morant Bay on the southeast coast of Jamaica. The militia fired at the protesters and captured and executed their leader, Paul Bogle. This incident unleashed a campaign in which more than four hundred peasants and their families were killed and hundreds jailed by the volunteer militia on orders from the colonial governor. The incidents are collectively known as the Morant Bay rebellion or massacre, and are today hailed as a major event in Jamaican history. It is a classic tale of imperial rule, colonial violence, the problem of land and labor control, and the close identification of economic and political interests—one small but telling chapter in the political economy of empire.[10]

Ironically, perhaps, a later British colonial governor of Jamaica wrote in 1936 that the peasants and small farming descendants of the former slaves were, and might again become, the ones who could make Jamaica self-reliant in feeding its population.[11] Had that been allowed to occur, perhaps Jamaica's transition to formal independence from Britain in 1962 would have provided some actual political and economic independence, or at least self-reliance, rather than the continued neocolonial dependency that the island suffers today.

Nicaragua

Nicaragua became independent from Spain in the 1820s. By the 1870s, the coffee boom had hit the country. Nicaragua's elites and politicians tended to see coffee as the engine of national progress. Nicaragua was also home to various Indigenous communities (*pueblos indios*) of peasant farmers who produced food for their families and the local markets. Getting the Indigenous communities to provide both land and labor for growing coffee became a part of the ruling elite's plan for making Nicaragua a modern nation-state.[12] Indigenous peoples and communities could not be allowed to grow their own coffee for export or sale. That would result in a patchwork of many different smaller communities and individuals dealing with the market, and Indigenous people might actually develop a base of economic power and ultimately political power if they were allowed to control this engine of progress. The coffee *fincas* had to be under the control of the ruling elite if the elite were to maintain political power.

Between 1870 and 1930, the Nicaraguan state abolished legal recognition of Indigenous communities, replaced Indigenous community landowning with private property, added taxes and other burdens and restrictions on Indigenous communities, and so created conditions that both impoverished these communities and exposed them to wealthy coffee planters who enticed or coerced them into debt peonage. In some areas of Nicaragua, Indigenous communities tried to make the most of this. In others (e.g., Matagalpa, 1881), they rose in rebellion against this transformation. For decades. this system of debt peonage on the coffee *fincas* remained in place.[13] Some scholars think the process resulted in the diminution of Indigenous identities into mestizo identities and the strengthening of patriarchy in Nicaraguan domestic and political life.[14] The planters were the patriarchs, the fathers. The *indios* were the children, the peons of debt peonage. The largest and most vivid example and symbol of this patriarchy arose near the end of this transformative period, in the 1930s when Anastasio Somoza Garcia seized power and ran Nicaragua as a de facto dictator, he and then his sons for forty-five years. Somoza was the patriarch, the father figure of the nation, who ruled by disciplining his children (the people) and occasionally rewarding a few. His sons continued this patriarchal dictatorship until 1979, when the Somoza family's rule was overthrown by a popular revolution led by the Sandinista Front.

Political opinion and nuance in Nicaragua has always been complex and sometimes apparently contradictory. When the Sandinista Front came to power, the Sandinista leaders, mostly urban and educated middle class and wealthy individuals, were divided about how to understand the rural communities of peasants and small farmers, many of whom had supported the revolution against Somoza. Some had suffered violence and repression under Somoza, while a few had been the beneficiaries of colonization schemes under Somoza that gave them land, albeit not always good land. Some of those who supported the overthrow of Somoza were also wary of the young Sandinistas who seemed to have Marxist ideas. The government expropriated the coffee *fincas* and other rural properties of Somoza supporters who had fled the country with the dictator, and it made these lands available to peasant communities if they agreed to act as production cooperatives rather than individual independent households and landowners. In other cases, the land was turned into state-owned farms that provided labor for rural people. These policies were accepted willingly by some rural people, grudgingly by others who wanted the land to be divided and title awarded to individual peasant families.[15]

SYSTEMS OF LAND AND LABOR CONTROL

Resource extraction and the forced displacement and movement of people have been features of life in Latin America for centuries. In the 1500s, Spanish colonial rule had two major forms of land and labor control. The *encomienda* system granted to individual Spaniards a portion of land and the right to the labor of Indigenous communities on that land. The *repartimiento system* grouped Indigenous peoples into communities under the control of Spanish authorities. In theory, the repartimiento system was supposed to curtail the abuses of Indigenous workers that the encomienda system might encourage. In practice, both systems led to abuse, and the Spanish Crown promulgated the New Laws in 1542 to abolish the encomienda system and strengthen direct rule by state authorities.[16] But the patterns established by these land-labor systems continued in some areas of Latin America after independence in the 1820s with locally governed *pueblos indios* and the *hacienda* system. In some cases, Indigenous populations were shipped as slave labor to other areas of Latin America; much of the Indigenous population of colonial Nicaragua was moved to other parts of Central America and beyond as forced or slave labor. Aside from the introduction of slave labor from Africa as the Indigenous population declined due to brutal treatment in the 1500s, much of the displacement of people was local or internal, allowing people to find ways of survival without moving too far afield.

Encomienda and Hacienda

In Latin America, the purpose of much government policy under both colonialism and independence—from the 1500s to the 1900s—was to control the movement of local populations and tie them legally and forcibly to particular areas. The traditional *hacienda* system that emerged in much of Latin America under late Spanish colonialism and continued in some areas into the 1960s, bound local populations, often Indigenous people, to particular haciendas, large tracts of land owned by elites or religious organizations. Local people provided the labor on the hacienda in a form of servitude that extended also to their children so that it continued for generations. Typically, workers had little contact with a world beyond the hacienda and the local market, and little or no education. In return for providing labor for the hacienda and its owner, they were usually given a small portion of hacienda land to cultivate for their own subsistence, sometimes being required to share a portion of whatever they produced with the hacienda owner.

The essentially exploitative nature of this relationship was masked by cultural practices that portrayed the relationship as familial. The owner (*patrón*) was a father figure, the locally bound worker (*peón* or *colono* or *pongo,* depending on the region of Latin America) was treated as a child that needed to offer obedience and deference to the patrón and needed to be disciplined as fathers discipline their children. In return for the peón's service, the patrón was supposed to represent and intervene for the peon in all dealings with the outside world, including civil and religious authorities.[17] The hacienda system and its variants had serious consequences for local populations. It severely restricted the movement of local people, physically, socially, and intellectually. It enforced a severely degrading image of hacienda workers as children and inferiors, and symbolized this with the most humiliating rituals. On some haciendas, workers were lined up each morning and individually forced to remove their hats, bow, and kiss the hand of the owner who was often a man younger than the workers themselves. Social stratification was strictly enforced. This did not prohibit the owner and members of his family from having (often forced) sexual relations with women among the workers' families. Such forced sexual encounters (rape) contributed to what became known as the *mestizo* or mixed-race (Indigenous and European) population in Latin America.

The hacienda system ensured that large numbers of people would never migrate far. It was not oriented toward production for foreign export on an international or global market. What was produced was usually geared to local or regional markets or was used by the hacienda owners themselves, including some religious institutions, for their own consumption or sale. Hacienda owners were often land rich but money poor. They owned large tracts of land but had little or no capital to invest in their land or the hacienda, no means to "modernize" their enterprise, and little incentive to do so as long as the external demand for raw materials remained low. For centuries, Latin America had systems of land and labor that had implications for the movement of people and for their own self-image: one that allowed the limited movement of potential workers, and another that bound workers in servitude in place for generations. Out of this came other forms of land and labor, especially as wage labor replaced forms of slavery and bound servitude in some areas of Latin America.

The "Rural Proletariat"

In the Caribbean island of Jamaica, when slavery was abolished in 1834, plantation owners tried to keep newly freed former slaves from leaving the plantations by making it difficult for former slaves to find land. The plantation owners were mostly unsuccessful, and the result was a system of self-reliant peasant villages composed of former plantation slaves. By the late

1800s, these villages formed the basis on which Jamaica could have become nearly self-reliant in supplying food to its entire population.[18] Having land to cultivate represented freedom and a measure of security. But many people supplemented their peasant farming with wages from seasonal or occasional plantation work.[19] In Central America in the late nineteenth century, as foreign companies established extractive industries based on paid labor, these enterprises attracted potential workers. In the 1870s, when U.S.-based Rosario Mining began gold mining in southern Honduras, men came to find work in the mine, sometimes leaving family members home to continue farming plots of land.[20] As the U.S.-based banana and fruit plantations began to expand across northern Honduras and in neighboring Guatemala, they attracted peasant farmers from surrounding communities who found work on the plantations as their family members remained at home to continue cultivating family land. Fruit companies expanded landholdings at the expense of peasant farmers, and thus managed to capture both land and labor.[21]

This system of engaging in independent peasant farming with plantation or mine work combined two modes and relations of production: one of local and relatively self-reliant livelihood, the other of dependent wage labor for (usually) foreign corporate owners. This had important consequences because it exposed traditional self-reliant and relatively unstratified local communities to the impersonal, distant, and hierarchically structured relations of the world market, resulting in a widening of thought, identity, and networks of relations and action that some scholars labeled *proletarianization.*[22]

The degree to which this transformation of thought, identity, relations, and action affected peasant populations depended on several factors, primarily the level of security that peasants had over their land and in their communities. Even into the 1970s in Jamaica, it was noted that those who had secure ownership of land were often able to limit their dependence on the plantations. Those who rented or sharecropped land and had less secure tenure tended, out of necessity, to embrace the realities of the corporate global economy in its local manifestation, usually the plantation.[23] In Central America, peasant communities learned lessons from the experience of plantation wage labor and the new networks and forms of organization it demanded. In Honduras, the great banana workers' strike of 1954 opened the way to legal recognition of labor organizing and unions (*sindicatos*). Peasant communities, trying to protect their land and gain more land to farm, followed suit in the 1960s and early 1970s, forming peasant unions to negotiate from collective strength that, despite much government repression and opposition, finally resulted in the Agrarian Reform Law of 1974 that recognized in law the right of all Hondurans to access to land.[24]

By the 1960s, as developmentalism in the form of modernization became a dominant force in Latin America, severe critiques condemned the *hacienda* system and the traditional landowning patterns on which it was based, as unjust, antiquated, and a major obstacle to development and progress. Land reform and agrarian reform (*reforma agraria*) became popular phrases, but they were understood and defined in law and policy in radically different ways. Some thought of land reform as a way of providing more land to peasant communities and small farmers, as a more just and effective way of providing food and promoting self-reliance.[25] This was one vision of what development meant. Others tended to see reform as a "rationalization" of agriculture, a sweeping away of peasant plots and an expansion of large-scale export agriculture using modern technology and geared to global or regional markets. This vision of development often used the term "economies of scale" to point out the presumed inefficiency of peasant and small-farming systems and the advantages of large, corporate agricultural systems.[26]

When scholars began to write critical studies of land reform and development in the early 1970s, they were faced with the reality of millions of former peasants now migrating across Latin America in search of work in large scale export agriculture or development projects such as construction of roads, dams, and other infrastructure that would open formerly remote rural areas to exploitation, and reconfigure the traditional social class structure of Latin America.[27] Traditional peasant communities all over Latin America were being invaded by foreign and global development projects. Those who could hold on to a bit of land might combine peasant farming with work in plantations, mines, or other enterprises. Those who became landless were no longer tied, even tenuously, to a particular location. Should these landless people be given land as peasants or small farmers, or used as a landless mobile labor pool? Or could they simply be ignored?

Development, Disappearing Peasantries, Superfluous People

To grasp the magnitude and importance of the transformation of peasants into a landless and mobile work force, it is necessary to understand something about traditional peasant life. Peasants were usually described as cultivators of land who tended relatively small plots using their own family labor, with simple, low-tech tools, and often animal manure for fertilizer. They cultivated crops primarily to feed themselves and their families, but ordinarily they also cultivated some crops to sell in the local market in order to have enough money to meet some basic demands—replacing tools and supplies they needed but could not make themselves; paying taxes to local, regional, or national government; tithes for the church; rent to a landlord if they did not own their land; and money for other legal and ceremonial demands. With limited land and labor resources, peasants had to decide how much production would go to feed their families and how much to meet these other demands. If taxes, rents, or other costs rose, peasants either increased production of their crops or reduced the portion they took for their own family consumption. There are strict limits on both of these strategies. Increasing production on their land meant more intense use of the land (risking depleting soil fertility); and there are physical limits to how hard a human can work, year after year. Cutting family consumption risked reducing the strength and work ability of family members, and their health. This difficult balance was sometimes referred to as the "peasant dilemma."[28] The dilemma did not affect all peasants equally. There were wealthier peasants who controlled more land or better quality land or had other resources that gave them an advantage over their more vulnerable neighbors.[29] It makes at least the poorest peasants vulnerable to losing their land. Peasant community production and consumption have always tended to be primarily local, not connected to larger national or global markets. Peasant communities that sell their produce in nearby cities may experience more exposure to a larger world, but even that tends to be limited to their stall or booth in a marketplace where other peasants sell. Peasants may crave, and occasionally obtain, items from the larger world, but often these items remain as unattained wants.[30] This depiction of peasant life, however, is subject to wide variation, even within one region or community, and certainly in global perspective.

Peasant communities have another important—and crucial—characteristic. Despite their local orientation, they have almost always been subordinate parts of larger political entities such as empires and nation states. They were relied upon to feed the population and as a source to be taxed for food or money to support the king, the army, or the state and church bureaucracy. Rulers, states, and empires derived much of their power from their ability to exploit a large peasant population to feed armies, bureaucracies, and to keep restive populations fed. The exploitative nature of this structure was traditionally masked under rituals, protocols, and an ideology of paternal protection, in a context of local life where people knew each other personally, and a sense of familiarity tempered the sense of exploitation. This mask often slipped, and peasants, *peones* on haciendas, and other locally exploited rural communities engaged in subversion or rose in revolt that might or might not lead to larger rebellions and movements of change.[31] But these incidents only tended to underscore the dependency of rulers and states on the peasants. For centuries in many areas of the world, traditional peasant life was, and was understood as, a fundamental asset to the power and function of rulers and states. John Bodley describes this in his schema of the three phases of food production and control: familial, political, commercial. In this depiction, familial food production is that of the family, tribal unit or small community not under the control of a larger entity. The transition from peasant to landless or land poor proletarian societies under development and commercial extractivism signals the move from political to commercial food production and control. The commercial and economic elite—not the feudal lord, the king—becomes the controlling entity, a situation characteristic of modern political economies.[32] This elite usually has international connections and networks.

By the 1960s, as developmentalism became a dominant ideology in Latin American governance, the role of the state changed and the power of rulers and states began to depend not on peasant production but increasingly on "development." Developmental models demanded not peasants but mobile workers and wage laborers. Governments in "developing" countries thought they had to decide whether to feed their populations through local—including peasant—food production, or by expanding large-scale export agriculture and extractive projects and use the income from these exports to import food for the population. The latter was a strategy that favored "economies of scale," creating a larger labor pool, and reducing or eliminating reliance on peasant farming.

In a country like Honduras, the consequences of this transformation have been far-reaching and multi-generational. As landless peoples came to cities seeking work that was scarce and poorly paid, their children and grandchildren grew up in a reality that was for many of them increasingly poor, insecure, precarious, and often violent. The destruction of local, relatively self-reliant, and closely-knit communities set several generations adrift and needing to find a new reality that gave them identity (personal, social, and political) and new meaning. This has happened at the same time, and in relation to the rise of a whole new and largely illegal export production sector in Latin America in the form of narcotics, arms, and human trafficking.

The 1960s and 1970s in Latin America was a time when movements for radical change clashed with determined efforts of elites to maintain control of wealth and power, this time by means of controlling and profiting from modernization and development. The political and economic elites often saw themselves as junior partners with elites in "developed' countries. For much of Latin America, the dominant developed country was the United States. The global transformation—or elimination—of peasant communities continues into the present, and it is by no means complete. The process continues to generate much conflict and repression in countries like Honduras, but is now much accelerated with the introduction of neoextractivism. The inclusion of Mexico and most of Central America into "free trade" regional agreements often accelerated the disintegration of local peasant communities. Thus, various forces met in unholy alliance to doom the widespread pursuit of peasant life and to ensure disappearing peasantries.

A MORAL TRANSFORMATION

The transformation from peasant to landless "proletarian" (or to a reality that straddles both) is not only economic. It also reshapes how people think of and identify themselves, how they cope with the loss of traditional rural community life and its social relationships, how they find or create new communities and forms of organization for survival, and how they interpret and manage a new reality not of their making and over which they seem to have little control, or "what it means to lose control over the means of production and to be controlled by them."[33] To some, development must have represented to some degree what Michael Taussig describes in a particular instance: the intervention of "an evil and destructive way of ordering economic life."[34] Yet, development also presented itself in various ways as opportunity, even as the new El Dorado (the city of gold) to many national and local elites who tried to sell to local populations the benefits of development projects. When salesmanship failed, force was employed.

As a form of development, neoextractivism represents to some extent a new ideology of governance and a new social morality. The older ideology claimed the right of a small elite to govern the development of the nation in the best interest of national sovereignty and the people. Neoextractivism replaces or obscures the goal of "development" with the priority of extraction of resources divorced from any coherent and sustainable program of "development." Extraction of resources—as many and as fast as possible—becomes in practice the purpose; national development is secondary. The emergence of this ideology of the priority of extraction over national development and sovereignty has laid increasingly bare the contradictions that were already visible before, between ideology and lived reality. The widening gap between what is presented as reality in the dominant ideology and what people actually experience in their lives is where criticism and resistance grow. "The breaking of the norms and values of a dominant ideology is typically the work of the bearers of a new mode of production, and not of subordinate classes such as peasants and workers."[35]

A new morality places a priority on extraction over other values such as human life and environmental health, and even discards the goals of national development and sovereignty.[36] The new ideology and morality shape the role and function of the state. Laws and political and legal institutions are now seen not so much as guardians of national order and more as instruments at the service of extractive enterprise—a "new institutionalism" reshapes governance to facilitate this end.[37] In the new morality that neoextractive frenzy promotes, violence and corruption are the means of governance. The scale of neoextractive investment and the profits expected from it increase the profit and wealth fetish. Taking cuts and bribes invades all aspects of society. Public officials siphon off money from the budgets of public services. The privatization of state services becomes an extension of the logic of privatization of profit instead of nationalization of benefit. It provides another avenue for corruption, enriching the owners of utilities and the officials who sell them the contracts. Government-private joint projects successfully obscure the flows of investment and profit. More profit is made as privatized services raise the prices of necessities like electricity and water while curtailing even basic maintenance of services. The public, especially the poor and marginalized, become yet another resource from which to extract profit. Corruption becomes "the operating system."[38]

As a result, public confidence and trust in the major institutions of society weakens across all social classes. Criminal gangs flourish among poor and disillusioned youth living in a society where the rulers themselves routinely disregard or re-write laws. Gangs become virtual proto-states within the state.[39] Government turns increasingly to fear and force to subdue popular discontent, relying more on police and military (militarization of daily life) and criminal gangs as proxy enforcers of fear and "governance" in many neighborhoods and areas.

All of this becomes the context in which children and grandchildren of the displaced rural communities of earlier developmentalism live with poverty and unemployment. The multiple effects of neoextractivism hit this already vulnerable population very hard, often leading to seemingly impossible living situations in which all avenues of change seem to narrow or disappear. Joining gangs and turning to criminality become paths to survival and identity, at least in the short run, and for some it can also be an expression of protest or resistance against the hypocrisy of the state and its institutions.[40] Others fall prey to internalized desperation and social pathologies of domestic, gender, and familial violence, alcohol and drugs, and quiet despair. Some turn to spontaneous or organized protest and resistance.[41] Many begin to see emigration as the path to survival.

This description does not apply everywhere in its entirety because of local and regional differences. It does apply in Central America, and especially to Honduras from which some of the largest numbers of immigrants and asylum seekers have come to the southern border of the United States in the years since 2010. There are historical and geopolitical events that have also shaped a unique context in Central America. This long history, of empire, capital investment, and development breaking down local self-reliant communities into large and shifting pools of landless workers produced in Honduras and in much of Latin America considerable internal migration of people seeking survival and identity. As this scenario worsened, it also began to produce flows of emigrants. Emigration has become another form of extractivism, extraction of human resources—human capital, talent, energy, and a source of wealth—not so much for the emigrants who are the "human commodities" in this extractive system, but for others who profit from the fears, desperation, toil, and miseries of the emigrants.

MIGRATION: LUCRATIVE EXTRACTIVE ENTERPRISE

Increasingly, emigration from Central America to the United States has become not simply an unfortunate consequence of neoextractive development but a necessary and integral feature of it, and a lucrative extractive business enterprise. Money is made on the removal of people, the human product, from the colony to the center of empire. Despite, or perhaps in part because of, the ongoing and often heated debates about how to reform immigration and asylum processes and resolve the "crisis," the current situation of migrant misery is lucrative for both the Honduran and the U.S. governments and for significant sectors of the business community and criminal enterprises in both countries. By 2019, the nearly one million Hondurans living in the United States were sending back to Honduras about four billion dollars in remittances annually, accounting for 21.5 percent of income for the Honduran economy.[42] Remittances come to Honduras in U.S. dollars that do not all go directly to the intended recipients—the families of emigrants. Some, at least, are funneled to the Honduran Central Bank or to a private bank. Through the bank, the families receive remittances in Honduran currency, *lempiras*, that have a smaller buying power than dollars. The bank loans income from remittances to larger entrepreneurs who need dollars to purchase and trade on the world market.[43]

In October 1998, Hurricane Mitch devastated much of Honduras, causing more than two billion dollars in damages and leaving several hundred thousand people homeless.[44] Honduran immigrants and asylum seekers already in the United States were among those granted Temporary Protective Status (TPS), a relief that acknowledges that conditions in the home country are not amenable to safe deportation or return due to natural disasters, wars, or other events. TPS must be renewed periodically and can be ended as conditions in the home country are assessed. Fifty-seven thousand Hondurans who enjoyed Temporary Protective Status in the United States faced termination of TPS. Together, they were contributing almost 15 percent of remittances send back to Honduras.[45] Their deportation would likely have increased the economic hardship of their families and relatives in Honduras who depend on them. Before the decision was made to terminate the TPS program, U.S. diplomats and embassy personnel warned that termination would send a flood of deportees back to El Salvador and Honduras that would further destabilize fragile economic and perhaps political security in those countries. The U.S. Administration ignored those warnings and terminated the program in May 2017. Two devastating hurricanes in 2020 led to the re-instatement of TPS for Hondurans. Meanwhile the Honduran government provided very little support for the families of emigrants or for returning deportees, although the emigrants had been a major source of income for the country.

Remittances enrich the Honduran economy in other ways, as well, even if they do relatively little to help the very families for which they are intended. Families that receive money periodically from relatives abroad are often poor, and the sums they receive from these remittances are often meager when compared to the needs. For many, remittances from relatives in the United States are the only means of support, and even that is often not enough to provide the minimum necessary for survival. Families that live with a constant, if sometimes subtle, sense of economic and social insecurity, powerlessness, and social inferiority may become targets of advertising, media propaganda, and a consumer culture that encourage the purchase of items that symbolize convenience, modernity, a small taste of "luxury," and control of at least a small part of one's life. This sort of "commodity fetishism" siphons off some of the meager incomes and remittances of families away from the longer-term goals of a better house (or even house ownership), educational support for their children, improving family health conditions, or even accumulating the capital to start a small business.[46] Consumer propaganda helps perpetuate the cycle of economic insecurity for families. More compelling is the awareness that attempts to save and invest in a better future are likely to be threatened by the daily bite of local gangs demanding extortion payments from families and small businesses, corrupt police and officials who must be bribed and appeased, prices that continue to rise, and a host of other dangers. What is the use, then, of dedicating remittance money to longer-term plans? In this way, the work of emigrants in the United States ends up benefiting not so much their families in Honduras but others who control parts of the economic system.

Criminal enterprises, gangs, and drug traffickers launder money through the system of remittances and the Honduran Central Bank. Coyotes offering to guide Hondurans to the United States are entrepreneurs in a big business that benefits directly from the flow of migration and circular (repeat) migration. Migrants are used as mules for drug trafficking and are victims of human trafficking. This only exacerbates the tendency to identify migrants and deportees as criminals instead of victims.

The United States benefits from the immigrant Hondurans as a cheap labor force, but also as a more educated work force. Hondurans who have lived in the United States for years are often contributing to the U.S. economy and society as professionals and service providers, and as parents whose children also become active contributors to the economy.[47] But they are also used as symbolic figures in the arguments over immigration that U.S. politicians and governments wage to further their own political fortunes. Immigrants and asylum seekers become political fodder to increase the political capital of certain politicians and government figures. Central American immigrants are criminalized by U.S. authorities and the media, and so also enter the public discourse as criminal suspects. This makes them useful both for the personal agendas of politicians and also for the promotion of fear among the U.S. population; fear that is a basis of the national security mentality. The U.S. response to immigrants and asylum seekers like the Hondurans reveals a tension or contradiction between the economic and social contributions they provide and the short-term political advantage of using them as scapegoats for the country's problems. Thus, immigrants and immigration can be politically as well as economically profitable. Immigrant bodies and lives are traded for political gain, as politicians in the United States play on immigration policy to appeal to their base.

Recent Honduran asylum seekers in the United States are also likely to become part of the large population of detainees in detention centers awaiting a hearing and/or deportation. Most of the centers are prison-like, and by 2015 many were operated by private corporations on contract with the U.S. government.[48] The government paid the corporations based on the number of detainees in the centers that they managed. These corporations have a financial incentive to spend as little as possible on the living conditions and welfare of each detainee, and to inhibit for as long as possible the rotation of detainees out of detention.[49] Asylum-seekers fortunate enough to have knowledge of their rights and to secure legal representation (things not always provided to them) may wait months or years for a hearing to determine their status.

These are some of the many ways that the increasing flow of immigrants from Honduras and other Central American countries becomes another lucrative extractive industry, one created largely by the rapaciousness of neoextractivism itself. In this sense the so-called "immigration crisis" is an integral component of the imperial relationship between the United States and Honduras.

CRIMINALIZING IMMIGRANTS

Historically, criminalization of immigrants has been a feature of social thought and politics during much of the history of the United States.[50] There are several reasons for this, but immigrant criminalization is a critical aspect of the U.S. imperial relationship to Central America. Criminalization supports the production of "colonized identities" that make "them" different from "us"—a crucial form of control and regulation in imperial systems.[51] It can be accomplished through racial stratification and invented standards of "respectability," or by granting formal citizenship without substantive citizenship—denying some citizens the full benefits of citizenship. It can also be attempted through depicting the inevitable flows of migrants from client countries as something to be feared—criminals, terrorists, anarchists, invading hordes, or as pawns manipulated by our enemies. To admit that immigrants in large numbers are worthy of integration into their new home would be to undercut the idea of their "otherness" and threaten one of the ideological and cultural pillars of the imperial relationship. While anti-immigrant sentiment is not new in the United States, it takes on a special role and importance in a neo-colonial relationship such as that between the United States and Central America. Criminalization helps to perpetuate the immigration crisis and tries to render immigrants powerless and dependent. This is, perhaps, a response to the realization that migration is an embarrassment and a form of resistance. The fact that the United States is itself a "country of immigrants" is in part the reason why there is also a strong empathy that fuels "pro-immigrant" sentiment in the United States—the myth of unsuitable difference has already (historically) been disproven in practice throughout the history of the United States.

Hondurans are declared criminals by their own government before they leave Honduras if they try to defend their land or resources from extractive development projects. Human rights and environmental activists are subject to being criminalized for their actions; the case of Berta Cáceres is emblematic. They are declared criminals if they engage in peaceful protest or popular resistance, since there are laws in place in Honduras to criminalize forms of public protest and, in any case, police and military regularly detain peaceful protesters.[52] High school and university students are increasingly treated as criminals by arbitrary acts of police violence perpetrated against them, including police invasion of schools to arrest students and, in the process, the use of tear gas against fleeing students.[53] University students are special targets of government suspicion since some are critical activists who care about building a better future for their country. Young people, teenage males especially, are considered or treated as if they were already criminals if they have the misfortune to live in certain areas of cities that are considered especially violent or gang-controlled. Since many youth in such areas must agree to do the bidding of gangs in order to survive, this fact lends the label of "criminal" a veneer of plausibility. What is criminal behavior in a context where a person must survive by any means available? Young men in Northern Triangle countries are subjects of "chimeric" or shifting identities, portrayed as both perpetrators and victims of gang violence. This follows them if they become migrants and asylum seekers, and plays into the narratives of both U.S. and

Honduran authorities that these youth, and by extension other migrants, are "criminals" and "rapists." This deflects the embarrassing question: What horrific conditions must they be fleeing in their countries of origin?

The process of "criminalization" in Honduras is achieved through diffuse means. Newspapers report gang violence, replete with photos of young men from poor neighborhoods in police detention as perpetrators of violence, or as accomplices, or as victims—but even victims are assumed to have become victims because of something they did. Government and police officials regularly declare their intent to combat youth violence with enforcement or education and training. Religious leaders reinforce messages of personal guilt and responsibility for the violence in Honduras. Criminalization of the poor and vulnerable and of the defenders of land and water in Honduras serves to promote a sense of insecurity that aids political control of the population and militarization of society and to distract attention from the criminal behavior of government officials, official corruption, and violations of the Constitution and laws by state actors.

Migrants are often criminalized as they leave Honduras—it is often one of the reasons why they leave since it seems that all peaceful means of change in their home country are repressed as criminal behavior. As they move north toward Mexico and the United States, migrants are subject to another set of accusations. This involves imposing on them what one scholar calls "chimeric identities"—identities that define people in several apparently contradictory ways simultaneously. They are vulnerable victims that need forms of protection. Everyone, it seems, cares for their safety; the journey north is dangerous and the migrants should abandon it and return to the safety of their home countries. Some wondered why governments were suddenly so solicitous for their security outside Honduras but cared so little for their security in Honduras or once they reached the U.S. border. This attempt to depict migrants as needy victims allowed the authorities of both Honduras and the United States to downplay the dangers of remaining in Honduras and to dissuade people from coming to the United States since conditions at home were not so bad as to warrant migration.

Simultaneously, however, migrants are also painted as criminals and people of dubious moral character—drug dealers, gang members, mothers who cared little for the safety of the children they dragged along on a perilous journey, people with diseases, young men who were looking for an easy life rather than doing the hard work of building their home countries—an invading horde, even terrorists. The chimeric identity of migrants as both victims and criminals has deep roots in racialized thinking in the United States. It provides a flexible tool for maintaining a wall of separation between us and them.

Immigrants and asylum seekers leaving a country in large numbers signal an embarrassing truth to the world: there must be something very wrong in their home country. For the United States in the twenty-first century, caravans of asylum seekers from Central America pose a threat, not to the security of the United States but to its imperial relationship to Central America. Their colonized identities make them "unsuitable," which really means that if we allow them to become us, there is no difference between them and us, and the whole imperial enterprise, or at least a prime rationale for it, collapses. We can tolerate a few, but not too many. The presence of so many Honduran immigrants and refugees in particular is an embarrassment to the United States, since they are fleeing conditions in a country that the United States has had a dominant hand in shaping for more than a century. Conditions from which Honduran emigrants flee undermine the legal distinction in U.S. immigration policy between "economic immigrants" seeking better opportunity and "asylum seekers" fleeing for their lives. In Honduras, poverty makes one much more vulnerable to violence of all kinds. When Hondurans say they migrate because of poverty, they are likely also to be fleeing vulnerability to extreme violence. To confer on immigrants a possible chimeric identity as both economic migrants and asylum seekers would imply admitting a much larger number of migrants into the United States. One mechanism for deflecting this possibility is to criminalize and trivialize migrants.

IDEOLOGICAL BREAKDOWN AND SURVIVAL

Development became the new name and the new ideology of imperial reach. Development ideology was hegemonic inasmuch as it claimed that there were no viable alternatives to it. Then the most recent iteration of development, neoextractivism, introduced new modes of production in intensity and extent beyond what had characterized the older extractivism practiced for centuries in Latin America. Extraction for profit became the end, the purpose, the priority in itself more imperative than national development, sovereignty, or the common good. This became increasingly apparent to people who saw and lived the consequences of this breakage of the development ideology in their own lives. Under the name of extractivism as development, the very moral values that development always touted were violated—widening poverty and insecurity instead of prosperity, and the subordination of national sovereignty to private and foreign interests over land, resources, and economic institutions through mining contracts, privatization, and other means. In a sense, extractivism's abandonment of any semblance of common-good "development" opened a pandora's box of consequences, that finally formed the context, the perfect storm in which large numbers of marginalized people decided that the only path to survival led out of Central America to the north. This perfect storm did not break over all of Latin America, but it did in Central America where other actions coming from the north, the United States in the 1980s—deportation of gang members, arms sales and trafficking, use of gangs and drug traffickers in proxy wars in Central America, and more—gave an increasingly lethal character to the damage caused by neoextractivism.

Development created the conditions of precarity that made large numbers of Central Americans vulnerable. Extractivism worsened those conditions and removed even the hope of better that development had, however feebly, promised. Increasing popular resistance was one response. Emigration became another response, one that was at once an attempt to escape the hegemony of the rich, a threat to that hegemony, and even a form of collective resistance. "The rich, the precondition of their new wealth has been the systematic dismantling of the practices that previously rationalized their wealth, status, and leadership. Their economic domination has come at the cost of having broken their own hegemony."[54]

Development policies and the actions and assumptions that constitute them do not displace people in a vacuum. People displaced by war and political conflict, for example, are living within conditions that are shaped by struggles for economic and political power that result in open conflict. Development is undertaken and functions almost always in the context of a particular political economy. In its simplest sense, the term political economy is used to define the structured relationship between economic and political power, usually within the structures of a modern nation state. Wealth or the means to generate wealth and political power are interchanged or integrated in particular persons or institutions. The one who has the gold makes the rules. The one who makes the rules does so in order to increase wealth for oneself or to regulate and distribute wealth for others or for the nation. The development policies pursued by a national government are likely to affect and be affected by the nature of the relationship between economic and political power. The conditions and forces that promote much emigration are created and shaped by development policies operating within the dynamics of the political economy of a nation state. Whether development is an instrument to increase the wealth and political power of a small group at the expense of others, or is an instrument of increasing prosperity and security for an entire nation—the decisions about development's purpose are shaped largely by issues such as whether a small group holds both wealth and the monopoly of political power and wants to maintain their privileged position. We see this dynamic at work in Honduras, and it is extant in other Central American countries. There is conflict in this that at times has erupted into open warfare in Central America, but is mostly seen as local or regional violence in which development practices clash with local needs and autonomy—a sort of ongoing low-level warfare waged by the economic and political elite against others who seem to stand in their way.

But there is still one more level to which our awareness of the situation must rise. The nation-state is the usual structure within which political economy functions, but at least since the beginning of modern imperial/colonialism, the political economy of the state is influenced, shaped, and ultimately controlled by a global political economy. Our understanding of "the state" itself has changed from an image of a monolithic player to a diverse set of people, interests, and institutions that do not always function in harmony.[55] This allows us to shift our attention from nation-states to a larger context in which it is not "the state" but rather individuals and groups (and perhaps institutions) within the state that operate within a global network that shapes development. In reality, "what develops are not countries but a global pattern of domination and distribution of power."[56] This pattern is exercised through the creation of chains of dependencies in which national elites in countries such as Honduras and the rest of Central America are linked to foreign elites. In the next chapter, we explore all of this as it operates in Honduras, between Honduras and countries such as the United States, and how it contributes to emigration.

NOTES

1. Eric R. Wolf, *Peasant Wars of the Twentieth Century* (New York: Harper and Row, 1969).

2. Savva Dmitrievich Purlevski, *A Life under Russian Serfdom: The Memoirs of Savva Dmitrievich Purlevski, 1800–1868*, trans. Boris B. Gorshkov (Budapest: Central European University Press, 2005), Open End Edition Books, 2013, https://books.openedition.org/ceup/488; John MacKay, trans. and ed., *Four Russian Serf Narratives* (Madison: University of Wisconsin Press, 2009).

3. For example, Elizabeth Teresa Newman, *Biography of a Hacienda: Work and Revolution in Rural Mexico* (Tucson: University of Arizona Press, 2014), https://uapress.arizona.edu/book/biography-of-a-hacienda; Julio Cotler, "Traditional Haciendas and Communities in a Context of Political Mobilization in Peru," in *Agrarian Problems and Peasant Movements in Latin America*, ed. Rodolfo Stavenhagen (Garden City NY: Anchor Books, 1970), 533–558.

4. Wolf, *Peasant Wars*; Robert Buijtenhuijs, "Peasant Wars in Africa: Gone with the Wind?" in *Disappearing Peasantries? Rural Labour in Africa, Asia, and Latin America*, ed. Deborah Bryceson, Cristóbal Kay, and Jos Mooij (London: Intermediate Technology Publications, 2000), 112–122.

5. James C. Scott, *Seeing Like a State: How Certain Schemes to Improve the Human Condition Have Failed* (New Haven CT: Yale University Press, 1998), 2.

6. Vandana Shiva, *Monocultures of the Mind: Perspectives on Biodiversity and Biotechnology* (New York: Palgrave Macmillan, 1993).

7. Orlando Patterson, *The Confounding Island: Jamaica and the Postcolonial Predicament* (Cambridge MA: Belknap/Harvard University Press, 2019), 40; Gordon K. Lewis, *The Growth of the Modern West Indies* (New York: Modern Reader Paperback, 1968), 49–53; Eric Williams, *Capitalism and Slavery* (Durham NC: University of North Carolina Press, 1944), 207.

8. Eric Williams, *From Columbus to Castro: The History of the Caribbean 1492–1969* (London: André Deutsch, 1970), 280–292.

9. Catherine Hall, "White Visions, Black Lives: The Free Villages of Jamaica," *History Workshop*, no. 36 (Autumn 1993): 100–132; Hugh Paget, "The Growth of Villages in Jamaica and British Guiana," *Caribbean Quarterly* 10, no. 1 (1964): 38–51; Sidney Mintz, "Historical Sociology of the Jamaican Church-Founded Free Village System," *New West Indian Guide* 38 no. 1 (January 1958): 46–70.

10. Patterson, *The Confounding Island*, 49–54; Williams, *From Columbus to Castro*, 400–402; Sydney Olivier, *The Myth of Governor Eyre* (London: L and Virginia Woolf, 1933).

11. Sydney Olivier, *Jamaica, the Blessed Island* (London: Faber and Faber, 1936).

12. Elizabeth Dore, *Myths of Modernity: Peonage and Patriarchy in Nicaragua* (Durham NC: Duke University Press, 2006), 149–163.

13. Dore, *Myths of Modernity*, 3–4 and throughout.

14. Jeffrey L. Gould, *To Die in This Way: Nicaraguan Indians and the Myth of Mestizaje, 1880–1965* (Durham NC: Duke U Press, 1998).

15. Salvador Martí y Puig and David Close, *Nicaragua y el FSLN 1979–2009* (Barcelona: Edicions Bellaterra, 2009).

16. Lewis Hanke, *The Spanish Struggle for Justice in the Conquest of America* (Boston: Little Brown, 1965), 83–105.

17. Paul Doughty, "Ending Serfdom in Peru: The Struggle for Land and Freedom in Vicos," in *Contemporary Cultures and Societies of Latin America*, Third Edition, ed. Dwight B. Heath (Prospect Heights IL: Waveland Press, 2002), 225–243.

18. Olivier, *Jamaica the Blessed Island*.

19. Patterson, *The Confounding Island*, 49–50.

20. Marvin Brahona, *Honduras en el siglo XX: Una síntesis histórica* (Tegucigalpa: Editorial Guaymuras, 2005), 31–32; Dario Euraque, *Reinterpreting the Banana Republic: Region and State in Honduras 1870–1972* (Chapel Hill NC: University of North Carolina Press, 1996), 5–6.

21. Barahona, *Honduras*, 52–57; Euraque, *Reinterpreting*, 5–9.

22. Sidney Mintz, "The Rural Proletariat and the Problem of Rural Proletarian Consciousness," *Journal of Peasant Studies* 1, no. 3 (1974): 291–325; Cristóbal Kay, "Latin America's Agrarian Transformation: Peasantization and Proletarianization," in *Disappearing Peasantries? Rural Labour in Africa, Asia, and Latin America*, eds. Deborah Bryceson, Cristóbal Kay, and Jos Mooij (London: Intermediate Technology Publications, 2000), 123–138.

23. James Phillips, "Democratic Socialism, the New International Economic Order, and Globalization: Jamaica's Sugar Cooperatives in the Post-Colonial Transition," *The Global South* 4, no. 2 (Fall 2010): 189.

24. James Phillips, *Honduras in Dangerous Times: Resistance and Resilience* (Lanham MD: Lexington Books, 2015), 72–77; Longino Becerra, *Evolución histórica de Honduras* (Tegucigalpa: Editorial Baktun, 1983).

25. For example, Ernest Feder, *The Rape of the Peasantry: Latin America's Landholding System* (Garden City NY: Doubleday and Company, 1971).

26. For detailed discussions of contrasting viewpoints see, Rodolfo Stavenhagen, editor, *Agrarian Problems and Peasant Movements in Latin America* (Garden City NY: Doubleday and Company, 1970).

27. James D. Cockcroft, André Gunder Frank, and Dale L. Johnson, editors, *Dependence and Underdevelopment: Latin America's Political Economy* (Garden City NY: Doubleday and Company, 1970); Stavenhagen, *Agrarian Problems.*

28. For different perspectives on the meaning of peasant, see Deborah F. Bryceson, "Peasant Theories and Smallholder Policies: Past and Present," in *Disappearing Peasantries?* 1–36; George M. Foster, "What Is a Peasant?" in *Peasant Society: A Reader*, eds. Jack M. Potter, May N. Diaz, and George M. Foster (Boston: Little Brown and Company, 1967), 2–14; Eric R. Wolf, *Peasants* (Englewood Cliffs NJ: Prentice-Hall, 1966).

29. Kees Jansen, "Structural Adjustment, Peasant Differentiation, and the Environment in Central America," in *Disappearing Peasantries?* 192–212.

30. Mary J. Weismantel, *Food, Gender, and Poverty in the Ecuadorian Andes* (Philadelphia: University of Pennsylvania Press, 1989).

31. James C. Scott, *Weapons of the Weak: Everyday Forms of Peasant Resistance* (New Haven CT: Yale University Press, 1985); Wolf, *Peasant Wars*. The literature of studies devoted to particular peasant revolts is large.

32. See, for example, John Bodley, *Anthropology and Contemporary Human Problems*, Sixth Edition (Lanham, MD: AltaMira Press, 2012), Chapters 4 and 5.

33. Michael Taussig, *The Devil and Commodity Fetishism in South America, Thirtieth Edition* (Chapel Hill NC: University of North Carolina Press, 2010), 17.

34. Taussig, *The Devil*, 17.

35. Scott, *Weapons of the Weak*, 318.

36. Claudia Mendoza, "El sol, el agua, un fusil en la frente," Centro de Estudios para la Democracia (CESPAD), September 29, 2020, http://cespad.org.hn/2020/09/29/el-sol-el-aguao-un-fusil-en-la-frente/.

37. Maristella Svampa, *Las fronteras del neoextractivismo en América Latina: Coflictos socioambientales, giro ecoterritorial y nuevas dependencias* (Guadalajara: Universidad de Guadalajara, 2019), 40–45.

38. Sarah Chayes, *When Corruption Is the Operating System: The Case of Honduras* (Washington DC: Carnegie Endowment for International Peace, 2017).

39. Max Manwaring, *State and Nonstate Associated Gangs: Credible "Midwives of New Social Orders?"* (Carlisle PA: Army War College Strategic Studies Institute, 2009), https://apps.dtic.mil/sti/pdfs/ADA499689.pdf.

40. Jon Wolseth, *Jesus and the Gang: Youth Violence and Christianity in Urban Honduras* (Tucson: University of Arizona Press, 2011); Jon Horne Carter, "Gothic Sovereignty: Gangs and Criminal Community in a Honduran Prison," *The South Atlantic Quarterly* 113, no. 3 (Summer 2014): 475–502.

41. Phillips's *Honduras in Dangerous Times* describes the culture of popular resistance that has evolved in Honduras.

42. World Bank, "Personal remittances, received (% of GDP), Honduras (1974–2019)," 2021, https://data.worldbank.org/indicator/BX.TRF.PWKR.DT.GD.ZS?locations=HN.

43. From my interviews with staff members of the Honduran Reflection, Investigation, and Communication Team (ERIC-SJ), who research remittances, September 2019.

44. Pan American Health Organization, "Impact of Hurricane Mitch in Central America," *Epidemiological Bulletin* 19, no. 4 (December 1998), https://www.paho.org/english/sha/epibul_95-98/be984mitch.htm; James C. McKinley Jr., "Honduras' Capital: City of the Dead and the Dazed," *New York Times,* November 5, 1998, https://archive.nytimes.com/www.nytimes.com/library/world/americas/110598honduras-destruction.html.

45. Latin America Working Group, "Negative Consequences of Ending Temporary Protective Status (TPS) for U.S. Investment in El Salvador and Honduras," March 2019, https://www.congress.gov/116/meeting/house/109000/documents/HHRG-116-JU00-20190306-SD021.pdf, a report presented to the U.S. Congress.

46. From my interviews with staff members of the Honduran Reflection Investigation and Communication Team (ERIC-SJ), who research remittances, September 2019.

47. Eric L. Olson and John Wachter, *What If They Return? How El Salvador, Honduras, and the United States Could Prepare for an Effective Reintegration of TPF Beneficiaries*, Wilson Center (n.d., but later than 2019), https://www.wilsoncenter.org/sites/default/files/media/documents/publication/lap_olson_and_wachter_.pdf.

48. Detention Watch Network, "Immigration Detention 101" (n.d., but later than 2019), "https://archive.nytimes.com/www.nytimes.com/library/world/americas/110598honduras-destruction.html.

49. Detention Watch Network, "Financial Incentives" (n.d., but later than 2019), https://archive.nytimes.com/www.nytimes.com/library/world/americas/110598honduras-destruction.html.

50. José Luis Rocha's *Expulsados de la globalización: Políticas migratorias y deportados centroamericanos* (Managua: Instituto de Historia de Nicaragua y Centroamérica, 2010) is entirely devoted to describing the ways in which immigrants are criminalized in the United States. See also Alejandro Portes and Rubén Rumbaut, *Immigrant America: A Portrait,* Fourth Edition (Oakland CA: University of California Press, 2020), 1–47 and 371–393.

51. Walter D. Mignolo, *Local Histories/Global Designs: Coloniality, Subaltern Knowledges, and Border Thinking* (Princeton NJ: Princeton University Press, 2000).

52. Héctor Silva Ávalos, "Honduras' New Criminal Code Will Help Impunity Prosper," InSight Crime, June 29, 2020, https://insightcrime.org/news/analysis/honduras-new-criminal-code/.

53. For example, Telesur, "Honduran Police Fire Tear Gas, Water Cannon at Student Protest," July 25, 2017, https://www.telesurenglish.net/news/Honduran-Police-Fire-Tear-Gas-Water-Cannon-at-Student-Protest-20170725-0029.html. Also see a short film of Honduran military police responding to student protest in Tegucigalpa at https://www.youtube.com/watch?v=rNYBX3BwrMQ.

54. Scott, *Weapons of the Weak*, 345.

55. Jordan Levy, "Schoolteachers and National 'Public' Education in Honduras: Navigating the Reforms and Refounding the State," *Journal of Latin American and Caribbean Anthropology* 22, no. 1 (2017): 137–156.

56. Anibal Quijano and Michael Ennis, "Coloniality of Power and Eurocentrism in Latin America," *Nepantla: Views from South* 1, no. 3 (2000): 533–580.

Chapter 5

Evolution of the Honduran Political Economy

In January 2020, the Honduran journalist Jennifer Ávila wrote:

> In Honduras, doing independent journalism means constantly running into a wall. This wall is built by mafia-run institutions that have silenced and terrorized whole communities. To simplify a complex reality, the media has labelled the country a narcostate. It's not hyperbole, but it also doesn't capture all the complicated factors. We live in a reality where drug trafficking and political power complement each other, where institutions are meant to launder money and where a president can get himself reelected by using money made from drug trafficking and political robbery. . . . But Honduras is also more than a narcostate. Before, when there were no drug cartels to control the country, it was a corrupt group of elites, as well as a fruit company, that wielded power over the president. The state was designed to facilitate crime and the enrichment of a select few. In both setups, silence is golden. Silence is a form of survival.[1]

This chapter outlines some of the ways in which the political economy of modern Honduras developed, and how economic and political power were formed and integrated. Honduras is controlled by a small group of "elite" families tied to networks of international capital and influence (including illegal enterprise), channeled through the overarching historical hegemony of the United States. With this chapter, we begin a more focused and detailed examination of modern Honduras and the major forces that have created the conditions driving some of its citizens to seek asylum elsewhere.

A CRUCIAL REALITY: NORMAL LIFE

To begin, it must be emphasized once again that there is significant danger in what anthropologists often term "essentializing." It is a danger often encountered by those who provide expert witnessing in asylum hearings. How is one to describe adequately and convincingly the scope of the problems and negative forces at play in Honduras without inadvertently contributing to the sense that the negative forces are all there is to the country, the whole story? Honduras, as everywhere, is overwhelmingly a land of ordinary people trying to lead normal lives and to survive. It is important to understand the difficulties described here not in a vacuum but in the context of these good and ordinary lives. One of the major questions that animates the story of life in Honduras and the flow of emigration from there is the apparent deterioration over several decades of what people considered normal, replaced by a more violent and warped image of reality.[2] Projects of life and death vie for dominance. Amid this imperial debris, parents try to provide a sense of the good and the normal for the next generation. Without the realization of this foundational, ordinary, normal pursuit of daily life, the question of why people flee makes little sense. The message delivered daily to Hondurans through the media and government officials is that the current conditions of violence, corruption, and repression are the new normal. Some Hondurans worry aloud that the rising generation of Honduran youth will accept that violence rather than the rule of law is how one must live. From this perspective, asylum seeking is born in the attempt to seek the conditions for a normal life—a life before or beyond or better than the current situation—that seems increasingly evasive or threatened in one's own land. Ideas of what "normal life" has been, or would be, is a factor in determining how far conditions must stray from this image before people begin to think of emigrating.

SOME FOUNDATIONAL ASSUMPTIONS
OF THE MODERN HONDURAN STATE

For the Spanish colonial conquerors who wanted to impose a regime of land and labor control over Indigenous peoples in Central America, the region that is now Honduras posed a difficult challenge. The country was rugged and mountainous in the west, with dense tropical forest in the east. The many Indigenous peoples in the region pursued different subsistence patterns, some based on sedentary farming, others based on hunting, gathering, and temporary villages. The Spanish colonial mind seemed to consider the more sedentary groups as more "civilized," the more mobile as "uncivilized." These designations reflected a Eurocentric perspective, but they also suggested that the more sedentary peoples might be easier to subjugate and their land and labor to control.[3] The reality proved more complex and difficult. Under the leadership of Lempira, Indigenous peoples—the Lenca in particular—put up a fierce armed resistance to Spanish control. This resistance became a combination of sporadic attacks and flight into the more inaccessible regions, the mountains and the tropical forests. Some Indigenous groups in the western areas were brought under Spanish "control" and gathered into settlements (*pueblos indios*) where Spanish colonial authorities permitted internal self-government in limited fashion, if land and labor were turned also to supplying a surplus for the colonial authorities. In these *pueblos indios,* resistance took the forms of hiding surpluses, economic sabotage, and playing into the Spanish stereotype that native peoples were lazy.[4] Even here, flight to the mountains was possible. In the east, in what became known as the Mosquitia, control remained sporadic or absent throughout most of the colonial period.

The inability in Honduras to impose an effective and widespread regime of land and labor control, to harness the lands and work of Indigenous peoples more securely, must have been especially frustrating to the colonial rulers inasmuch as they seemed to perceive Honduras as a region potentially rich in resources, a land that could yield great wealth, a promise unfulfilled for lack of a reliable regime of land and labor control to extract the wealth.[5] The problem was laid to the ruggedness of the land that isolated communities, prevented transportation and communication, and provided safe havens for Indigenous peoples who did not want to work for the colonial rulers. A stereotype of Indigenous communities as "lazy" and rebellious became a weapon in the conflict to compel Indigenous people to submit to colonial authority. In addition, "vast amounts of land were simply outside the control of the elites, and were thus understood as empty."[6] This convenient fiction mirrored a colonial mentality that local peasant and Indigenous populations were inferior or not quite human, and that they did not deserve to control and manage the land and resources of the areas in which they lived. This fiction allowed colonial authorities, and later the incipient independent state, to justify any action to control how the land and resources of the country were controlled and used, for the state always knew better than the people. As important, it meant that the state could allow outsiders to encroach on the lands of Indigenous peoples and peasant communities with impunity. It promoted the idea of a more efficient and focused reliance on the unfettered inflow of foreign (global) capital and investment. Soon the myth of empty land and unproductive Indigenous land practices, "facilitated the adoption of a discourse of efficiency and exclusion in the name the dynamics of global capital."[7] The state and foreign investors knew better than the people how to manage the land and resources. The same fiction of empty or unused lands was also used to rationalize plans for the placement of charter or model cities (*ciudades modelos*), essentially foreign enclaves on Honduran soil already inhabited by Garifuna Indigenous communities on the Honduran Caribbean coast, or the displacement of farming and fishing communities on the Honduran Pacific coast.[8]

The establishment of a Honduran state with a strong central government and institutions was always a work in progress, and it was often subverted by the inability to establish effective control over the entire national territory and to reap the assumed wealth of the land. This, too, became a concern that fueled both the tendency to turn to absolutist political control—as in the national security state of the 1980s or the current virtual dictatorship and militarization of the country—and a pervasive concern about national sovereignty, especially as the country became increasingly infiltrated by foreign investment and political influence in the late nineteenth and twentieth centuries. Honduras was seen as a country with a strong ruling elite and a weak central government and state institutions. In the twenty-first century, the rise of powerful local and national criminal gang networks has allowed or forced the Honduran state to cede areas of control to the gangs and to establish a co-existent regime of control, corruption, and impunity using gangs as an extension of elite, if not state, control—"*fuerza paraestatal desde abajo*" (parastate force from below).[9]

EXTRACTIVE DEVELOPMENT, STATE POWER, AND FOREIGN INFLUENCE

How did the rulers of a newly independent Honduras try to create the economic and political basis for a strong centralized and modern nation state during the late nineteenth and early twentieth centuries? How was the political economy structured? Since the small ruling elite did not have the capital and sufficient resources to develop industry or commerce, they thought to attract and open Honduras to foreign investment in developing extractive industries so as to accumulate wealth for themselves and the national treasury.[10] This would provide an economic base for developing state institutions and political power. Extractive industry would appeal to foreign investors—the promise of gold, metals, minerals, precious mahogany and other wood, and good conditions for plantation export agriculture. In the last decades of the nineteenth century, the liberal government that was undertaking a serious attempt to found a modern Honduran state opened the country to mining companies from the United States. The Rosario Mining Company and others developed mines in the central areas around the old capital of Comayagua, and the new capital of Tegucigalpa, which was not much more than a small mountain town at the time.[11] But the wealth was there. The Honduran government and the elite that controlled it received income from granting mining concessions to foreign companies. There was also lumber extraction from the country's extensive mountain groves of precious mahogany.

At the end of the nineteenth century, U.S.-based fruit companies were beginning to enter Honduras. A combination of generous concessions and legal support from the Honduran government, and the backing of U.S. military power (the occasional gunboat off the northern coast of Honduras), allowed United Fruit and others to gain vast acreage in the north of the country, displacing peasant and Indigenous communities and hiring some of the displaced.[12] This system provided advantages for both the Honduran ruling elite, foreign corporations, and the United States. It allowed, even promoted, the extension of foreign economic and eventually political influence into Honduras. Political influence over Honduran affairs could also be exercised through members of the elite who were closely allied with U.S. business and economic investment interests. An example of this was that, for a period, the Honduran attorney general was also a legal adviser to United Fruit in Honduras.[13] Members of the Honduran elite benefited from their role as power brokers and gatekeepers for foreign investment. That role was valuable in giving Honduras links to the larger global economy and markets. The economic value of this function enhanced the political power of the elite as the most essential members of Honduran society. In order to buy into this belief, one must also buy into the belief that foreign investment and linking the national to the global economy were good things in themselves.

This elite strategy for strengthening and extending state power had several serious drawbacks. The most egregious was the displacement and disruption of life it caused for rural peasant and Indigenous communities that were displaced—sometimes by "legal" fictions, sometimes by violence—to make way for mining or the fruit companies' plantations. The displaced who found jobs on the foreign plantations became dependents of the companies and were paid low wages to work in difficult, often horrendous, conditions. Life as a workers on the fruit plantations was starkly described in *Prision Verde* (*Green Prison*) published in 1950 by Honduran writer/journalist and plantation worker, Ramón Amaya Amador. The introduction of large-scale U.S. and other foreign investment and political influence in Honduras also created tensions within the Honduran elite around concerns for economic competition and national sovereignty.[14]

As long as the Honduran elite was unable to create its own industrial or commercial economic base, foreign investment could be seen as a blessing. But by the early decades of the twentieth century, a new commercial and industrial center was developing in and around the fruit plantations of the northern coast. A new group of entrepreneurs, mostly immigrant families of Middle Eastern origin, brought capital and developed service industries that catered to the needs and wants of the plantation communities of managers and workers, and the populations of the growing towns in the area. Construction and building supplies, cement manufacturers, breweries, banks, newspapers, were among the enterprises developed by this group of entrepreneurs. This new elite gradually became an economically and politically powerful presence.[15] By the mid-twentieth century, Honduras had a ruling elite whose interests and economic bases included both "landed" and "commercial" interests—wealth generated from exploitation of the earth and natural resources; and wealth generated from serving the daily needs of expanding human communities. In time, these interests became integrated to some extent, with commercial elites becoming landowners, and landowners entering product manufacturing. A major example—the Facussé family developed a small economic empire with political clout based on their position as the country's largest landowners and their control of a group of companies (Dinant Corporation and others) making products derived from palm oil from their African palm plantations in northern Honduras.[16] One of the family members, Carlos Flores Facussé, served a term as Honduran president (1998–2002).

So it was that several thematic assumptions became normalized and pervasive in Honduran history, and continue to shape Honduran political economy today. The colonial rulers or their successors in independent Honduras assumed the right to conquer and subjugate Indigenous people, claiming their land and coercing their labor for the elite and the Crown, or later the Honduran state. The ruling elite included large-scale landowners and the owners of commercial and service industries. This elite assumed from colonial times a sense of their exclusive right to manage the affairs and "development" of the country and to control state institutions. Honduran lands promised great wealth, a promise that seemed always to remain unfulfilled, and thus became one of the driving forces behind extractivism and neoextractivism as the engine of prosperity and state power. In this scenario, Indigenous peoples and local peasant communities who should have been laborers for producing wealth for the rulers, the elites, were instead always a source of resistance and an obstacle that must be tamed or removed, resulting in endless conflicts over land and resources. Areas that did not meet the rulers' standards of productiveness, were hard to control, or were outside the elite's and the state's control might be considered empty (*vacio*). In modern Honduras, these areas are heavily populated by Indigenous and small-farming communities, but are designated for hydroelectric dam projects, mining, export agriculture, tourist development, and model/charter cities. They are considered empty or must be made empty by forcibly removing those who live there and denying their legal and moral right to be there.

The state evolved with an economically and politically powerful elite and weak national political institutions.[17] The elite systematically blocked attempts to broaden decision-making and political participation to include a wider popular participation in the affairs of state or to strengthen political institutions as instruments of democratic participation. The eventual outcome of these tendencies in the political economy of Honduras was described by historian Marvin Barahona in 2017.

> The mythical glorification of private initiative and economic growth as motors of development has led to individual dependency, political co-optation . . . without any actual political rights. The State dissolves the political even as it divides society into clients and citizens, and simultaneously expels thousands of other citizens from its borders. . . . These contradictions [of neoliberal extractive development] make it so that the political disappears and, with it, the free individual.[18]

The elite also relied on police and military that became, thereby, the most powerful of the institutions of state. Military coups and governments, or civilian governments that relied heavily on military support, became a feature of twentieth-century Honduras. The military became another part of the political and economic ruling elite.[19] The dominance of the United States in the economy and political life of Honduras was increasingly clear as extractive industries, including mining and export plantation agriculture, became the preferred bases of the economy. To maintain its power, the Honduran elite became increasingly dependent upon the United States and was obliged to accept its dictates. These tendencies became increasingly salient as Honduras entered the world of modern "development."

THE HONDURAN DEVELOPMENTALIST STATE
(*ESTADO DESARROLLISTA*), 1957–1980

The effort to make Honduras into a modern nation state began in earnest in the 1870s. The result was what one Honduran historian called a "liberal oligarchic state."[20] It was liberal in the classic sense of economic liberalism, promoting private enterprise and encouraging foreign investment, with minimal state intervention. The state's role was to encourage a modern economy oriented to the wider international market. This state was oligarchic inasmuch as it also promoted a national identity, an official history, and a political imaginary that emphasized the dominant role of the small elite and ignored or marginalized the presence and importance of the rest of the population.[21] This effort co-opted or explicitly ignored Indigenous actors in the country's life, and consciously restricted political power and decision-making to a small elite. It was during this long period (1870–1950) that U.S. and foreign mining and banana enterprises became prominent in the economic and political life of the country. The small Honduran military was the enforcer for the oligarchy and the foreign interests in eliminating popular resistance that mostly took the form of labor strikes.

By the 1930s, the liberal oligarchic state had devolved into a virtual dictatorship. Tiburcio Carías Andino exercised the power of the elite and the military. His regime was technically a limited electoral democracy engaged in active repression against all opponents. By 1947, Carías was forced to cede power, due to popular discontent with lack of participation, rising demands for greater rights, and concerns within his own National Party that his unpopularity would injure the Party itself. Worse, Carías' personal interests in maintaining power sometimes seemed to conflict with the interests of foreign investors, banana and mining companies that much of the elite considered essential players in the political economy of the Honduran state.[22]

It is worth noting that the dictatorship of Carías coincided with dictatorships elsewhere in Central America. In El Salvador, the military-controlled government were engaged in an active genocide against what remained of the Indigenous populations there. In Guatemala, Jorge Ubico ruled as dictator while welcoming U.S. fruit companies. The popular uprising that overthrew Ubico in 1944 installed two reformist governments that increased the rights of workers (Juan José Arévalo, 1944–1950) and attempted a land reform to curb the power of the U.S. fruit companies (Jacobo Arbenz, 1950–1954). Arbenz was overthrown by a coup engineered in Washington and launched from Honduran soil, so that the interests of the fruit companies and other foreign investors in Guatemala could be maintained.[23] This lesson in a neighboring country was not lost on Hondurans. In Nicaragua, the United States actively supported the establishment and continuance of the Somoza family dictatorship. When Nicaraguans overthrew the Somoza dictatorship and installed a revolutionary government in 1979, the United States and the Honduran elite considered this a serious threat.

After the fall of Carías, the Honduran military assumed an increasingly powerful political role as a liberalizing and reformist force. It received support from the United States that saw the Honduran military as the force to push through the reforms necessary to preserve the essential features of a political economy that favored U.S. companies and would at least pay lip service to some of the demands of rising popular organizations, workers, peasant communities, and a growing intellectual middle class.[24] Liberal reform was better than popular revolution. The banana strike of 1954 and rising demands for worker and peasant rights were features of this period. Honduran workers and peasants became a rising political voice. U.S. support for the "reformist" role of the Honduran army increased after the triumph of the Cuban revolution in 1959, which was seen as another example of what could happen if mild reform was not entertained. The Honduran army was a new ally for the

United States, especially after the old ally, the National Party was discredited with the fall of Carías.

The new wave of reformism led to the recasting of the role of the state, moving away from a hands-off to a more active, interventionist role in the economy, with some attention to the demands of workers and rural peasant communities.[25] The major objective of the new model of the state was to ensure the growth of economic and social forces in order to accelerate the growth of capitalism. A new constitution was promulgated that institutional-ized this role. It contained this statement:

> The principal objective of the state in promoting the economy will be to promote a growing and orderly level of production, employment, and income, distribut-ing income equitably among the factors that contribute to its formation, in con-ditions of reasonable monetary stability, with the objective of giving the entire population a dignified and decent existence.[26]

The Constitution of 1957 also assigned to the state powers and responsibility to promote, stimulate, and support private initiative and private enterprise based in rational and systematic economic planning.[27]

This emphasis on the state's active promotion and regulation of private industry as an engine for social development and general prosperity—and a space for allowing but not actively supporting labor, peasants, and others to advance their demands—opened Honduras to the new discourse of "develop-ment" that was emerging in the centers of global economy and political power in the 1950s. It engaged the state as an active agent of "development" in ways that the old economic liberalism did not. Honduras became a developmental-ist state (*estado desarrollista*).[28] Modest moves toward reform of the econ-omy were begun, including a limited agrarian reform law passed in 1962.[29]

In 1963, the military deposed the mildly reformist civilian government and assumed direct control of the state. This coup reflected a fundamental source of conflict in the political economy of the developmentalist state between the reformists who wanted reform in order to "develop" the country, and those who opposed change. During this period, opponents of change were found among the ruling politico-economic elite. The military government was ambiguous and weak in its reformism, with paper decrees that increasingly were not carried out, and increasing repression against labor and peasant unions, the Catholic church, and middle-class intellectuals. Senior military ranks seemed uncertain whether they were of the people or of the elite. During military rule, the 1974 Agrarian Reform Law that promised more land to peasants was approved, but it was followed in 1975 by the killings at the hacienda of Los Horcones, in which twelve leaders of the National Union of Peasants (UNC) along with two Catholic priests who worked with them were killed. The perpetrators of this "massacre" were large landowners and military officers. The military government arrested, imprisoned, and executed peasant leaders and raided the headquarters of the UNC. This "massacre" and the crackdown that followed were intended to send a clear message to those who still wanted reformism. In reality, democracy and social justice were not the principal objectives of the state, so they became the principal objectives of other Hondurans in popular organizations, student, labor, and peasant groups, and one portion of the Catholic church.

The manner in which the 1974 Agrarian Reform Law was (and was not) implemented demonstrates further the state's role in "modernizing" the more "backward" sectors of the economy while actively supporting private and foreign investment in large-scale extractive industries—roles of a modern developmentalist state as envisioned in the 1970s. The state's policy toward implementation of the agrarian reform was largely expressed by granting land to peasant cooperatives that officially registered with the state; these peasant cooperatives became the core of agrarian reform.[30] This fit well with the new international discourse of development that touted cooperatives as a means for peasant economic and social advancement.[31] Cooperatives also made state control of peasant land use easier than monitoring hundreds of thousands of individual peasant farmers. The cooperative requirement forced peasant farmers who wanted or needed land to submit to a certain dependency on the goodwill of the state that controlled whether peasant cooperatives were registered and approved, and thereby entitled to land.

The lower Aguan Valley in the north of the country was part of the banana kingdom of the foreign fruit companies until Panama disease, a banana blight, in the 1940s forced the companies to reduce operations and retreat to their core areas to the west in the Sula and Ulua river valleys. During the 1960s and 1970s, the Honduran military government promoted the Bajo Aguán Project (BAP), encouraging the formation of farming cooperatives among the population of former fruit company workers, Salvadoran immigrants, and Garifuna communities in the region, resulting in the formation of more than 150 peasant cooperatives and making the Bajo Aguán the center of peasant cooperative activity in Honduras and one of the most important areas of peasant cooperative activity in Latin America.[32] By or even before 1990, this accommodation to peasant demands for land was already threatened by the government's embrace of neoliberal development policies that increasingly privileged large scale export agriculture and the growing international market for palm oil, a shift that actively encouraged wealthy landowners to expand their palm oil plantations at the expense of peasant communities and cooperatives. The land controlled by peasant cooperatives and peasant and Indigenous communities was increasingly circumscribed, and the lower Aguán region became the scene of more frequent and intense land conflicts, as this "agrarian counter reform" moved forward.[33] The El Astillero massacre (1991) involving a deadly conflict between a peasant cooperative group and a landowning army colonel was only one of the more infamous events of this period.[34]

The failure of the government to fully implement the promise of agrarian reform provoked peasant groups to increase land takeovers and other actions by which peasant organizations tried to make reform not a piece of paper but a living reality. "We are the agrarian reform," they said.[35] In Honduras, demanding reform or change became a matter of embodying and living the demand. The political economy of Honduras was now based not only on the misery of development but also on the power of human bodies to transform into living realities the broken promises and the ideologies of progress propagated by elites. This reclamation of land and resources and of group agency was another source of potential economic and political power to counter that of the elites.[36]

FROM NEOLIBERAL TO NEOEXTRACTIVE STATE

The new neoliberal development policies that encouraged this "agrarian counter reform" in the Aguán and elsewhere in Honduras were introduced in full force with the presidency of Rafael Callejas (1990–1994). They were the product of development plans introduced by the Honduran business elite and the Reagan Administration in the early 1980s, but delayed until the end of the regional wars in 1990. The so-called *paquetazo* (package) of changes introduced during the early 1990s included policies that strongly favored large-scale export agriculture and reduced support and protection for peasant and Indigenous small producers and cooperatives. The Agricultural Modernization Act especially contradicted and undermined the 1974 Agrarian Reform Law without actually repealing the law. The introduction of this neoliberal shift in development policy effectively ended the period of reformist development, not simply by abandoning modest concession to peasant and Indigenous communities but by actively promoting aggressive elite and foreign corporate takeover of the lands and resources that happened to be under the control of these communities. This all-out assault was led by extractive projects in the name of national development, and continued with only two brief periods of pause—during the governments of Carlos Roberto Reina (1994–1998) and Manuel Zelaya (2005–2009).[37]

The coup that deposed Zelaya in June 2009 was in part a reaction to his tendencies toward reform. The political and economic elite that promoted and carried out the coup (*los golpistas*) fully embraced the frenzied exploitation of land and resources—neoextractivism. This grab, that increasingly privatized the country's resources and wealth in a few hands, abandoned any serious pretense of national development for the benefit of the country. It effectively marked the end of the older reformist developmentalism that at least pretended to address the demands of various sectors of the population. The role of the state became nearly identical with the promotion of individual wealth. Predictably, pervasive official and private corruption became the "operating system."[38] This is the significance of the 2009 coup as a major inflection point in the political economy of Honduras, along with a tsunami of misery, precarity, and conflict for much of the population.

POWER BROKERS AND RESISTERS
IN A GLOBAL ECONOMY

Scholars of the modern state often caution that "the state" is not monolithic and does not act as a single person. It is a composite of many individuals in many roles and many institutions, often with different, even divergent agendas.[39] Thus "the state" operates at various levels in the lives of individuals and communities, often with inconclusive or even conflictive results. The state implies a stratification of power, with some individuals acquiring more importance because of the resources—material, informational, social—that they control. In an increasingly globalized economy, the Honduran elite is composed largely of those who control the links to international economic investment and "development." These are the power brokers of Honduran society.[40] They control the institutions of state for their own purposes. The global economy itself is to some extent stratified with levels of dependency upon the elites, institutions, and forces that act in the global economy. Modern imperial powers such as the United States differ from the older empires in several ways, including the degree to which they are controlled by and attempt to control global forces and thus also to control local elites.

An important aspect of developmentalism is its ability to establish interdependent links between national and international elites. These linkages allow international elites some control over the political economy of a country, and they enhance the political and economic "value" and power of the national elite, those who controls the precious link to international investment and global markets. Thus, depending on one's perspective and place in the system, the value of a particular extractive industry can be measured in terms of: (1) what it actually brings into the national treasury; (2) what it puts into the private pockets of national elites; (3) the degree to which it strengthens the nation's connection to foreign capital, investment, and markets; (4) the degree to which it opens and smooths the path of international enterprises and elites to enter, influence, and even control the national economy and political policy-making; and (5) the degree to which such linkages enhance the political power of the national and local elites in the country. There is another dimension that elites prefer to ignore unless they perceive that it threatens the system: the degree to which extractivism and, more generally development projects, produce "externalities" or costs that can detract from, and ultimately make unsustainable the bases of "development." The costs can be measured in terms of diminishing economic returns, degraded environments and exhausted resources, destruction or degradation of human capital and potential (labor and human misery), the deterioration of confidence and trust in national institutions and especially in the elites who control these institutions, and the rise of popular unrest and resistance to extractive projects and their human and environmental costs. All of these "costs" undermine the longer-term sustainability of extractivism and development policies and projects. Finally, the urgent embrace of neoliberal extractive development as national policy can have consequences over time that produce conditions making life unbearable to the point where people contemplate emigration. Such has been the case in Honduras.

NOTES

1. Jennifer Ávila, "The Difficulties of Reporting in Honduras," *El Faro*, January 7, 2020, elfaro.net/en/201912/internacionales/23899/Seen-as-Either-a-Sell-Out-or-a-Rebel-On-the-Difficulties-of-Reporting-in-Honduras.htm.

2. Adrián Pérez-Melgosa, "Low-Intensity Necropolitics: SlowViolence and Migrant Bodies in Latin American Films," *Arizona Journal of Hispanic Cultural Studies* 20 (2016): 217–236.

3. Marvin Barahona, *Pueblos indígenas, Estado y memoria colectiva en Honduras* (Tegucigalpa: Editorial Guaymuras, 2009), 91–95. See also Linda A. Newsome, *The Cost of Conquest: Indian Decline in Honduras Under Spanish Rule* (Boulder CO: Westview Press, 1986).

4. Jeffrey L. Gould, *To Die in This Way: Nicaraguan Indians and the Myth of Mestizaje, 1880–1965* (Durham NC: Duke University Press, 1998); Barahona, *Pueblos indígenas,* 100–107.

5. Andres Leon, "Rebellion under the Palm Trees: Memory, Agrarian Reform and Labor in the Aguán, Honduras," (PhD diss., City University of New York, 2015), 31–35.

6. León, *Rebellion*, 36.

7. Maristella Svampa, *Las fronteras del neoextractivismo en América Latina: Coflictos socioambientales, giro ecoterritorial y nuevas dependencias* (Guadalajara: Universidad de Guadalajara, 2019), 40–45.

8. James Phillips, *Honduras in Dangerous Times: Resistance and Resilience* (Lanham MD: Lexington Books, 2015), 33–36; Arthur Phillips, "Charter Cities in

Honduras," *Open Democracy*, January 7, 2014, https://www.opendemocracy.net/en/opensecurity/charter-cities-in-honduras/; Danielle Marie Mackey, "I've Seen All Sorts of Horrific Things in My Time, but None as Detrimental to the Country as This," *The New Republic,* December 14, 2014, https://newrepublic.com/article/120559/ive-seen-sorts-horrific-things-time-none-detrimental-country-this.

9. Svampa, *Las fronteras de neoextractivismo,* 74; Max Manwaring, *State and Nonstate Associated Gangs: Credible "Midwives of New Social Orders"* (Carlisle PA: Army War College Strategic Studies Institute, 2009), https://apps.dtic.mil/sti/pdfs/ADA499689.pdf.

10. Marvin Barahona, *Honduras en el siglo XX: Una síntesis histórica* (Tegucigalpa, Editorial Guaymuras, 2005), 32–33.

11. Guillermo Molina, Chocano, *Estado Liberal y desarrollo capitalista en Honduras* (Tegucigalpa: Universidad Nacional Autónoma de Honduras, Editorial Universitaria, 1982), 24–30; Darío Euraque, *Reinterpreting the banana Republic: Region and State in Honduras, 1870–1972* (Chapel Hill NC: University of North Carolina Press, 1996), 8–9.

12. The introduction and expansion of the "banana empire" in Honduras is well-documented. See, for example, Euraque, *Reinterpreting,* 24–25 and throughout; Charles D. Kempner and Jay H. Soothill, *The Banana Empire: A Case Study of Economic Imperialism* (New York: Russell and Russell, 1967); Barahona, *Honduras en el siglo XX,* 52–58.

13. See Barahona, *Honduras,* 56–57, for a brief discussion of major Honduran political and government figures who were on the payroll of United Fruit Company.

14. Barahona, *Honduras,* 57; Euraque, *Reinterpreting,* 41–60.

15. Euraque, *Reinterpreting,* 5–40 and throughout; Barahona, *Honduras,* 52–58.

16. Banktrack, "Dinant Honduras" (March 27, 2016), https://www.banktrack.org/company/dinant; Leon, "Rebellion," 4–5 and 177–179; Tanya Kerssen, *Grabbing Power: The New Struggle for Land, Food, and Democracy in Northern Honduras* (Oakland CA: Food First Books, 2013), 31–33.

17. James Phillips, "The Misery Financing Development: Subsidized Neoliberalism and Privatized Dependency in Honduras," *Urban Anthropology* 46, no. 2 (Spring–Summer 2017): 54. The Sarah Chayes publication, *When Corruption Is the Operating System: The Case of Honduras* (Washington DC: Carnegie Endowment for International Peace, 2017), describes in detail a system where the elite use the institutions of government for their own purposes.

18. Marvin Barahona, "Auge de decadencia de la ideología de la desigualdad: Un cuestionamiento necesario a la hegemonía neoliberal," *Envío* 15, no. 2 (May 2017): 31, English translation mine.

19. Chapter 7 details the role of the Honduran military and its part in creating the conditions that encourage emigration.

20. Barahona, *Honduras,* 27–47.

21. Barahona, *Honduras,* 34–44.

22. Euraque, *Reinterpreting,* 68–70.

23. Stephen Schlesinger and Stephen Kinzer, *Bitter Fruit: The Untold Story of the American Coup in Guatemala* (New York: Doubleday, 1983); Piero Gleijeses,

Shattered Hope: The Guatemalan Revolution and the United States, 1944–1954 (Princeton NJ: Princeton University Press, 1991).

24. See chapter 7.

25. Margarita Oseguera de Ochoa, *Honduras hoy: Sociedad y crisis politica* (Tegucigalpa: Centro de Documentación de Honduras, 1987), 53–63; Barahona, *Honduras,* 187–191.

26. Quoted in Barahona, *Honduras*, 190, translation mine.

27. Barahona, *Honduras*, 190–191.

28. Historian Marvin Barahona uses the term *estado desarrollista* (developmentalist state) to characterize this period in Honduras and includes a detailed discussion in his *Honduras*, 185–232.

29. FIAN International, "Agrarian Reform in Honduras," 2015, https://www.fian.org/fileadmin/media/publications_2015/Agrarian-Reform-in-Honduras-2000.pdf; Barahona, *Honduras*, 192–193.

30. Michael J. Martin, "Agrarian Reform Cooperatives in Honduras" (PhD diss., University of Florida, 1996), https://ufdc.ufl.edu/AA00029921/00001; Kerssen, *Grabbing Power*, 18–21; Andes Leon, "Rebellion under the Palm Trees," 110–115 and beyond (which describes in detail the beginnings of the Bajo Aguán Project and the cooperatives).

31. For example, Peter Worsley, *Two Blades of Grass: Rural Cooperatives in Agricultural Modernization* (Manchester UK: Manchester University, 1971).

32. Kerssen, *Grabbing Power*, 18–21.

33. León, "Rebellion," 4–5; Kerssen, *Grabbing Land*, 28–33.

34. Elias Ruiz, *El Astillero: masacre y justicia* (Tegucigalpa: Editorial Guaymuras, 1992).

35. Douglas Kincaid, "We Are the Agrarian Reform: Rural Politics and Agrarian Reform," in *Honduras: Portrait of a Captive Nation*, eds. Nancy Peckenham and Annie Street (New York: Praeger, 1985), 135–142.

36. Phillips, *Honduras in Dangerous Times*, 128–133.

37. Phillips, "The Misery Financing Development," 14–18.

38. Chayes, *When Corruption Is the Operating System*.

39. Jordan Levy offers a useful discussion of state theory in practice in Honduras in his "The Politics of Honduran School Teachers: State Agents Challenge the State" (PhD diss., Western Ontario University, 2014), 12–14, and throughout, https://ir.lib.uwo.ca/cgi/viewcontent.cgi?article=3603&context=etd.

40. Harald Waxenecker, *Redes de poder político-económico en Honduras: Un análisis post-golpe* (San Salvador: Fundación Heinrich Boll Stiftung y Equipo Maíz, 2019), https://sv.boell.org/sites/default/files/2020-03/Redes%20en%20Honduras%20HW%202019.pdf.

Chapter 6

Characteristics and Consequences of Neoextractive Development in Honduras

This chapter critically and more closely examines some of the major consequences of three kinds of extractive industry in Honduras—mining, logging, and export agribusiness. Mega-projects for damming rivers to produce hydroelectric energy are also discussed. In the political economy of Honduras these extractive industries very often result in physical displacement of communities, but also in social and cultural fragmentation and political exclusion of those most affected, as well as increasing gender inequality, militarization, climate change and environmental degradation, criminal gangs and official corruption, and the growth of poverty and the "informal" economy. All of this, in turn, creates conditions that, over time, encourage several responses, including emigration. It does not have to be so.

MINING

Foreign and Honduran corporations control the bulk of mining in Honduras. Canadian companies are the most prominent, but the list includes corporations based in the United States, China, and western Europe. Some mining is done by Honduran-foreign partnerships. The following are only a few of many true tales that reveal some of the issues at stake for local communities facing mining projects in Honduras. If anything, the pressure and the audacity of companies and the Honduran government have increased over the years.

Some Cautionary (and Illuminating) True Tales

Cerro San Cristobal. In the 1950s, a U.S. citizen started a gold mining operation near an area known as Cerro San Cristobal in the Department of El Paraíso. He used mercury, other chemicals, and local water sources to process the gold, contaminating the local river and the rivulets that were used by people and animals. He plowed a dirt road through the mountains to transport gold from the mined areas. Today, the road is in disrepair, almost unused. Except for a very few scattered households, almost no one lives in the area and no one farms there. Much of the area, which is quite mountainous, has been determined to contain gold, perhaps enough to be economically exploitable. But it is part of the watershed for the city of Danlí, and its streams and water sources remained highly polluted in 2020 from the gold mining of the 1950s. The water is discolored and sometimes foul smelling. Where once there were year-round flowing streams, now there are only trickles of fetid water. The silence of the area is striking, as is the apparent absence of birds and animals that would normally flourish in abundance in this tropical environment. Local people say the area around Cerro San Cristobal may never heal from the mining that took place almost seventy years ago.[1]

El Barro. In 2010, in the community of El Barro (pseudonym) in southern Honduras, a foreign mining company was trying to get land for mining operations. They offered a local small farmer, a respected community leader, two million dollars for his land and his public approval of the mining project. He refused because, as he said, he knew that the company was trying to use him in an attempt to divide the community, and he did not want other community members who opposed the mining to consider him a traitor. In any case, he said, he knew the company would never give him, a peasant farmers, such a sum. He and others wondered if the mining company was using tempting offers to gauge the temperament of the community. This concern seemed to be confirmed when the company and the government send a psychologist along with their representatives to negotiate with the community. Local people said this "negotiation" consisted mostly of the company making promises about the benefits that would accrue to the community, but not the potential damages the mining operation could inflict. But people in El Barro were well organized in their response, often citing their rights under Honduran law and international conventions, which legally demanded that the company and the government provide them with a full explanation of the proposed project before anything was begun, and that their approval or opposition was to be without pressure from the government or the company. Community members were critical of the company's failure to fulfill these legal obligations, and they especially felt unduly pressured to approve the mining. Local people said their opposition to mining was partly the result of a visit that a group of community members had made to see the impact of mining operations in the valley of Siria, not very far from their own community. With human rights and environmental groups, and in the lore of various communities faced with mining operations, the Siria case had become a telling example of the destructive potential of unrestricted mining. The destruction wrought in Valle de Siria by mining and the failure of the mining company to compensate the community, and to clean up and help to restore some of the environment after the mine was closed became a cautionary tale.[2] There was also a local history of organized community resistance around El Barro, part of the local ethos; many of the older residents had been involved in successfully blocking a commercial logging operation in the area during the 1970s. According to one local resident, compared to then the change now was "triste" (sad).[3]

Azacualpa. In August 2020, despite the opposition of much of the local population in the small western Honduran community of Azacualpa, the Canadian mining company Aura Minerals (known in Honduras as MINOSA) was again setting dynamite explosions on the hill where the community's cemetery was located, in order to extract gold. The company had been engaged in trying to get the bodies exhumed from the cemetery in order to mine the hill. Beyond all the concerns—about how the explosions and resultant landslides would threaten most of the 600 homes in the area, block access roads to the community, destroy the local environment, shatter the tranquility, and fray people's nerves—much of the community regarded the invasion of their cemetery as a profound desecration. For several years, residents of Azacualpa had been engaged in protests and legal action to stop the exhumation of their cemetery and the gold mining, but the national government continued the company's concessions and its support for mining. The image of a foreign company invading a cemetery in order to extract gold with the support of the central government sent the clear message that in the world of neoextractivism nothing was sacred, neither the safety and wellbeing of the living nor the peace of the dead.[4]

The Importance of Mining

For much of Honduran history, the purpose of mining was to generate wealth. Gold has remained a source of wealth today that feeds the global financial markets and generates profits for foreign corporations and some well-capitalized individuals. By the 1870s, Honduras was also a site of mining for iron ore and exploration for other metals and minerals that had gained increased strategic importance in the global economy. The Honduran elite—the small group that controlled the government—derived some or much of its wealth from selling concessions for mining exploration and exploitation, and from other financial spinoffs of mining. The wealth went into the pockets of the elite, but it also went to servicing the formation of national institutions and as capital to finance the further expansion of a national economy.[5]

As a basis of the national economy, however, mining became less important with the expansion of export plantation agribusiness after 1900, driven by the foreign banana/fruit companies and the new commercial elite that serviced the needs of the staff and workers of these plantations in the Chamelecón, Sula, Ulua, and Aguán river valleys that spread across much of northern Honduras. Increasingly, elite wealth was derived from diversification and integration of enterprises, including landowning, plantation agriculture, energy production and sale, commercial interests, building supplies, banking and media ownership, and more.[6] Some of these enterprises also served to establish links to foreign capital and markets.

As a primary source of national income mining declined in importance over the years. By the 1990s, it represented barely 5 percent of the national product, far outstripped by export agriculture, manufacturing and commercial sales, and tourism. But mining still had economic, political, and emblematic value. It provided links to foreign investment, especially from countries with major mining industries, such as Canada. These links also put Honduras in the sights of foreign investors in other industries, such as tourism and those seeking cheap labor for assembly plants (maquiladoras). Indirectly at least, mining seemed important, for attracting foreign investment, economic diversification, and job generation in other industries. Its political importance was enjoyed mostly by members of the Honduran elite who were in positions to act as brokers with foreign investors, and thus to enhance their own apparent importance to the country. Mining also signaled to the world that Honduras held some resources important for the global economy, and was therefore a country of some potential importance in the global political economy. Historically and culturally, mining was a primary emblem of the potential wealth of Honduras, and the lure of a modern El Dorado. Economically, however, mining employed 0.57 percent (less than 1 percent) of the employed population in the country in the period from 2009 to 2018. The benefits of mining did not extend to employment for the Honduran population.[7]

Mining remained an important component of the neoliberal development model embraced by Honduran governments beginning in earnest in 1990. After the package (*paquetazo*) of neoliberal reforms implemented in the early 1990s, the Congress passed a new mining law in 1998, replacing the 1868 mining code.[8] The 1998 law (*Ley General de Minería,* Decree 292–98), was soon followed by the approval of 155 mining concessions covering 35,000 square kilometers of territory. The law was a gift to mining enterprises. It diminished environmental regulations for mining projects, allowed mining companies almost unrestricted use of water sources and property rights, regardless of the cost to local communities, and reduced the degree of the state's legal control over mining operations. This unrestrained embrace of mining and the deliberate abdication of state control occasioned this observation in a report on the impacts of twenty years of mining operations in the Valle de Siria.

> [Mining] concessions, both for exploration and for exploitation, are granted in a context that implies a disarticulation of the State and a privileging of foreign or private national capital ahead of social and human interests, led by a doctrinaire neoliberalism promoted since the 1990s, that continues promoting and facilitating a process of transferring natural and community resources to foreign private investors.[9]

The resultant rise in conflicts between mining companies and local communities helped to persuade the Zelaya government to impose a temporary moratorium on new mining concessions. Those in the Honduran government and elite, and foreign governments with major mining interests in Honduras supported the coup (*golpe*) that removed Zelaya from power in June 2009. The mining moratorium was not the only grievance the *golpistas* had with Zelaya, but the coup sent a clear message that nothing would be permitted to slow or stop the expansion of mining and other extractive industries in Honduras.[10]

Post-coup governments wasted no time in canceling the mining moratorium, and then passed another mining law in 2013. The new law allowed the practice of open pit mining (*mineria a cielo abierto*, mining to the open sky), opening the way for a new level of environmental destruction. The 2013 law also allowed mining operations to use all the water they needed even if the water source was outside the area of the mining concession, and regardless of the needs of neighboring communities. Additional laws and modifications in the next few years reduced further the ability of the state to legally regulate mining operations or to uphold the rights of local communities. Existing legal instruments such as ILO Convention 169—that guaranteed the right of Indigenous communities to refuse to allow mining operations in their areas—were re-interpreted to mean that communities had the right only to negotiate the methods used by a mining operation, not the right to reject the project altogether.[11]

With the flurry of mining laws and regulations in the years after the 2009 coup, the Honduran government effectively handed over the regulation of mining operations to the companies that ran them. Such a retreat was a symptom of what most Hondurans already knew. National development was intended not for the nation but for the few; not for the majority of Hondurans, but for foreign interests and the rulers of the global political economy. The intensification of mining's impact on local communities wrought by these legal maneuvers was matched by an extension of areas granted to mining concessions.

Local Concerns: Nueva Esperanza

The physical effects of mining operations included removal of the often fertile layer of topsoil; destruction of trees and vegetation, promoting soil erosion and changes in microclimate; air pollution from dust and fumes; contamination of land; and intensive water use and pollution. All of this rendered the land useless for the traditional small farming of local communities. In the northern community of Nueva Esperanza where a local struggle over mining had been ongoing since at least 2011, a local resident expressed this concern in 2016.

> With this problem of the miners, yes we were really concerned because . . . it would contaminate the water and the resources we need, both for us and the animals and plants [that we need]. That's something that troubles us a lot because we see that if we harvest very little today because the earth cannot produce as before [*ya no es igual*], . . . if the miners came in we were worried we wouldn't have food.[12]

Contamination is not the only water problem with mining. As a rough indication of scale, a Honduran geologist familiar with mining once commented that a medium-sized mining operation in Honduras can use as much water in a few hours as a rural peasant family might use in several years.[13] Honduran mining law is interpreted to give prior water rights to the mining operation, not the peasant or the community. In Honduras and internationally, the case of so-called Guapinol water defenders (see chapter 1) became emblematic of the abuse of water and the popular demand that water is a human right. The local people of Guapinol and fourteen other communities who formed the Comité Municipal de Defensa de los Bienes Comunes (Municipal Common Goods/Resources Defense Committee) were concerned especially about mining operations destroying the region's water sources. For this, some of their members were criminalized and imprisoned, but the Committee won the 2019 Letelier-Moffitt Human Rights Award. One of its members placed their protection of water in a larger frame:

> The planet Earth has limits, but the extractive economic model does not recognize limits. The North has channeled the land, natural resources and hydroelectric energy of the South into its own storehouses. Our land has been fenced off, given in concession, militarized, and colonized; and our brothers and sisters have been criminalized, jailed, and murdered in the violence produced by this kind of capital accumulation.[14]

While the Honduran state retreated from its enforcement of restrictions on mining companies, it was quite zealous in restricting the rights of local communities to access the most basic necessities of life.

Health concerns were also associated with mining, especially open pit mining—air and water pollution, reduced ability to produce crops, increased hunger. People reported increased respiratory illnesses, malnutrition, and other conditions, and expressed fears for the health of their children who play outside. These concerns might be quite familiar to people in many other places, including Navajo communities in the United States where children played in the dust generated by nearby uranium mining. People rely on their own sense that there is something dangerous about mining operations.

> Many of us in this community [Nueva Esperanza], we've been educated in matters related to mining. It is known that these projects are contaminators. And even apart from what the people have studied, they feel it in their blood that these projects are damaging, that they are death, and that they have never and nowhere been beneficial.[15]

Psychological health emerges as a primary concern in many communities where resistance to mining has been strong. The major concern here is the devastating effects of a climate of pervasive fear generated by the armed defenders of mining operations. These include private company "security guards" and police and military that are provided by the state or hired by the company to protect mining operations. They also include armed gangs that terrorize local people known to oppose mining projects. The retreat of government control over mining enterprises allowed fear to increase. A man in the community of Nueva Esperanza experienced this fear as a loss of the right to oppose the mining operation.

> I have lived in these communities for 35 years. For 14 years we've been fighting these threats of mining exploitation, but especially since 2011 there has been tremendous pressure here from the mining companies. At the beginning, the local authorities listened to us and were with us, but in 2012 the Mayor of Tela (the municipal center) went against us, allied with the government that we have now, with the Congressional deputies all in support of mining and approving a new mining law. And in communities like ours where they had come before, they began to pressure and force us without community consensus about what we wanted. You see, this is a really fertile zone. It is a great place to live. Our fear right now is their coming by force, the mining company with the police and private armed men. That is our greatest concern. We feel completely unprotected. Our own government and our own authorities are complicit in this situation that for us, the poor who live here, brings no benefit. What we are protesting is that this only brings death.[16]

Other Nueva Espeanza community members were more explicit about their fears.

> We live terrified, they shoot off guns in the middle of the night, there are armed men hiding near our houses. Sometimes the school is closed. . . . Yes, more than anything it's lack of trust, because now we still don't have any trust. . . . I didn't have peace in my house, I lived thinking that at any moment they would break down my door, and if I went out to do an errand or to work, I didn't feel at peace (*tranquilo*). . . . I had to leave my house because the miners were menacing me a lot to make us hand over our land. And when you don't want to sell your land, they want to pressure you to do so. I invited a few foreigners to my house, and then men sent by [the mine owner] came and took these folks from my house and kidnapped them. So I had to leave because I felt that I was running a lot of risk.[17]

This last comment referred to an incident in 2013 in which three human rights observers from Europe had come to visit the people of Nueva Esperanza. While they were visiting in the house of a local resident who opposed the mining operations, the house was surrounded by an armed group that ordered them into the back of a truck, and drove them down the road—apparently a kidnapping. Some of the local people tried to chase the truck, and to make the abduction known. Before long, the human rights observers were dropped off by the side of the road some distance from Nueva Esperanza. Local people said the kidnappers were employees of the mining company, and that the incident was intended to heighten fear in the community with the message that international solidarity is not an option.[18]

The social fragmentation of community is a frequently expressed concern. Families become divided as some members see possible benefits from mining operations—job opportunities, the company's offers of new schools, roads, and improvements. Community leaders and local political authorities are also subjected to special offers (bribes) if they publicly support mining projects. Opposition to mining is sometimes denounced as selfishly hindering "progress." Opponents sometimes feel that community members who support mining projects are supporting the terrorist tactics of the companies and their armed enforcers, and so cannot be trusted. Mining also alters the position of women in a community. In small farming communities, both men and women have important traditional functions. In mining, women have no productive place, but are relegated to marginal support, or even to prostitution or other degrading situations.[19]

> The growth in the number of extractive industries is reflected in significant harm to the health of women, who in their domestic tasks caring for the family are exposed in greater proportion to illnesses caused by environmental

contamination in their communities; skin conditions from contaminated water, respiratory illnesses from exposure to the dust coming from dynamite explosions on hillsides [from mining operations], etc. Even more, extractive industries are spreading new scenarios of violence against women, with the presence [in the community] of men as private company guards and other strangers in the area who, according to local women, are spreading prostitution, ill treatment of women, and sexual aggression.[20]

The income a man can gain from a mining job may be many times more than a woman can gain from selling her farm produce locally. Mining also introduces rural communities to outside cultural influences that can further exacerbate tensions between parents and their sons and daughters who want a different life. If the bearers of these new influences—the mine employees who come from elsewhere—also carry an attitude of disdain toward the local community, the encounter may not be a happy one.

A large portion of the mining concessions granted by the post-coup governments were granted in the territories of Indigenous communities who claim the land as a result of continuous occupation for many generations or by treaties with the Honduran state in the 1860s. Because the culture, traditions, and life-ways of Indigenous people are usually grounded firmly in the land, the disruptions caused by mining pose a particular threat to an entire way of life and a worldview for Indigenous and tribal peoples everywhere, and in Honduras for the Lenca, the Tolupanes, and others. Indigenous people in Honduras are at particular risk from extractive industries, but they also possess cultural, social, and legal resources that other communities often lack, and they are recognized by other Hondurans as the frontline in defense of the country's natural resources.[21]

Political Displacement and Legitimate Knowledge

Mining in particular causes another kind of displacement that is not physical but rather political—a loss of legal and political identity. The mechanisms used to achieve this displacement are the privileging of certain kinds of knowledge and the intentional exclusion of local individuals from negotiation and decision-making. The mining laws of 1997 and 2015 attempted to narrow the rights of local communities solely to the negotiation of technical issues such as the methods to be allowed and the mitigations to be put in place, effectively stripping local people of the right to argue the larger political issue—whether the project should be permitted at all. The views, concerns, and opinions of local people about mining projects were countered with "scientific" answers, or were discounted altogether as being unscientific or based on emotion and belief rather than technical knowledge. Fabiana Li recounts this from the conflict between a mining operation and a local community in Peru:

> Concerns of local residents over the ways in which water and land would be transformed were quickly countered by the company with environmental studies, water monitoring programs, technical parameters and risk assessments. In the course of what Li stresses was a *scientization* of the conflict, engineers were hired to study the complaints of canal users, discrediting the latter's perception of risks as not scientific.[22]

In a review of Li's book, Barbara Hogenboom points out that there may be a "logic of equivalence" at work here.

> The term equivalence refers to forms of expertise and technical tools used to make things quantifiable and comparable and the negotiation process over what counts as authoritative knowledge. The engineers hired by the company hold a "logic of equivalence" in which water from a natural source is interchangeable with water from a treatment plant. In addition, in their eyes the effects of mining on the canals can simply be compensated with payments, temporary jobs and local projects.[23]

The privileging of "scientific" knowledge over the lived knowledge and needs of local communities (instead of attempts to integrate these two forms of knowledge) reflects a colonial attitude and constitutes a powerful weapon for controlling and discrediting opposition. It forces local people to seek their own "experts" who can translate the risks sensed by local people into a language that can do battle on equal "scientific" grounds with the companies and the government representatives. Some of these local concerns are cultural and spiritual, and are not easily translated into technical, scientific terms. Together with this discounting of local knowledge is the marginalization of local community representatives. People often complain that companies and government representatives talk only with local government representatives while ignoring or shutting out the rest of the community. In effect, the company talks only with the government. Members of the local community affected by a mining operation are disenfranchised in this way, denied the right of citizens to determine the policies and practices that affect their lives.

Conclusion: Mining's Characteristics

According to a study conducted by the Reflection, Investigation, and Communication Team (ERIC, a well-known social analysis and community development group in Honduras) mining in that country has four major characteristics. It represents and normalizes a practice of accumulation by dispossession (*acumulación por desposesión*). Mining represents the process of deterritorialization, shipping the natural resources of the country to foreign owners abroad. Mining fractures the social fabric of a community and a nation (*la fractura del tejido social*). And mining introduces technologies and methods that can overwhelm both the normal life patterns and the knowledge base of communities.[24]

Mining projects create physical and psychological conditions of deterioration, fear, and insecurity in local communities that make impossible, or nearly impossible, the continuation of small farming and traditional life-ways dependent on the earth. Inasmuch as mining projects tend to bring in their own workers from outside the community, the displacement from farming is seldom replaced by an availability of local mining jobs, despite promises sometimes made to local people. The displacement of local people does not usually result directly in patterns of emigration abroad but rather of migration within Honduras. Sometimes people find unused land in more remote areas in which to farm and set up a household, always with the fear of being evicted yet again. More often they migrate to plantations and export agroindustries or to cities in search of jobs. This migration to the cities over the past few decades has contributed to the burgeoning of urban neighborhoods where the next generations of displaced rural communities live in poverty, gang violence thrives, and people contemplate emigration out of Honduras as a means of survival.

Zealous support for mining leads the state to abdicate control over mining companies and their operations, and to abandon to the companies the treatment of the local communities in which mining projects operate. This *deterritorialization* effectively removes mining areas from the control and responsibility of the state, an abdication of national sovereignty in areas where extractive industry is concentrated. At the same time, the state makes available the security forces—police, military, law enforcement entities—to put down local opposition and bolster the control of companies. The state and its agencies operate not as national institutions addressing the needs of the population but as servants of extractive industries and their owners. National development is no longer development, but rather kleptocracy. In this situation, it is little wonder that many Hondurans regard their politicians and government officials as complicit in *vendepatria,* selling the country.

Mining under these conditions also promotes a fragmentation of the social fabric (*la fracture del tejido social*) of local communities, but also ultimately of the entire society. Families and communities are divided between supporters and opponents of the mine. People live in heightened fear and distrust spreads. The position of women declines in relation to that of men. Laws are broken and disregarded. The state fails to protect people, and even supports their dispossession, so that people no longer trust the government and its institutions. This pervasive loss of trust becomes a powerful underlying factor in the calculus of deciding whether survival requires emigration. Mining is not the only force undermining popular trust, but it, together with other forms of neoextractivism, is an important one.

Mining in the context of a neoliberal political economy as in Honduras introduces and legitimizes technologies and methods of extraction that privatize the wealth derived and socialize the costs incurred in the extractive process. This theme—the massive transfer of national resources and wealth from public to private hands—is a major characteristic of the political economy of neoextractivism, and of modern imperial systems that no longer pretend to be for the advancement of the nation but rather for the social class that controls the means of wealth production. Imperialism under the name of national development discards even the pretext of national development, becoming an instrument of power and wealth for a transnational elite. This elite includes, as junior members, the small set of families that form the economic and political elite of Honduras.

To these characteristics of mining in Honduras must be added one more. Mining as it has been described in the words of people in local communities tends to objectify them, disregarding or marginalizing the voices, opinions, and demands of local people, even engaging in or promoting violence against the lives of people. This is a step toward the normalization of the idea that most Hondurans are simply resources, objects, to be used or discarded in the pursuit of the well-being of elites; and that violence is a normal way to "negotiate."

LOGGING

Logging has been an important extractive industry in Honduras for a long time. In the eighteenth and nineteenth centuries, British interests engaged in clandestine logging of mahogany along the Caribbean coasts of Honduras and Belize. Mahogany (*caoba*) is a particularly precious and desired hardwood considered beautiful and resistant to insect infestation. Honduras today still has sizable groves of mahogany. Pine was another desired wood for many purposes, including its by-product, pine sap, that had various important uses. Today, the legal and illegal logging of these woods creates much conflict, and has been a source of environmental degradation, corruption, crime, violence, displacement, fear, and uncertainty.

Government and Logging

Concerns about illegal logging and deforestation have plagued Honduras since at least the 1970s. A government agency (Honduran Forestry Commission, COHDEFOR) was created in 1974 to oversee and regulate logging. In 1988, COHDEFOR's director was so alarmed at the pace of deforestation that he warned of emerging and irreversible desertification of areas under intense logging.[25] The same year, however, the government proposed building a road through part of the Department of Olancho, an area especially desirable to logging companies for its stands of pine. The proposal spurred protests from local groups, especially Indigenous communities that feared destruction of areas in what was a regional biosphere reserve. Cattle ranching, often the sequel to logging, was also a concern. To Indigenous communities, environmentalists, and others, the commitment of the government to protecting forest areas and communities seemed less than wholehearted.[26]

In 1991, as the Callejas government was structuring its neoliberal *paquetazo*, government agencies entered into negotiations with Stone Container Corporation, one of the world's major producers of cardboard, to grant logging concessions giving the cardboard-maker forty years of rights to log 320,000 hectares of land in Olancho and Mosquitia, in eastern Honduras—a significant portion of the national territory that was a region of rich biodiversity and the home of several Indigenous communities. When the deal was revealed to the Honduran Congress and the public, there were large protests bringing together Indigenous communities, environmentalists, forestry professionals, students, peasant groups, and others.[27] By this time, COHDEFOR, the government agency, had a reputation for bias in favor of logging companies

Undaunted, the government expanded its policies of extractive development after 1990, creating new laws to expedite the exploitation of forests and to criminalize protests against exploitation. In 2001 came the misleadingly named Forestry Law of Protected Areas and Wildlife (*Ley forestal de areas protegidas y de vida silvestre*). This legislation transferred to government control some forest areas that had traditionally been within the territories and under the stewardship of Indigenous communities. The rationale for this was that government agencies could better manage the forests than Indigenous communities that lacked the scientific and technical expertise to do so—the same technocratic and "privileged knowledge" argument used to marginalize local communities in negotiating mining operations. It ignored centuries of Indigenous stewardship that had safeguarded the integrity of the forests, as various studies showed. The actual effect of the law was to weaken Article 347 of the Constitution that had granted Indigenous communities rights over the management of their traditional territories, and to make it easier to grant logging and mining concessions in those areas. As if to undercut the government's claim to good forest stewardship, the independent Honduran Documentation Center (CEDOH) estimated in 2006 that one hectare of forest was cut (deforested) every five minutes in Honduras.[28] The granting of logging concessions became the responsibility of the government Institute for Forestry Conservation and Development (ICF). This agency was supposed to "develop" the forests—to regard forest management and logging concessions as part of a national extractive development model.[29]

Political Question: Deforestation, Crime, Human Rights

Concerns about the rate of deforestation prompted various studies and speculations. A 1988 report stated that more than 811,000 hectares of forest had beed destroyed by fire in an eleven year period, 80,000 hectares of forest were degraded by slash-and-burn peasant farming, and six million cubic feet of firewood extracted for fuel by poor rural communities.[30] These causes emphasized the activity of peasant farmers and poor communities, and implied that they were responsible for much of the deforestation. A second report shifted the focus and provided more insight by mentioning cattle ranching, natural disasters, peasant relocation in forest areas, and urbanization in addition to the earlier list. Poor peasant communities were considered responsible for significant deforestation, but this obscured the primary role of large scale agroindustry and plantation agriculture in forcing peasants off their land and onto more marginal land in or at the edges of forested areas, a problem that increased with the government's expansion of extractive agriculture at the expense of peasant communities.[31]

By 2000, this assessment, that peasants were major culprits in deforestation, had clearly begun to change. Illegal logging emerged as a major concern, linked not only to environmental degradation but to a range of serious economic, social, and political problems. In 2001, an international organization issued a report on Honduran logging that found:

> The illegal timber trade costs governments a fortune in lost revenue, corrodes State mechanisms of formal governance at all levels and leads to increased violence, as income from illegal timber is invested in small arms. As well as important economic costs, there are wider social losses due to poor governance. . . . 75–85% of hardwood timber production and 30–50% of the coniferous wood extraction in Honduras is clandestine. . . . The trade is frequently linked to criminal syndicates and feeds administrative corruption at national and local levels.[32]

An investigative news report published in 2003 targeted the crucial role of "illegal" logging as a primary cause of deforestation. The report described how crews cut and hauled truckloads of precious hardwoods without obtaining government concessions, and made unauthorized and unregulated shipments of logs originating in remote forest areas. The particular importance of this newspaper article was that it also reported the murders of Indigenous leaders and environmentalists who tried to halt the illegal trade and the degradation of natural resources related to logging. Lives were lost, crimes were committed, and illegal logging was a human rights issue as well as an environmental threat.[33]

A report published in 2005 offered the most complete assessment of the scope and impact of illegal logging in Honduras, and specifically traced its ties to the lumber market in the United States. This report, the product of collaboration between a UK and a U.S. organization, found that in Honduras:

> Mahogany, a prized and increasingly rare hardwood, could be gone in as little as 10–15 years. The Rio Platano Biosphere Reserve, a UNESCO World Heritage site, is under immanent threat, its surrounding buffer zone under daily attack from deforestation. The park's protected core zone is infested with illegal loggers seeking mahogany and other valuable hardwoods.[34]

Illegal logging on a commercial scale is enormously damaging to environmental sustainability by promoting soil erosion, dessication (including the loss of an estimated 60 percent of the water supply of western Olancho Department), local and micro-weather changes, topsoil erosion, landslides, and destruction of habitat for plants and animals that local communities depend upon for food, medicine, and other needs. Local peasant and Indigenous communities cited these effects as serious problems that threatened the stability and sustainability of local farming and traditional community life, and would alone be enough to force the dislocation or relocation of communities. But there were still more problems.

> EIA [UK's Environmental Investigation Agency] investigations, documented in this report, have unveiled a far-reaching web of corruption and illegalities involving politicians, the State Forestry Administration (COHDEFOR), timber companies, sawmills, transporters, loggers, mayors, police, and other officials. Illegal timber trade is also used to smuggle narcotics and to launder drug money. . . . The underground timber trade is too powerful and entrenched, corruption and nepotism too rife to be challenged easily, even if the political will existed within the Honduran government.[35]

Several other reports prepared by international organizations in collaboration with Honduran partners documented the expansion of illegal logging and its many destructive effects.[36] These reports highlight illegal logging, but they also raise several questions. They invite one to ask whether there is a level of integration, a gray area, between illegal and legal logging. Does legal logging also generate some of the same destructive patterns as illegal logging? If government officials, politicians, and members of the elite are in charge of regulating legal logging and are also implicated in illegal logging, what is the line? The situation tends to blur the difference between legal and illegal, so that in terms of practical results the difference may be irrelevant to Honduran rural communities.

Logging and (Under)development

An important difference between mining and logging as extractive industries is that logging is often easier to do clandestinely. Large scale mining, especially open pit, in Honduras is difficult to hide. Remote forest logging is often easier to conceal, and it can act as cover for a variety of criminal enterprises in ways that would be more difficult with mining. Illegal logging emerges as an important extractive industry that both produces and attracts very destructive forces for Honduras. But is illegal logging an integral part of the extractive development model for Honduras?

As earlier assessments of the causes of deforestation in Honduras described, illegal wood extraction is not done solely by large corporations of wealthy entrepreneurs. Peasant and Indigenous communities and poor families living near forests do use the forests for sources of firewood or other essentials, or to carve out a plot of land when there is none available elsewhere. While the impact of these activities can be significant, these familial and communal practices tend to be conservative in both method and intent, and their impact is dwarfed by the footprint of logging—both legal and illegal. Poor people can be recruited into gangs whose purpose is to engage in illegal logging on a commercial scale for profit. But for the poor and for rural communities, much of the benefit this "employment" affords is part of a devil's bargain, inasmuch as it invites both environmental degradation and criminal violence.

Illegal logging is often a cover for gang activities, narcotics enterprises and drug transshipments. It is an enterprise attractive to politicians and government officials, both local and national because, as a significant export industry that aids national "development," it can also be a cover for various illegal and lucrative practices to an extent that mining cannot—especially narcotics trafficking and transshipment and money laundering. Thus, illegal mining promotes illegality, criminal activity, and official corruption.[37]

One of the poorest countries in Latin America, Honduras is losing up to $18 million a year in lost stumpage fees and other forest-based revenue. Yet this is only the tip of the iceberg of a massive, nationwide, resource rip-off by major timber and wood product producers and their high level political backers. An estimated

80% of mahogany and up to 50% of pine—Honduras's main timber export—is produced in violation of government regulations . . . a far reaching web of corruption and illegalities involving politicians, the Stat Forestry Administration, timber companies, sawmills, transporters, loggers, mayors, police, and other officials. Illegal timber trade is also used to smuggle narcotics and to launder drug money. Additionally, tax evasion is widespread by companies that fail to declare the total volume or value of their wood exports to evade paying corporate taxes.[38]

In terms of Honduran relations to the global market economy, there may be little difference between legal and illegal logging. Honduran wood, both "legal" and "illegal," is sold to foreign companies, lumber and building suppliers, and consumers in the United States that do not or cannot differentiate between legal and illegal lumber.[39] Questions can be raised about whether logging as currently practiced in Honduras actually benefits national development, or is in fact more destructive than developmental. The money from illegal logging remains in private hands and is considered a loss to the state, since the state receives neither the concession fees nor the income from illegal logging. The money from legal logging comes from the concessions granted to logging companies. Given the generosity of these concessions, the profits from legal logging also tend to remain largely in private hands. If concessions are granted with the understanding that companies will pay government officials for granting a concession, the profits remain in private hands, and the amount accruing to state coffers is reduced or absent. In its effects on the prosperity and security of local communities, almost all logging enterprises have consequences that include short and long term environmental degradation and the potential for threat and violence. This is true whether or not the logging enterprise has a government concession.

The upshot of these considerations is that there is little real difference between "legal" and "illegal" logging as a component of extractive development; and that it is questionable how much logging under current conditions supports national development rather than simply contributing to private fortunes. The cost of logging and its tendency to extractive underdevelopment is felt especially and deeply in the lives of local communities. The Honduran state under neoextractivism has become a very protective advocate for logging. That this can provide cover for drug trafficking is a bonus to some government officials who are themselves, or are in collusion with, major drug traffickers. One might consider whether it is not logging but narcotics trafficking that is the real enterprise, while logging is simply a convenient cover that can be portrayed as a legitimate extractive enterprise and part of the plan for national development. When Honduras is labeled as a narco-state, the implication is that narcotics is the real engine of development, but one that develops not the national weal but private bank accounts.

The Human Cost of Logging

Logging in Honduras comes with considerable human cost to local communities such as Dulce Nombre de Culmí, a small town on the edge of the Rio Platano Biosphere in eastern Honduras. From there, the forests and rivers stretch for many miles in a vast area to the Caribbean coast and south to the border with Nicaragua. The region contains several important rivers and many Indigenous communities. The area, that includes eastern Olancho Department and most of the Department of Gracias a Dios (aka La Mosquitia) has long had a reputation as a region where government law enforcement and institutions are weak or non-existent. The region has historically been densely forested with mahogany and pine, a perfect area for logging, both legal and illegal. The Rio Platano Biosphere is supposed to be a protected area.

Aside from the extensive destruction of a world-class environmentally diverse biosphere, the particularly insidious element of this system is its effects on local populations. Illegal loggers and drug traffickers can enlist poor people in local peasant and Indigenous communities to cut wood or to clear a road for illegal logging and drug shipment.[40] Local people live in fear of at least three drug trafficking rings that control the forests and many of the roads through the region. People become forced labor, or they live under the threat of punishment from drug traffickers.[41] They sometimes complain that fear of entering the forests or even going to their fields to cultivate prevents them from farming, even as logging accelerates local climate change and the degradation of environmental support structures. Hunger, in addition to fear, is a product of this cycle.

Local people cannot rely for protection on police or government authorities who are very often providing protection for the narco-traffickers and the illegal logging companies. If local community people complain to police or courts, they run the risk of retaliation and criminalization. When two leaders of a community in Olancho went to the public prosecutor to ask that illegal logging in their community be investigated, the prosecutor's office instead notified the businessman who owned the logging operation. The businessman then pressed charges against the community members, accusing them of trespass (*usurpación*). Later, the case was dismissed, but the lesson was reinforced: to protest logging is to risk criminalization, or worse.[42]

Much of the eastern side of the Department of Olancho is covered by bio-reserves that are protected by law. But politicians and landowners buy plots of land, log them, sell the logs and put the money into cattle raising, laundering dirty money. In this way, they illegally log and clear the forests and expand cattle raising. Major families and others engaged in this practice also use deforested plots as a base for drug transshipment. Logs and cattle go to local markets or for export—often mixed with legally obtained shipments—while narcotics travel north on forest roads, paths, and by river through sparsely populated areas to the Caribbean coast for shipment to the Caribbean and the United States. Along this northern route, drug traffickers pay or force local community people to work for them in transporting the narcotics. Illegal logging, cattle ranching, and drug trans-shipment form a system that includes bribed and corrupt police, prosecutors, and local authorities. The system integrates at least three illegal enterprises and numerous other criminal activities—bribing officials, threatening local people, deforesting protected biospheres. Logging is the platform and the cover for all of this.[43]

Money from drug trafficking and illegal logging needs to be laundered through a "legal" enterprise. Cattle ranching has been an especially favored choice.[44] Ranching has a long history in Latin America and in Honduras going back to Spanish colonial times, and beef and leather products have served as important exports for Central American countries. But cattle ranching has also been decried for its destructive impact on local environments, the elimination of forest cover, pollution of waterways, and the tendency to hold large areas of land in private hands in areas where many peasant farmers lack land to grow food. Like mining and logging, cattle ranching has been a source of much conflict and popular protest in local communities. As a means for illegal money laundering for some, it becomes part of an exploitative system that makes life harder for local communities.[45]

Communities in the Departments of Olancho and Gracias a Dios (La Mosquítia) find themselves tainted by their association with or proximity to these illegal and criminal enterprises. As forced labor for criminal enterprises such as illegal logging and drug trafficking, communities are targeted by police, state authorities, and United States enforcement agencies working with Honduran security forces. This situation can have fatal consequences. Around midnight on May 11, 2013, an anti-drug raid descended by helicopter near Ahuas, an Indigenous Miskito community near the Patuca River. The river is the major highway in the area; local communities use it to travel by boat to market. The raid was a combined operation of Honduran police and the U.S. Drug Enforcement Agency (DEA). The DEA's semi-permanent presence in Honduras reflects the intent of the United States to fight the "drug war" in Central America, rather than to deal with the causes of the drug addiction epidemic in the United States. But many Hondurans believe that the DEA is itself involved in the narcotics trade. This joint Honduran-U.S. anti-drug campaign was appropriately called Operation Anvil. Probably unintentionally, the name reflected the reality of local communities caught between drug traffickers who threatened to kill them if they did not cooperate, and police enforcement that tended to criminalize them by association.[46]

In the Ahuas raid, the joint raiding force was looking for a boatload of narcotics that they thought had set off down the river from a local community. Instead, they fired on a boat carrying local people to market and to other riverside communities. Four people (including a pregnant woman) in the boat were killed by gunfire from the hovering helicopters. Others were injured, including a fourteen-year-old boy who escaped by jumping into the river. The boy's best friend, another teenager, was killed. According to accounts of local people, the anti-drug raiding party then landed in the community and spent several hours searching houses. Local people said the Honduran police and the DEA agents treated everyone as if they were drug traffickers.

The advantages afforded by logging operations facilitate the criminal narcotics transshipment enterprise through eastern Honduras. The ability of state authorities to criminalize any local protests against logging is an enormous help to the drug lords, and yet another misery for local communities that live in fear. This fear also serves a convenient purpose for the Honduran government and private developers. Several of the large rivers running through Olancho and Gracias a Dios were targeted for major hydroelectric dam projects that are in stages of completion and are disrupting the life of local communities.[47] Oil reserves were discovered off the coast, and the government awarded contracts for exploration and exploitation. Some Hondurans, including many local residents, say the people of these areas have an array of powerful elites against them: government security forces, logging barons, drug traffickers, and private companies—all with an agenda of exploitation of the region's resources and, perhaps, the labor of its people. In these conditions, an exodus of communities from eastern Honduras is not unlikely.

Tolupán Experiences

The Tolupán Indigenous people of Yoro and western Olancho have several thousand years of history in the territory now known as Honduras. Official government figures place the number of Tolupanes at about ten thousand, organized into as many as thirty groups (*tribus*). Their ancestral title to their territory was ratified by the Honduran state in 1864.[48] The area is rich in minerals, water sources, and extensive forests of mahogany and pine. This natural wealth has been both a blessing and a curse, with outsiders, including government agencies, private Honduran entrepreneurs, and foreign companies, maneuvering to secure mining and logging rights in Tolupán communities. Tolupanes have a long and particularly uneasy experience with logging as an extractive industry.

Before 1974, local Tolupán leaders (*caciques*) granted rights to outsiders for some of these extractive enterprises and the community had some control over the granting of permission. In 1974, the Honduran government established the Honduran Forestry Development Corporation (COHDEFOR) and the local leaders found themselves at the mercy of government bureaucrats who could reward leaders who were docile and ignore those who tried to act independently. This politicization of the management of Tolupán lands posed dangers for the preservation of the land's resources and of the people's relative autonomy. There followed a period of tension and conflict between Tolupán communities and government and private interests that was marked by several murders of Tolupán leaders. To address this situation, some leaders got the idea that their people needed their own organization to represent and advocate for them in a way that could withstand government control. They formed the Federation of Xicacaque [Tolupån] Tribes of Yoro (FETRIXY) in the early 1980s. For a while, FETRIXY leaders and activists became targets of assassination because they led resistance to logging and mining in Tolupán territory. Between 1988 and 1993, at least five Tolupán leaders and activists were killed, including FETRIXY's president, Vicente Matute.[49]

In 1988, Tolupán leaders complained to the National Agrarian Institute (INA) that had allowed a non-Tolupán peasant cooperative to resettle in one of the "best regions" on Tolupán territory. In another incident, peasants were accused of killing a Tolupán in a land dispute, but neither Indigenous nor peasant leaders were willing to declare war on each other. Some peasant organizations demanded instead that the government honor the Agrarian Reform Law of 1974 and grant land to peasants on unused corporate and private estates rather than in Indigenous territories. After the Honduran government's embrace of neoliberal extractivism as the model of national development in the early 1990s, the government succeeded in co-opting FETRIXY leadership and in compromising FETRIXY in the eyes of some Tolupanes, thereby exacerbating divisions within Tolupán communities between those who favored the promised benefits of logging and mining and those who opposed these extractive projects.[50]

Throughout the early 2000s, there was resistance in Tolupán communities to logging and mining enterprises. Despite the government's claims that it had abided by the mandates of ILO Convention 169—providing full information to Indigenous communities and asking for their consent without coercion prior to letting companies begin mining or logging in the community— Tolupanes argued that the government almost never abided by this mandate. After the 2009 coup, several outside entrepreneurs obtained government concessions for logging, and they pressed criminal charges against several members of the Tolupán community of San Francisco Locomapa for blocking access to the logging sites and obstructing logging operations. The district court dismissed the case and released the Tolupanes who had been jailed.[51]

In 2013, the Locomapa community was facing demands to expand antimony mining and logging in and near their community. (Antimony is in demand as a component in the manufacture of cell phones.) Locomapa community members regarded themselves as protectors of the extensive groves of mahogany (*caoba*) on the mountainsides around the community; they thought of mahogany as a resource for the future, not for wholesale present exploitation. On August 25, 2013, three members of the Locomapa community were shot and killed. Two of them—Armando Fúnez Medina and Ricardo Soto Fúnez—were guarding a roadblock that members of the community had set up to stop the passage of mining and logging trucks and machinery. The third victim, María Enriqueta Matute, was a seventy-year-old woman who had come out of her kitchen when she heard the shooting. All three died. The shooters were quickly identified by community members as employees of the antimony mining operation nearby, but the police did not detain any suspects. According to local people, the shooters continued to move about freely and to threaten community members for months after the shooting. They also threatened to kill any international human rights or solidarity observers or visitors to the community. It was clear to the Tolupanes and others who resisted mining and logging that they would be subjected to a reign of terror until they acquiesced to government and company demands—and then they might be in for more terror as the rule of law was ignored in favor of extractive development. The bodies of the victims that day were taken to the public morgue in San Pedro Sula, several hours away, where supporters of the Tolupán community accompanied them, bought caskets, and accompanied the bodies on a return to Locomapa, where an all-night vigil was held in the presence of community members and at least one international observer.[52]

In the years after this triple assassination, Tolupanes were active in the protests organized to support other Indigenous groups such as the Lenca and the Garifuna, and in national protests in Tegucigalpa. Seven Tolupanes from Yoro participated in a protest fast with others in the capital. Protesters in these large demonstrations linked the miseries that communities were suffering from extractive industries to the corruption of the central government itself and the prioritizing of extractive enterprises and private profit above human life, the environment, and the nation's preservation of its natural resources.

All the while, Tolupán communities in Yoro were subjected to displacement from their land by powerful landlords with close ties to local authorities and politicians. These displacements (*desalojas*) were carried out by groups of heavily armed men who arrived unannounced in Tolupán villages, often at night, and told the villagers to leave if they did not want to be killed. The land was wanted not only for logging and mining but also as a base for narcotics transshipments; powerful landowners and politicians in the region were actively involved in the drug trade, according to both local sources and news articles. Displaced Tolupán community members found temporary shelter with church groups in Yoro city and elsewhere.[53]

In 2019 and 2020, several more Tolupán leaders and community members were killed or criminalized and detained for resisting mining and logging operations.[54] The Tolupán people have experienced a range of extractive projects and the kinds of miseries these projects have brought. To call them "activists" misses the point. They are ordinary people trying to save their communities and way of life. Some have begun to place their local struggle in a larger national and international context. What is extraordinary is the level of destruction—physical, environmental, social, political—that extractive industries seem to have wrought against Tolupán communities.

Industrial Export Agriculture and Tourism

In 2005, the Tela Railroad Company (official name for United Fruit in Honduras) began efforts to evict the Tierra Nueva Peasant Movement from lands the peasants had occupied for several generations in the north of Honduras. The company wanted to grow African palm and enter the global palm oil market. Threats and legal maneuvers continued for two years. On July 14, 2007, the peasants were forcibly evicted by the company with the help of state security forces. The evicted were 74 families numbering 178 individuals, including 45 children.[55]

In Honduras, large-scale plantation agriculture is an extractive industry. Sugar, fruits, and palm oil have been the major export plantation crops of Honduras. Export plantation agriculture monopolizes large expanses of land, uses huge amounts of water, dumps tons of toxic pesticides, and displaces small farmers in order to produce crops. Beyond corporations and their owners, who actually consumes or benefits from this production is a complicated question.

For the first half of the twentieth century, bananas and other fruit crops dominated export plantation agriculture in Honduras. Today, palm oil has become a dominant crop. Palm oil is used in commercial baking and food products, soap manufacture, as a biofuel—a "clean" energy source that has severe social consequences—and much more. Demand for palm oil in the global market grew rapidly in the first decades of the twenty-first century. From 2000 to 2020, palm oil production increased more than fivefold, making Honduras the eighth largest producer in the world. Fifteen foreign and Honduran companies controlled most of the palm oil production. In 2017, palm oil was the fifth largest export from Honduras. Large areas of northern Honduras, including the great Aguán Valley, are dominated by African palm plantations and dotted with factories that render oil from the palm nuts. Foreign fruit companies have shifted some production to palm oil, but a very few wealthy Honduran families and family companies dominate much of the production.[56]

Peasant cooperatives also started to grow African palm and produce palm oil or sell the palm nuts to large owners who could process them. This peasant cooperative sector experienced considerable pressure from the large growers and the Honduran government in which large growers often have a dominant voice. Some cooperatives disbanded and their members sought work on the palm oil plantations where the work was usually brutal and unhealthy. Local peasants and small farmers expressed interest in producing other kinds of crops, like cacao (chocolate) that are far less damaging to soil quality than African palm. For a few years, under the presidency of Manual Zelaya, such alternatives for peasant and local communities seemed possible. But the 2009 coup and its aftermath made almost every kind of local peasant initiative more difficult or impossible in the Aguán Valley and the northern Caribbean region. For several decades, foreign and Honduran owners have been expanding their African palm plantations into land claimed by local small farming communities. The experience of the Tierra Nuestra peasants has been repeated many times since 2000. Communities are evicted at the point of police or army guns, their houses and crops burned, to make way for corporate palm oil production. By 2020, the expansion of African palm plantations and palm oil production—with full government, police, and military support—had taken the place of fruit and sugar plantations as the most serious threat to the land and livelihood of many peasant communities and small farmers in northern Honduras.[57]

Large-scale export plantation agriculture and tourism development promised employment to local people but delivered threats, evictions, and killings of those who dared to lead or participate in resistance. The Garifuna Indigenous communities experienced all of this, beginning after Hurricane Mitch in 1998 and in accelerated and more deadly fashion in the decade after the 2009 coup when the Honduran government put extractive development on steroids. Poisoning of fishing lagoons, gunfire around Garifuna communities at night, burning of homes of Garifuna who agreed to testify before an international fact-finding commission, exclusion from traditional land and maritime resource areas, and the kidnapping and disappearance of young Garifuna men prompted parents and community leaders to allow or even encourage many Garifuna youth to flee the country.[58]

Tourism is an extractive industry. In Honduras, it can monopolize land and beachfronts, created major pollution problems, and sell local "culture," turning "locals" into servants and dependents in their own lands. Along the Caribbean coast, foreign tourism enterprises have opened luxury tourist resorts, pushing aside Garifuna communities that have farmed and fished for generations. Garifuna youth fled not only the physical danger and appropriation but also the debasement of their identity and self-worth, and the destruction of their future.

In the south of the country, around the Gulf of Fonseca, the Pacific coast, and Zacate Grande, other local communities began experiencing displacement from lands and waters they had traditionally farmed. The government, in partnership with foreign investors, was developing a series of projects to produce "clean energy," including solar and wind farms covering many acres. Local people organized to resist and they complained that, while "clean" energy was a good thing, their lands and resources were being taken from them without compensation, and they would not benefit from the energy that might be produced. Fishermen and shrimp farmers were also concerned about restrictions on their activities and possible pollution of the Pacific waters in the area. A group of wealthy political and business leaders supported the developments and began to claim beach areas for personal use or tourist development. In addition, plans to locate a model city (charter city, *ciudad modelo*) on the coast nearby promised more eviction, disruption of livelihood, pollution, and repressive political control over local communities.[59]

(Not So) Clean Energy

The energy sector of the Honduran political economy is a major ancillary industry for mining and other extractive projects and for the growing maquiladora industries. The energy sector has been largely privatized, and it has been a focus of criticism for corruption. Privatization is advanced in several ways, including the development of hydroelectric power. Private companies contract to build and maintain dams and to control or share with government the control of energy production and sale. Much of this energy goes to other development projects, including mining. Some reaches urban households that must pay higher prices for often erratic service. Honduran development policy has promoted the expansion of hydropower as a cleaner and greener source of energy. Unfortunately, the reality is far more complex.[60] In an unpublished paper in 2011, anthropologist Barbara Johnston, writing about the Chixoy Dam Project in Guatemala, could as well have been describing hydroelectric river damming projects in Honduras.

> The disaster that is large-scale hydrodevelopment is, for far too many, a structural violence sanctioned and imposed by the state and other powers, in theory for a common good, in reality fort short-term gain. The nation trades the lives, community, well-being, and the happiness of certain citizens to generate and

deliver water and energy to other distant, privileged interests. Some profit. Many pay the price.[61]

As Berta Cáceres, COPINH, and Lenca communities were trying to stop construction of a hydroelectric dam on the Gualquarque River (see chapter 1), Desarrollos Energeticos (DESA), the private company that had the contract to build the dam, published statements describing hydroelectric energy as clean and environmentally friendly, a component in the overall energy development plan of Honduras into the future. The company accused the Lenca of being selfish, short-sighted, and unpatriotic by trying to deprive other people and the country of this important source of clean and dependable energy. DESA also threatened a lawsuit against COPINH to collect financial losses to the company caused by months of opposition to the dam and the withdrawal of some foreign investment. "Green neoliberalism," is the use of environmentally friendly ideas and policies to hide "dirty" development and the violation of community rights. Much of the energy to be generated by the dam projects along Honduran rivers would likely be channeled to mining, tourism, or maquiladoras—development projects far more likely to pollute than to keep the environment clean, or more likely to displace communities and their rights. Damming a river has been described as an attempt to colonize the river.[62]

Green neoliberalism also came in the form of government laws and policies that removed areas from Indigenous control and stewardship by declaring these areas environmentally protected zones. As we have seen, this legal mechanism was used to exclude Garifuna communities along the Caribbean coast from land and sea where they had sustainably farmed and fished for almost two centuries.[63] In the fetish of neolibral extractivism, green and environmentally friendly discourse framed an excuse to remove opposition to extraction and exploitation. Again, in southern Honduras, along the Pacific coast, government-private partnerships promoted wind and solar farms and tourism. Local people have criticized all of these projects because they displaced local communities and restrict areas that have been freely used for generations. One wonders who will actually benefit from the energy derived from wind and solar farms in the area, and what the displaced will do.

There is an argument to be made that Honduras needs more internally generated energy to support greater employment opportunities in a country with an unemployment rate of more than 50 percent (the rate is so high, in part, because of the dislocation and eviction of rural communities in the face of extractive projects). For example, energy is needed for the assembly factories that have multiplied around cities such as San Pedro Sula, even though these do not generate enough jobs, working conditions are usually poor or unhealthy, and the jobs are low wage, often not enough to support a family. Most of the assembly plants are located in or near urban areas. But the Honduran state's assumption of the mantle of protector of clean, environmentally friendly development usually ignores both the obvious disruption and repression of Indigenous and other rural communities and the state sponsored violence that this often necessitates; and that much of this "clean and sustainable" energy will be used to enable the most environmentally disruptive and unsustainable sorts of development projects, such as mining and logging.

SOME OTHER CONSEQUENCES OF NEOEXTRACTIVE DEVELOPMENT

Neoextractive "development" in Honduras has had other consequences. Several of the most salient are briefly described here. All of them, in different ways, create conditions that encourage some Hondurans to emigrate.

Environmental Degradation

Green neoliberalism represents itself as a way of preserving natural resources and addressing the growing threats posed by climate change. Those threats—droughts, floods, wildfires, coastal flooding, extreme heat, and perhaps more intense dengue fever epidemics—are real enough in Central America. The region is considered among the most vulnerable to those effects. The vulnerability is a result not only of the region's geography but also of specific development policies and practices and the corruption and weakening of state institutions. As these initiatives in extractive development and energy generation moved forward, water resources were drained or polluted, areas were deforested, and monocrop plantations replaced more sustainable forms of food production. Honduras experienced prolonged periods of drought that forced coffee farmers in western highlands to consider quitting and moving or emigrating.

Honduras, and much of Central America, became more vulnerable to devastation from hurricanes such as Mitch in 1998 and Eta and Iota that struck Honduras one week apart in November of 2020. In Honduras, these hurricanes displace hundreds of thousands of mostly poor people, destroyed thousands of acres of crops, further contaminated water supplies, and created conditions for disease and other miseries to spread. During and after Eta and Iota, people complained that the government was absent or extremely slow in providing even minimal assistance. Some reported that government agents even tried to stop local people from helping each other. People adopted the phrase "Here the people help the people," as a critique of government failure to assist its citizens.[64] Others reported that flooding displaced local gangs along with their victims, and gang members were invading less flooded areas to prey on other populations. People sought shelter wherever they could, often by the side of roads or underneath highway overpasses, crowded together for shelter in the middle of a Covid-19 pandemic. State institutions weakened by corruption and privatization were unable or unwilling to assist. The dislocation and challenges to survival wrought by the 2020 hurricanes in Honduras were followed by the formation of yet another migrant caravan that departed from San Pedro Sula a few weeks later, bound for the United States and Mexico.

Racial and Ethnic Inequality

Extractive projects in Honduras tend to be located in areas where Indigenous communities are concentrated. Much of the mineral deposits and especially the forest reserves are in areas long claimed and inhabited by Indigenous communities. Lenca, Tolupán, and Miskito peoples bear the brunt of much of the extractivism from these industries. Garifuna communities have the misfortune to be located in Caribbean coastal areas suited for palm oil production and much desired by tourist developers. Underlying this geographic pattern is a strain of historic racial and cultural stereotype against Indigenous peoples as "underdeveloped," backward, and vulnerable. The pressures, threats, and violence against some Indigenous communities, for example the Garifuna, have pushed adults to allow and even encourage the emigration of their young people rather than subject them to more violence, gangs, and drug traffickers. Extractivism covets the "wealth" that lies in the lands of Indigenous people, and rationalizes the seizure of that wealth by perpetuating or expanding negative stereotypes of Indigenous people. Government agencies, courts, and companies collude in this effort.

Socioeconomic Inequality

In Honduras, decades of neoliberal extractive development resulted not in greatly increased living standards for the population, but rather in spreading poverty and widening the poverty gap. By 2019, Honduras had one of the widest wealth gaps and income inequalities in the world.[65] When extractive projects are not locating on Indigenous lands, they are usually pushing into rural areas where peasant communities live, some of the poorest people in the country. Privatization means transferring the sources of wealth into a few private hands and eliminating state responsibility for basic services to everyone else. Prices for necessities such as electricity rise as the dependability and quality of services falls. The poor and increasingly the middle class bear the burden in the cities and towns.

Gender Inequality

The "frontier town" mentality that mining projects bring to a rural farming community threatens women in several ways, and exacerbates some older strains of patriarchy and machismo in Honduran society. In Honduras, as in many other places, women have been the conspicuous leaders in resistance to mining projects. Women are also confronted with domestic violence in a country with one of the higher indices of femicide in the world.[66]

> Globally, El Salvador and Honduras stand out with rates of more than 10 female homicides per 100,000 women. The level of violence affecting women in El Salvador and Honduras exceeds the combined rate of male and female homicides in some of the forty countries with the highest murder rates in the world, such as Ecuador and Tanzania.[67]

It seems as if poverty, dependency, and powerlessness in the face of neoliberal extractive development exacerbate the reach and power of patriarchy and machismo. The maquiladora industries, fed by the influx to the cities of landless and displaced people, employ women in work that is low paying, often damaging to health, and fraught with conditions facilitating sexual harassment.

Corruption and the Confusion of Legitimate and Criminal

The opportunities that extractive industries offer for illegal enterprises such as drug trafficking and violent crime have been mentioned, including the opportunities for money laundering—cattle ranching, for example—that provide a legitimate cover. In cities, ill-gotten drug and gang money can be laundered in other legitimate ways such as car wash enterprises (literally, a case of money laundering).

There are other dimensions to the confusion of legitimate and criminal activity as well. With the Honduran state's wholesale embrace of neoliberal extractivism in 1990, and increasingly after the 2009 coup, public-private partnerships became part of the development strategy. In 2010, a few months after the coup, the government passed Law Decree 143–2010 for Promoting Public Private Partnerships (PPP), and created an entity for coordinating such partnerships, that is known in Honduras as the Coalianza. In the following decade, Coalianza was involved in promoting infrastructure projects in cities and extractive projects in other areas of the country. The relationship between government funding and private investment funds became a "known unknown" for the Honduran public and even members of the Congress. Concerns and accusations of corruption increased as infrastructure projects failed to meet completion dates and costs mounted well beyond projections. Where did the money go? At the same time, a lengthening list of revelations of corruption and the private pocketing of state and investment funds was reported in the Honduran press and by brave journalists and prosecutors, some of whom were killed outright or imprisoned for "defamation" when they named names. All of this strengthened a widespread sense of rampant corruption.[68] In 2019, the Honduran government announced the disbanding of Cozlianza and the formation of a new structure to promote public-private enterprise. To observers, it seemed that very little had changed. The prosecution case against the killers of Berta Cáceres, in which evidence seemed to indicate collusion between DESA company and government officials, became emblematic of state-private corruption and illegality, a stand-in for the many similar cases involving extractive projects and government officials across the country. When there is little or no attempt to prosecute these officials, the absence confirms for some the "culture of impunity" that enables the corruption to spread. Impunity is the consort of corruption. Legitimate infrastructure projects became also channels for corruption.

The impunity that shielded government officials, powerful families, and corporation, and their alleged associates in drug trafficking and gang activity, did not extend to other Hondurans, certainly not to those who resisted extractive projects. In 2018, the Honduran Congress undertook a revision of the country's penal code. This revision represented an inversion of the standards of guilt and punishment. The revision added new legal categories of crimes that included aspects of popular protest and increased the prison penalties for some categories of popular protest or "disturbances of the peace." Simultaneously, the revisions lowered the prison penalties for categories of gang and drug trafficking offenses.[69] It became another emblematic moment for many, showing clearly the two-faced nature of impunity that looked kindly on crime and corruption, but sternly on peaceful opposition to crime and corruption. The take-aways from this for many Hondurans were distrust and despair. Confusion of legitimate and illegitimate, the apparent inversion of legal and illegal, were a concern for many Hondurans who worried that the situation made it much more difficult to teach that corruption and violence were not the new normal.

Militarization of Honduran Society

The militarization of Honduran society is yet another consequence of neoextractivism. In Honduras, the militarization of national development, national institutions, and everyday life has a long historical evolution. It is perhaps the most denounced and yet controversial feature of Honduran life, and it is a major force in maintaining the conditions that promote emigration. The next chapter examines the militarization of Honduran society in some detail.

CONCLUSION: EXTRACTIVISM AND EMIGRATION

Extractivism cannot be held responsible for all the corruption that plagues Honduras; that has a long history. But the intensification of extractivism as national development policy provided much increased opportunity, temptation, and cover for confusing legitimate and criminal activity. As we noted earlier, neoextractivism altered the political economy of Honduras and vitiated the meaning of national development. Political and economic power became not only integrated but necessarily bound together in a national corrupt enterprise that replaced and violently repressed any sense of development as improving of condition of the nation and its people. Therein lies a major impetus for emigration.

NOTES

1. My interviews and site visit, Honduras, August 2013.
2. Environmental Law Alliance Worldwide (ELAW), "Honduras: Holding the Mining Industry Accountable," Winter 2008, https://elaw.org/es/node/5169.
3. My interviews with El Barro resident, Honduras, August 2013.
4. Centro de Estudios para la Democracia (CESPAD), "Azacualpa, MINOSA, Copán," August 18, 2020, http://cespad.org.hn/2020/08/18/alerta-minosa-comienza-de-nuevo-a-dinamitar-cementerio-de-azacualpa-y-pone-en-riesgo-decenas-de-familias/; Claudia Mendoza, "Azacualpa," Centro de Estudios para la Democracia (CESPAD), September 29, 2020, http://cespad.org.hn/2020/09/29/el-sol-el-aguao-un-fusil-en-la-frente/.
5. Marvin Barahona, *Honduras en el siglo XX: Una síntesis histórica* (Tegucigalpa: Editorial Guaymuras, 2005), 31–33; Guillermo Molina Chocano, *Estado Liberal y desarrollo capitalista en Honduras* (Tegucigalpa, Editorial Guaymuras, 1982), 24–30.
6. Barahona, *Honduras*, 52–58; Darío A. Euraque, *Reinterpreting the Banana Republic: Region and State in Honduras, 1870–1972* (Chapel Hill: University of North Carolina Press, 1972), 27–35.
7. Honduran Social Forum on the External Debt (FOSDEH), "El presupuesto público: Danza multimillonaria que bailan los pobres," *Realidad Nacional* (February 2020), https://fosdeh.com/tag/honduras/; Extractive Industries Transparency Initiative (EITI), "Honduras," February 4, 2021, https://eiti.org/honduras; *Conexihon*, "Privilegios fiscales en energía y minería agudizan desigualdades en Honduras," July 2, 2019, http://www.conexihon.hn/index.php/transparencia/1140-privilegios-fiscales-en-energia-y-mineria-agudizan-desigualdades-en-honduras.

8. Center for Latin American and Caribbean Studies, University of London: "1998–2013 Honduran Mining Laws," 2020, https://ilas.sas.ac.uk/research-projects/legal-cultures-subsoil/1998-2013-honduran-mining-laws. For a brief review of recent mining legislation in Honduras, see Equipo de Reflexíon, Investigacíon y Comunicacíon (ERIC), *Impacto socioambiental de la minería en la región noroccidental de Honduras a la luz de tres estudios de casos,* (Tegucigalpa: Editorial Guaymuras, 2016), 29–56.

9. Instituto de Derechos Ambientales de Honduras, *La Mina San Martin en el Valle de Siria, exploración, explotación, y cherries: Impactos y consecuencias* (Tegucigalpa: Instituto de Derecho Ambiental de Honduras, 2013), 13, translation mine.

10. Lynn Holland, "The Dangerous Path toward Mining Law Reform in Honduras," Council on Hemispheric Affairs, December 18, 2015, https://www.coha.org/the-dangerous-path-toward-mining-law-reform-in-honduras/.

11. Center for Latin American and Caribbean Studies, University of London, "1998–2013 Honduran Mining Laws," 2020, https://ilas.sas.ac.uk/research-projects/legal-cultures-subsoil/1998-2013-honduran-mining-laws.

12. Equipo de Reflexión, *Impacto socioambiental*, 85, translation mine.

13. From my interviews and field notes in Honduras, August 2017.

14. Juan López quoted in *Earth Rights International*, "Criminalized Earth Rights Defenders Should Be Immediately Released," February 27, 2020, https://earthrights.org/blog/criminalized-guapinol-earth-rights-defenders-should-be-immediately-released/.

15. Equipo de Reflexión, *Impacto socioambiental*, 87.

16. Equipo de Reflexión, *Impacto*, 90–91.

17. Equipo,de Reflexión, *Impacto*, 82–83.

18. Personal communication from Honduran Accompaniment Project and Comité de Familias de los Detenidos/Desaparecidos en Honduras (COFADEH), 2013.

19. For example, Echart Muñoz and Maria del Carmen Villareal, "Women's Struggles Against Extractivism in Latin America and the Caribbean," *Contexto Internacional* 41, no. 2 (May/August 2019): 303–325.

20. Nancy García and Lucía Vijil, unpublished report of investigations by Red Nacional de Defensoras, a Honduran network of women defenders of the environment, 2019.

21. James Phillips, *Honduras in Dangerous Times: Resistance and Resilience* (Lanham MD: Lexington Books, 2015), 93–97.

22. Fabiana Li, *Unearthing Conflict: Corporate Mining, Activism, and Expertise in Peru* (Durham NC: Duke University Press, 2015).

23. Barbara Hogenboom, "Latin America's Transformative New Extraction and Local Conflict," *European Review of Latin American and Caribbean Studies* 99 (October 2015): 147.

24. Equipo de Reflexión, *Impacto*, 16–18.

25. Jorge Arévalo Cárcamo quoted in the Honduran daily *El Tiempo*, September 7, 1988.

26. Honduran daily *El Tiempo*, August 26, 1988.

27. Comité para la Defensa de los Derechos Humanos en Honduras (CODEH), *Boletín* 85 (February 1992): 8; Hannah C. Riley and James K. Sebenius, "Stakeholder

Negotiations over Third World Resource Projects," *Cultural Survival Quarterly* 19, no. 3 (1993): 39–43; James Phillips, "Resource Access, Environmental Struggles, and Human Rights in Honduras," in *Life and Death Matters: Human Rights and the Environment at the End of the Millennium*, ed. Barbara Rose Johnston (Walnut Creek CA: Altamira Press, 1997), 180–182.

28. Centro de Documentación de Honduras, *25 Años de Reform Agraria* (Tegucigalpa: Centro de Documentación de Honduras, 1988).

29. Susan Stonich and Billie R. DeWalt, "The Political Ecology of Deforestation in Honduras," in *Tropical Deforestation: The Human Dimension*, ed. Leslie E. Sponsel, Thomas N. Headland, and Robert C. Bailey (New York: Columbia University Press, 1996), 187–215.

30. Cárcamo, *El Tiempo*, September 7, 1988.

31. Mayra Lisset Fuñez Martinez, *Problematica ambiental en Honduras* (Tegucigalpa: Asociación de Ecología, 1989).

32. Overseas Development Institute UK, *Governance and Poverty Impacts of the Illegal Timber Trade in Central America* (London: Overseas Development Institute, 2002), https://www.odi.org/projects/1187-governance-and-poverty-impacts-illegal-timber-trade-central-america.

33. Maria Fiallos, "Honduran Indigenous Community in Standing Forest Area," *Honduras This Week*, June 9, 2003.

34. Environmental Investigation Agency and Center for International Policy, *The Illegal Logging Crisis in Honduras* (Washington DC: Environmental Investigation Agency, 2005), introduction, https://eia-international.org/wp-content/uploads/Honduras-Report-English-low-res1.pdf.

35. Environmental Investigation Agency, *Illegal Logging Crisis*, introduction.

36. For example, Global Witness, *Illegal Logging in the Río Plátano Biosphere: A Farce in Three Acts* (Washington DC: Global Witness, 2009).

37. Environmental Investigation Agency, *Illegal Logging Crisis*, 13–18.

38. Environmental Investigation Agency, *Illegal Logging Crisis*, introduction.

39. Environmental Investigation Agency, *Illegal Logging Crisis*, 26 and 38–40.

40. Fiallos, "Honduran Indigenous Community."

41. Héctor Silva Ávalos, "The Logging Barons of Catacamas, Honduras," *InSight Crime*, September 18, 2020, https://insightcrime.org/investigations/logging-barons-catacamas-honduras/.

42. Riccy Ponce, "Sobreseimiento definitivo para ambientalistas querellados por defender el bosque," *Defensores en Linea*, February 10, 2020, http://www.defensoresenlinea.com/sobreseimiento-definitivo-para-ambientalistas-querellados-por-defender-el-bosque/.

43. InSight Crime, "Los Cachiros: Honduras," October 23, 2019, http://www.defensoresenlinea.com/sobreseimiento-definitivo-para-ambientalistas-querellados-por-defender-el-bosque/; Silva Ávalos, "Logging Barons."

44. InSight Crime, "Los Cachiros."

45. Silva Ávalos, "Logging Barons." Environmental Investigation Agency, *The Illegal Logging Crisis*, 1–4.

46. Annie Bird and Alexander Main with Karen Spring, *Collateral Damage of a Drug War: The May 11 Killings in Ahuas and the Impact of the U.S. War on Drugs in Honduras* (Washington DC: Rights Action and the Center for Economic and Policy Research, August 2012).

47. The basic elements are summarized and well documented in Sarah Chayes, *When Corruption Is the Operating System: The Case of Honduras* (Washington DC: Carnegie Endowment for International Peace, 2017): 40–47.

48. Marvin Barahona, *Pueblos indígenas, Estado y memoria colectiva en Honduras* (Tegucigalpa: Editorial Guaymuras, 2009); pages 49–61 offer a useful brief history, and pages 56–57 explain the modern Honduran state's territorial agreements with the Tolupanes, dating from the mid-1800s.

49. James Phillips, *Honduras in Dangerous Times: Resistance and Resilience* (Lanham MD: Lexington Books, 2015), 98–99.

50. Anthony Stock, "Land War," *Cultural Survival Quarterly* 16, no. 4 (1992): 16–18; Comité para la Defensa de los Derechos Humanos en Honduras, *Boletín* 80 (September 1991).

51. James Phillips, "Tolupanes Put Their Lives on the Line Defending All Hondurans," *Cultural Survival Quarterly*, July 12, 2015, https://www.culturalsurvival.org/news/tolupanes-put-their-lives-line-defending-all-hondurans.

52. Information provided by Locomapa community members and Honduran and international human rights workers who accompanied the Locomapa Tolupán community throughout these events (per my interview with an international observer of these events).

53. My site visit and field notes, Yoro, Honduras, August 2013.

54. Meghan Krausch, "Fighting to Protect the Forest in Honduras," *The Progressive*, May 15, 2019, https://progressive.org/dispatches/forest-protection-under-dictatorship-honduras-krausch-190515/ (The first lines of this article is "Many in the U.S. are unaware of the connection between refugees fleeing Honduras, and the struggle there for environmental justice."); Meghan Krausch, "Honduran Indigenous Protesting Logging Killed," *The Progressive*, October 3, 2019, https://progressive.org/dispatches/Honduran-indigenous-protesting-logging-killed-Krausch-191002/.

55. *Intercontinental Cry,* July 14, 2007, and my field notes, Honduras, 2013.

56. Tanya M. Kerssen's *Grabbing Power: The New Struggle for Land, Food, and Democracy in Northern Honduras* (Oakland CA: Food First Books, 2013) is entirely devoted to the rise and consequences of the palm oil industry in Honduras. See also Max Radwin, "'It's Getting Worse': National Parks in Honduras Hit Hard by Palm Oil," *Mongabay Series Forest Trackers*, April 11, 2019, https://news.mongabay.com/2019/04/its-getting-worse-national-parks-in-honduras-hit-hard-by-palm-oil/; Andres Leon, "Rebellion under the Palm Trees: Memory, Agrarian Reform and Labor in the Aguán, Honduras" (PhD diss., City University of New York, 2015), 144–204.

57. For example, Elizabeth Díaz, "Honduras: Criminalization of the Garifuna people defending their territory from the advance of the African palm," *World Rainforest Movement*, Bulletin 206 (September 26, 2014), https://wr m.org.uy/articles-from-the-wrm-bulletin/section1/honduras-criminalization-of-the-garifuna-people-defending-their-territory-from-the-advance-of-the-african-palm/.

58. Interviews with and personal communications from members of international human rights organizations in Honduras.

59. Giorgio Trucchi, "Zacate Grande: 'Nos desalojan en nombre de desarrollo,'" *AlbaSud*, December 31, 2018, http://www.albasud.org/noticia/es/1080/zacate-grande-honduras-nos-desalojan-en-nombre-del-desarrollo.

60. Barbara Rose Johnston, "Water and Human Rights," in *Life and Death Matters: Human Rights, Environment, and Social Justice*, Second Edition, ed. Barbara Rose Johnston (Walnut Creek CA: Left Coast Press, 2011), 443–453; Barbara Rose Johnston, "Dam Legacies: Guatemala's Chixoy Dam-Affected Communities," in *Life and Death Matters*, 460–465.

61. Barbara Rose Johnston, "Healing in the aftermath of development-induced displacement: The anthropology of reparations," unpublished paper presented at the Society for Applied Anthropology annual meeting, Seattle, April 1, 2011.

62. Vandana Shiva, *Water Wars: Privatization, Pollution, and Profit* (Boston: South End Press, 2002), 53–86.

63. Keri Vacanti Brondo, *Land Grab: Green Neoliberalism, Gender, and Garifuna Resistance in Honduras* (Tucson: University of Arizona Press, 2013).

64. Jeff Ernst, "'Everything Buried in Mud': Hurricane Eta's Devastating Blow to Honduras," *The Guardian*, November 11, 2020, https://www.theguardian.com/global-development/2020/nov/11/everything-buried-in-mud-hurricane-etas-devastating-blow-to-honduras.

65. "Why Honduras Remains Latin America's Most Unequal Country," *World Politics Review* (January 6, 2017), https://www.worldpoliticsreview.com/insights/20856/why-honduras-remains-latin-america-s-most-unequal-country; Raiesa Ali, "Income Inequality and Poverty: A Comparison of Brazil and Honduras," *Council on Hemispheric Affairs*, July 1, 2015, https://www.coha.org/income-inequality-and-poverty-a-comparison-of-brazil-and-honduras/.

66. Maria Fernanda Bozmoski, "The Northern Triangle: The World's Epicenter for Gender-Based Violence," *New Atlanticist* (March 3, 2021), https://www.atlanticcouncil.org/blogs/new-atlanticist/the-northern-triangle-the-worlds-epicenter-for-gender-based-violence/.

67. Global Americans, "Femicide and International Women's Rights: An Epidemic of Violence in Latin America," *Global Americans Report*, 2021, https://theglobalamericans.org/reports/femicide-international-womens-rights/.

68. Chayes, *When Corruption Is the Operating System*, 35–37; Javier Suazo, "Coalianza: Negocio de pocos," *America Latina*, December 5, 2019, https://www.alainet.org/es/articulo/203673.

69. Marlon Gonzalez, "Honduras' New Penal Code Lightens Sentences for Corruption," *Associated Press*, June 25, 2020, https://apnews.com/article/1efbd7e8a44f6c2458fb6a15c2950642.

Chapter 7

The Militarization of Honduras, Emigration, and the United States

Militarism is a necessary force in creating and supporting conditions of rampant neoextractivism that make life difficult for many. It thus promotes emigration. But it also thwarts immigration as international borders become militarized zones. Militarism pushes people to seek survival; then pushes them back to unsurvivable conditions. To understand the roots of emigration from Central America, and especially from Honduras, it is necessary to understand something of militarism in these countries and in the United States. It is an essential component in imperial enterprise.

Militarism is an ideology, not only a set of policies and practices but also and primarily a way of framing and depicting an alternative reality. In Honduras, militarism is depicted as the guardian of the interests of the nation and its people. In reality, it is the primary support for the interests of a privileged few. Neoliberal extractivism and the imperial project of the United States—and to a lesser extent other major powers—is greatly assisted by the militarization of Honduran society. From a critical anthropological perspective:

> militarism is a cultural system; it is shaped through ideology and rhetoric, effected through bodies and technologies, made visible and invisible through campaigns of imagery and knowledge production, and it colonizes aspects of social life including reproduction, self-image, and notions of community.[1]

The logic of militarism is constant threat and expansion. Security measures tend to move into every aspect of social, economic, and political life.[2] The history of Latin America evokes images of *caudillos* (strongmen) and military dictatorships. But modern Latin America has also suffered from the national security ideology, a variant of militarism.[3] Like the classic forms of national security in the Latin American military dictatorships of the 1970s, Honduran militarism really serves to protect the interests of a small elite and its foreign associates. In its upper ranks, the military is increasingly identified with the privileged elite. The strong connections between Honduran and U.S. military institutions is a core feature of the imperial relationship between these countries.

THE HONDURAN MILITARY

Since at least the 1950s or before, the Honduran military has been perhaps the most stable and important link between the Honduran government and the United States, via military-to-military collaboration and U.S. security aid. Civilian governments come and go, but the military institutions of the two countries continue to collaborate, ensuring a dominant relationship for the United States in Honduras. This has had some disturbing consequences for human rights and the principle of democratic civilian government. The military provides the muscle to push aside community rights and popular resistance and to facilitate and protect extractive projects. The economic and political power of the Honduran military as an institution whose high-ranking officers are also members of the country's elite arises in part from the military's crucial role in promoting neoextractive development.

In Honduras, neoextractive development takes on characteristics of a military campaign waged against a significant portion of the Honduran people who, as we have seen, are regarded as the enemy simply for being in the way of "development," physically or politically. Communities complain about the heightened military presence in areas such as the Bajo Aguán, where land conflicts are many and the military is regarded as if it were an occupying force. People say the soldiers are not there to protect them but to oppress them. In a study of the conflicts over water and mining in Guapinol (see chapter 1), three-quarters of the local population said that the presence of the military filled them with insecurity and terror. Add to this the increased use of the military police to repress peaceful popular protests in the cities, the violent control that criminal gangs enforce in many places, and the predations of corrupt police, and it can seem as if Honduran emigrants are fleeing a war zone.

Although the military continues to be among the more trusted institutions in Honduran society (along with the Catholic and Evangelical churches), by 2012 an increasing volume of reports out of Honduras detailing or alleging major human rights violations—killings; evictions of communities from their land; repression of peaceful protest; attacks on journalists, peasants, environmentalists, Indigenous and human rights leaders—prompted demands to investigate how U.S. aid to Honduras was used, and whether U.S. assistance to Honduran security forces supported or enabled actions that violate basic human rights. Since 2012, there have been attempts in the U.S. Congress to call attention to the need for such a review, through letters to the Secretary of State signed by Members of the House and Senate; hearings of Congressional committees in which Honduran human rights leaders and experts gave testimony; and bills in the House of Representatives, including in particular the Berta Cáceres Human Rights in Honduras Act, and in the Senate, the Honduras Human Rights and Anti-Corruption Act.

THE MILITARY IN HONDURAN HISTORY

What is referred to here as the Honduran military really signifies two realities.[4] Early on, the military was not so much a modern professional army as that is understood today, but an armed force that more or less did the bidding of whoever could pay, a force at the service of strongmen (*caudillos*). By the 1950s, the Honduran army had become more professional as the primary and official government institution of national defense.[5] This was due in part to its developing relationship with the U.S. military.

> The relationship with the United States served to professionalize and institutionalize the Honduran Armed Forces. The opening of the *Escuela Militar Francisco Morazán* in 1952 gave the military legitimacy and the needed training to be recognized and respected as a true military institution. With time, however, this relationship changed from one of cooperation to more of a transactional relationship; one in which cooperation seemed contingent on the ability of the United States to provide resources to the state.[6]

The Honduran military has continued to project a mission of national security while also serving the needs of the country's economic and political elite—in reality these two are considered the same—and even developing its own institutional interests, becoming itself a major economic and political power. At times, the military has been constitutionally independent of the civilian executive. At other times it has taken direct control of the executive power for itself in the form of military governments.

In the late 1800s and early 1900s, Honduran governments deployed the military to crush labor strikes and demonstrations. In 1909, workers at the San Juancito mine, owned by the U.S.-based Rosario Mining Company, went on strike. The Honduran military was called out to forcibly end the strike, and some miners were jailed.[7] That became a common pattern. Honduran governments called out the soldiers to forcibly put down labor or peasant unrest and protect foreign extractive and agricultural enterprises.

As the banana companies expanded their operations along the north coast of Honduras in the first half of the twentieth century, the Honduran military's role in crushing labor unrest for U.S. companies increased. The army broke up a strike at the Cuyamel fruit plantations in 1916, and sent four hundred workers to prison.[8] There were close ties between Honduran government officials and the foreign banana companies, including a period in which the Honduran Attorney General was also a legal consultant for a U.S. fruit company. The Honduran military and the U.S. military at times seemed to reinforce each other in their determination to eliminate popular opposition to extractive export enterprises. This was the era of "gunboat diplomacy." U.S. military force was called in, or was stationed offshore to supplement the Honduran military in case they were not zealous enough in defending U.S. investments.

During the height of the "banana empire" from 1920 to 1950, there was a series of labor strikes on the banana plantations—at that time still the backbone of the Honduran economy. For economic and political reasons (good relations with the U.S.) Honduran governments deployed the military to end these strikes, sometimes by force or intimidation, sometimes by overseeing negotiations between workers and management.[9] The banana workers' strike of 1954 was a pivotal event in Honduran history, and it transformed the political landscape by raising labor and then peasant communities to a voice in the country's political and economic development. In their demands, the strike leaders cited the United Nations Universal Declaration of Human Rights that had been adopted only six years earlier, and the Inter-American Charter of Social Guarantees, adopted the same year as the UN Human Rights Declaration.[10] The workers identified their strike as a struggle for rights. An end to the strike was finally negotiated on May, with the aid of two Honduran army generals and the looming threat that the army would intervene in force. In June, the Central Intelligence Agency and the U.S. military used Honduran land and air space to stage a coup against the Arbenz government in neighboring Guatemala, a government trying to impose a modest land reform that banana companies feared would threaten their interests.[11] The military was increasingly called on to control or repress the activities of new peasant organizations and peasant unions.

During the 1950s, the military's image of itself became increasingly professionalized and defined as the primary defender of national sovereignty and security. Eventually, military leaders decided to push aside the weak civilian governments they had served and take direct control of the state. In October, 1963, a military coup ended a mildly reformist civilian government by taking direct control of power and initiating a severe repression of labor and popular activism.[12] Honduras had military rule from then until 1980. In reality, the 1963 coup was only an open recognition of the fact that the military had been the real power propping up civilian governments for many years.

During the seventeen years of direct military rule (1963–1980) repression took direct form with arrests, imprisonment of labor and peasant leaders, and destruction of their organizations' offices. Some of the most heinous and notorious incidents were perpetrated by military officers collaborating with powerful landowning families to eliminate the power of peasant groups that were demanding land reform. Although peasant unions succeeded in pushing the military government to allow the Agrarian Reform Law of 1974, the law itself was not particularly strong, and its implementation was uneven, at best.[13] The head of the military government in1974, General Osvaldo Lopez Arrellano, said of the proposed land reform, "I intend to give the peasants what they want, but I want them to fight for it." The military's problem in this period was that it wavered between promoting reform and applying repression. Every step the military government took toward mild reform was met with fierce resistance from the landowning elites, and so the military finally opted for repression instead of reform.[14]

The infamous "massacre" at the hacienda of Los Horcones in 1975 became emblematic of the repression and the role of the military during this period. Twelve members of the National Peasant Union (UNC) along with two Catholic priests that supported their work were brutally killed in a manner that including burning and dismemberment. The two clerics were tortured and killed and their bodies thrown down a well. The perpetrators were reportedly several military officers and landowners. The Catholic church in the area had been supportive of the UNC and the peasants' efforts for land.[15] The military government responded to this incident by banning the UNC, hunting down is members, and destroying its offices. The government also ordered the deportation of all foreign Catholic priests in the Department of Olancho where Los Horcones was located. The bishop was forced to close the diocese entirely. He escaped persecution because he was out of the country at the time of the incident. In two ways, the military was deeply involved in this incident and similar ones: as individual members directly involved in the crime, and as government officials directing the persecution of peasant unions and members of the Catholic Church. Military governments sometimes employed the discourse of anti-communism to justify this repression. The rationale was the struggle against the "communist" influence of some peasant groups and sectors of the Catholic Church after the Church in the 1960s had haltingly adopted the reforms of Vatican II, including liberation theology, and the "preferential option for the poor."

The military returned power (at least nominally) to a civilian government in 1980, but the military command remained constitutionally independent of the civilian executive power, and the National Police remained under military command. The new civilian government was politically dependent upon the military and a group of powerful families controlling much of the country's economy. This group was represented by the Association for the Progress of Honduras (APROH), an organization still functioning in 2020. APROH, in conjunction with the U.S. Embassy in Tegucigalpa, dictated the outlines of the economic development policies the new civilian government was to follow.[16] But the regional conflicts of the decade prevented Honduran governments from fully implementing these policies until 1990.

During the 1980s, the role of the U.S. military in Honduras expanded and intensified, and with it, the relationship between the military of the two countries. The Reagan Administration's policy was to make Honduras the platform for U.S. military forward strike capability to counter the FMLN insurgency in El Salvador and especially the FSLN (Sandinista) popular revolutionary government in Nicaragua that overthrew the forty-five-year-long dictatorship of the Somoza family in 1979. The Nicaraguan revolution raised concerns among members of the Honduran political and economic elite who feared the example that Nicaragua might provide to many Hondurans. It also raised concerns in the Reagan Administration that portrayed the Sandinistas and the revolution as a communist threat to the hemisphere.

To transform Honduras into a military platform against revolution and insurgency in Central America in the 1980s, the Honduran government and the Reagan Administration signed a mutual aid agreement that effectively facilitated the transformation of Honduras into a national security state.[17] This was followed in 1983 by several military security agreements (*convenios*) between the Honduran military and the Reagan Administration.[18] These accords included agreement to joint use of the Honduran military base at Soto Cano (Palmerola) with the United States, and other installations in several areas of Honduras for military bases, intelligence posts, U.S. training of Honduran military, and facilities for surveillance and other military functions. The United States provided approximately $1.6 billion in economic and military aid to Honduras in the 1980s, stationed 1,200 U.S. military in Joint Task Force Bravo, and trained approximately 9,500 Honduran military officials at the U.S. Army School of the Americas (moved from Panama to Ft. Benning, Georgoa, in 1985).[19] The sharing of Honduran bases was an effort to circumvent the Honduran Constitution's prohibition against foreign military bases on Honduran soil, but it also cemented a closer working relationship between the military forces of the two countries. The U.S. military presence has become permanent without interruption since the early 1980s.[20]

In addition, areas of southeastern Honduras bordering Nicaragua were effectively cleared of civilian population in the 1980s and set off for training and sanctuary camps for the Nicaraguan Contra forces being equipped and trained by U.S. military, the CIA, and other U.S. government agencies and private contractors. The Honduran military also increased its presence in the border areas to assist the Contra-U.S. military presence and to control the increasing flow of refugees from Nicaragua and El Salvador that were arriving in southern Honduras. In private conversations, workers with the Catholic aid agency Caritas estimated that as many as ten thousand Hondurans were displaced by this joint military presence.

To deal with the influx of refugees and immigrants from El Salvador and Nicaragua escaping conflict in their countries, the Honduran government established a National Refugee Commission (CONARE) that was headed by a Honduran army colonel, not a civilian—an indication that the government regarded the refugees as a security risk. At this time in the early and mid-1980s, there were at least two notorious incidents in which eyewitnesses reported that units of the Honduran military joined in the killing of Salvadorans crossing into Honduras to find refuge from the civil war in El Salvador. As the refugees were crossing the Rio Sumpul that formed the border between El Salvador and Honduras, they were fired upon by Salvadoran soldiers as they fled and by Honduran soldiers as they approached the Honduran shore.[21] When Salvadoran army detachments pursued the fleeing refugees into Honduras, Honduran military seldom intervened.[22]

In the first years of the 1980s, the Honduran military under General Gustavo Alvarez encouraged a sense that the country was in immanent threat of military invasion from the Sandinista Army. Alvarez instituted some of the harshest practices of a national security state, essentially copying the practices of the Argentine, Brazilian, and Chilean military dictatorships of the 1970s. Military roadblocks and checkpoints were established throughout the country, where men were pulled off buses and vehicles to be searched at gunpoint. Mandatory military service was instituted for young Honduran males. In cities, army patrols entered movie theaters, pool halls, and other youth hangouts to arbitrarily conscript young men into the army or, in some cases, to detain them if they were deemed security risks. Arbitrary search and seizure by military units was practiced.[23]

Perhaps the most notorious of the military's practices was the formation of Battalion 316, widely known among Hondurans as a death squad.[24] Disappearances of Honduran human rights and political opposition leaders, including student activists, was a standard practice.[25] Today, many Hondurans who lived through the 1980s say that period was one of the two worst and most repressive in their experience. The other is the period of the past ten years since the 2009 coup, now often compared to the national security state of the 1980s, including the re-activation of the death squads that operated then.

The desire of Honduran governments and the military to obtain U.S. aid, diplomatic and political approval, and investment ensured that the Honduran military and the civilian governments would welcome the increasing U.S. military presence. The two countries engaged in a series of war games or joint trainings throughout the 1980s, designed both to strengthen the military relationship and to "send a message," a projection of power, to governments and people of the region, especially Nicaragua. The U.S. military presence that was at first described as temporary became in fact permanent. The close collaboration of Honduran and U.S. military ensured that Honduras would rely increasingly on U.S. military assistance, training, supplies, transport, communications equipment, and other materials. Despite the changes in civilian governments and policies, this practice remains. The "cooperative" relationship to the U.S. military facilitates access to U.S. military aid and to U.S. corporations and military contractors.[26]

As the regional conflicts in Central America formally ended, the government of Rafael Callejas (1990–1994) adopted the "neoliberal" economic development model advanced by APROH and the U.S. Embassy in the 1980s. A set of policy initiatives—Hondurans derisively called it *el paquetazo* (the package)—privileged extractive export industries at the expense of local production and subsistence.[27] It opened the way for more displacement of local communities by extractive projects, and probably contributed to an increase in hunger in the cities.[28] These policies gave the military more work in repressing popular resistance and protest, but they were criticized by various Honduran popular and human rights organizations and the Honduran Catholic Bishops' Conference. The bishops warned that this extractive development policy would result in a great increase in rural displacement, landless peasants, poverty, crime, violence, and human rights violations.[29] Today, thirty years on, these warnings have proven prescient. The Honduran military assumed the task of curbing popular protest against these neoliberal extractive policies.

The invasion of drug cartels and traffickers and the rise of criminal gangs in Honduras in the 1990s was in part the result and the legacy of U.S. policies that had used drug trafficking by Contra forces to finance the war against the Nicaraguan Sandinista Army in the 1980s; and the policy of deporting young Salvadorans living in the United States who brought gang organization with them to Honduras.[30] As poverty and displacement increased in Honduras under the extractive development model, gangs and drug trafficking increased. The Honduran military now had a new focus, and an added rationale for U.S. security aid—to combat drug trafficking before it reached the United States, and to control gang activity. These reasons for U.S. security aid replaced the "Communist Sandinista threat" of the 1980s. But since the 1990s, both drug and gang violence have greatly increased, despite ongoing U.S. security aid to Honduras. Instead of progress and success in eliminating narcotics networks and gangs, the Honduran security forces themselves have been implicated in collusion with these groups. By 2015, many Hondurans were saying that the United States should fight its own drug war in the United States, not in Honduras.

There was one attempt to reduce the power and use of the military in Honduras during the 1990s. When Carlos Roberto (Beto) Reina was president (1994–1998) his "moral revolution" managed to return the military to civilian control, reduce military intervention in the political life of the country, separate the National Police from military command, and end mandatory military service.[31] Gradually, these constraints on military reach were pushed back. In the following years, sectors of the military continued to be deployed to protect elite and major private economic interests. In the first years of the new century, the government touted its hard crackdown on gang activity (*la mano dura*, the hard hand), using police actions. But the economic extractive policies continued, drug and gang activity remained a major problem, and corruption among the police and the military became more public.

These trends were interrupted briefly, again, during the presidency of Manuel (Mel) Zelaya (2005–2009). Zelaya imposed a moratorium on extractive mining and began to invite the voices of local communities affected by extractive industries.[32] It seemed that his government was moving toward a re-assessment of the extractive development policies of his predecessors. This alone caused concern among powerful groups in Honduras and abroad that had a stake in the expansion and intensification of these extractive policies. But Zelaya also raised minimum wages for urban workers in some areas, and in his foreign policy created relationships with the ALBA group headed by Venezuelan president Hugo Chavez—all initiatives that made his government a matter of concern.[33] The actual events of the coup of June 28, 2009, that removed Zelaya from power are well documented.[34] The drama was captured in the description of an army unit, on orders from the Honduran Congress and the Supreme Court, arriving at the president's home in the early morning hours, pushing aside his guard, removing Zelaya, still in pajamas, and transporting him to the military air base at Palmerola, where he was placed on a U.S. (presumably military) aircraft and sent into exile in the Dominican Republic.

Much has been written about the June 2009 coup. In the days after the event, it was revealed that the Honduran Congress had written a resignation letter for Zelaya in order to pretend that he resigned voluntarily. The pretext for the removal was the assertion that Zelaya was planning to run for re-election, which would have been unconstitutional. But Honduran and international legal scholars argued convincingly that the coup itself violated several articles of the Honduran Constitution and was illegal.[35] After the coup, the head of the Honduran Congress. Roberto Micheletti, quickly assumed the presidency until regularly scheduled elections could be held a few months later. Many of the major actors in the coup—many Hondurans refer to them as *los golpistas*—were themselves large landowners or had major investments in extractive industries, and a few were high ranking military officers.[36]

The Obama Administration's public response to the 2009 coup has been much assessed and criticized. The expression "coup d'etat" was avoided. Secretary of State Hilary Clinton soon affirmed recognition of the post-coup interim government on the grounds of restoring order and normalcy to Honduras and Honduran-U.S. relations. This operation clearly required coordination between Honduran and U.S. military units under orders from their respective governments.[37] But in Honduras the situation was anything but normal. Some Hondurans accepted the coup leaders' rationale that Zelaya had to be removed because he was leading the country to a Venezuelan-style communist regime. Others were confused and did not know what to think of these dramatic events.[38] But the coup also provoked mostly peaceful but impassioned massive popular protests in many parts of the country, involving at times as many as one million Hondurans who demanded restoration of Zelaya's government, or condemned the illegality of the coup. The military was deployed to control and repress the protests. People were killed and injured.The coup created confusion, insecurity, division, and protest among Hondurans.

In November 2009, regularly scheduled presidential elections were held in Honduras. The interim government tried to portray the situation as a normal transfer of power, even as massive popular protests continued in the streets and the security forces continued to beat, arrest, disappear, and kill protesters.[39] Porfirio (Pepe) Lobo (one of the *golpistas*) was elected. Many Hondurans believed his government was illegitimate because it came to power after an illegal coup and in the middle of massive repression. Some Honduran analysts describe the years since the 2009 coup as a time when the re-militarization of Honduran society has accelerated. Acting on a proposal from the head of the Honduran Congress (Juan Orlando Hernandez, currently president of Honduras), Lobo's government created the military police (PMOP), partially reversing the separation of police from military, and arguably violating the country's Constitution (Leg. Dec. 168–2013).

Since 2009, the Honduran military have had a major role in protecting the expansion and intensification of extractive industries. There has been an intensification of conflict between local communities and the security forces over land and resources; repression of popular protest against two elections widely considered fraudulent and widespread official corruption; and an expanding governmental security structure that integrates military with judicial and police functions. Drug trafficking expanded into almost every corner of society and intensified, giving the military and the police both an enforcement rationale and a temptation to corruption.

MILITARIZATION AS HONDURAN
GOVERNMENT POLICY

The military dictatorships and national security states of Latin American countries during the 1970s that engaged in widespread and heinous human rights violations provoked a popular response during the 1980s and 1990s that reduced the political involvement of the military and brought back civilian rule. People had lost trust in the military, and the "communist threat" rationale for military control began to lose some of its persuasion. In the past two decades, however, the rise of criminal gang and drug trafficking violence has contributed to a widespread sense of fear and insecurity that has provided fertile ground for the resurgence of the military as a major force in national life in many countries across Latin America. Civilian governments now struggle with popular perceptions of corruption and weakness in facing the rising violence and insecurity. Governments respond by using the military for domestic policing in order to bolster their own legitimacy; and some take advantage of this to tighten the grip of their control through increasing militarization of national life. As Michel Foucault writes, security apparatuses "have the constant tendency to expand; they are centrifugal. New elements are constantly being integrated. . . . Security therefore involves organizing, or anyway allowing the development of ever-wider circuits."[40]

This pattern is reflected in recent Honduran history. The military governments of 1963–1980 were replaced by civilian government in 1980 while the military remained independent of civilian control, a period of "democracy under tutelage" (*la democracia tutelada*).[41] The Reina presidency in the mid-1990s retired the military from political life, eliminated mandatory military service, and separated the national police from military control, but the 2009 coup revived the power and importance of the military, and has led to a government policy of increasing militarization of Honduran life.

Militarizing the Police

There are at least fifteen different kinds of national police units in Honduras, each with its own particular function. Many of these are commanded by military officers, and several are actually military units acting as civil police. In 2012, while Juan Orlando Hernandez was head of the Honduran Congress and a candidate for the presidency, he strongly supported the creation of the TIGRES (*Tropa de Inteligencia y Grupos de Respuesta Especial de Seguridad*) to respond to crime and terrorism; and the PMOP (*Policía Militar del Orden Público*) to respond to popular protests and to maintain public order. These entities were a militarization of internal police functions in the face of rising crime and ongoing popular resistance. The government created the Inter-institutional National Security Force (FUSINA) that was intended to increase the efficiency of the government to respond to all threats. FUSINA and the National Security Council included leading functionaries from all three branches of the government as well as the military, under the direct control of the President of the Republic. In this way, President Hernandez assumed power over all branches of the government and elevated the military to a seat in governing policy. There remained no area of government that was actually independent of the President's control.[42] As of 2018, the PMOP had approximately 4,300 members in nine battalions, equipped with an array of military gear.[43] It was denounced by human rights and popular organizations as the Hernandez government's prime instrument of repression of peaceful political and social protest.[44]

In the past few years, the government has given to the military control over the daily functioning of the country's major prisons.[45] This means that in many cases the military now perform the functions of arresting, detaining (and sometimes interrogating, and imprisoning) individuals. The warden of one major prison, who was an active major in the army, denied that the military administer the prison where he was warden. When the contradiction was explicitly pointed out—are you or are you not a member of the military?—he had no answer. In Honduran law, the administration of prisons had been the function of an internal police unit, not the military. Whether the material conditions of prisoners are better or worse because of the military control of prisons may be a matter of discussion since, in any case, conditions in Honduran prisons generally do not meet basic international standards.[46]

Hondurans often see the police as corrupt and complicit in violence, including torture and extra-judicial killings. Many Hondurans will not go to the police to report an incident or to prosecute a crime. The February 6, 2015, edition of the Honduran daily newspaper *El Heraldo* quoted the Honduran National Commissioner for Human Rights:

> We have to recover the police . . . because we have given them complete permission as if they were the owners of the country. They kill, allow alleged culprits to go free, extort, and traffic weapons. The Honduran people must gain the civic control of this institution that is in practice perverted; it is even a menace and not a source of public security anymore.

Police corruption is noted by Hondurans at all levels of society. In July 2011, the (then) vice-president of the Honduran Congress stated publicly that local police chiefs had estimated that at least 50 percent of their police forces were involved in corruption and criminal activity. In 2014, the international organization Human Rights Watch reported at least 149 extra-judicial killings allegedly perpetrated by government security forces (mostly police) between January 2011 and November 2012. A former Honduran National Police Commissioner has admitted that these estimates are likely to be understated, since a significant percentage of such killings go unreported because of fear, intimidation, or simply because the victims are without survivors to report them.

Reform of the Honduran police, with a purge of corrupt officers, has been a talking point since at least 2013. As long as the Honduran government can rely upon the military and the military police to enforce order and put down resistance, it has little incentive to reform the police. The police purges announced by the government have been criticized by human rights, legal, and other organizations as illusory, with practices such as dismissing police officers who are about to retire or who have criticized government or police policy, rather than those accused or convicted of corruption and crimes.[47]

Militarized Budget Priorities and Food Control

The militarization of Honduras is reflected in the changing priorities of the national budget. Between the coup year of 2009 and 2020, the Defense Ministry budget increased by over 300 percent. The budget of the Security Ministry (including the police) increased by 152 percent.[48] Active or retired military officers also head or have leading roles in the Ministries of Defense and Security, the Ministry of Foreign Relations and International Cooperation, and the entity governing the Exclusive Economic Development Zones (ZEDES), a major development initiative.[49] The military presence in international cooperation reflects the importance of the military in maintaining the cooperation of the United States. The military presence in charge of the ZEDES reflects the increasing role of the military in economic development. This role continues to be one of repressing and sweeping aside popular resistance, but it now also includes direct economic and political stakes for the military in the success of such development projects. The ZEDES, zones of economic development, already have a history of forcible and illegal displacement of communities—notably in the Pacific coastal area of Zacate Grande and adjacent mainland areas, and the Caribbean coastal area near Trujillo—and have occasioned considerable criticism from both Honduran and international organizations.[50]

A shifting of funding in the national budget toward the military has been achieved at the expense of underfunding or defunding other public functions, especially public health and education. Proposals to further reduce the budget allotments for health and education, forcing school principals to seek private funding for schools in some areas, and the lay-off of hospital and medical workers and teachers in 2019 provoked sustained mass demonstrations that widened into protests against the Hernandez government in general.[51] Major medical personnel, including the head of the College of Physicians, decried the budget cuts and the near collapse of the public health system. Some Hondurans said the budget reductions were responsible for the deaths of several thousand poor people who relied on inadequate public health facilities. When the Covid-19 pandemic struck Honduras, the country's public health facilities were badly equipped to deal with the crisis. The military was given control of the functioning of the mobile hospital units (hospital tents) bought by the government from Turkey for use in the Covid-19 pandemic. The hospitals were purchased in March, but as of mid-October 2020, only a few had been delivered, and none were as yet opened for use. Accusations of irregularities and lack of transparency in the way the purchase was spent, as well as the long delays, have prompted popular protests behind the question, "Where is the money?" Two of the top civilian administrators of the entity in charge of this transaction (INVEST-H) have been indicted, partly to assuage popular opinion that believes that delays and corruption have cost more lives to the pandemic.[52]

As for public education, in the two years *before* the pandemic struck there were estimates that as many as one million Honduran youth were not in a school or educational institution, partly because of fears for safety and partly because of the poor quality or limitations of schools in many areas that exacerbated the limitations that poverty placed on poor families to fund their children's schooling; most of these out-of-school youth were also unemployed.[53] Criminal gangs drew potential recruits from this vulnerable population. In these and other ways, the shift in budget priorities toward military and security has had widespread and quite harmful effects on the Honduran people, both in the deterioration of public services and in the increased potential of the security forces to repress peaceful popular protest. By weakening the possibility for poor youth to obtain an education, it has also created conditions that are likely to lead to more gang recruitment or more youthful emigration.

The Honduran military has effective control over a significant portion of the country's food production and reserves, and the Hernandez government has shifted several hundred million dollars to the military to finance its expansion into the agricultural production sector of the economy. There is concern among human rights leaders and some Honduran economists that the militarization of a significant portion of the country's food security combined with the forced removal of small farming communities from the land to make way for extractive industries will result in even more severe food insecurity, especially in a time of climate change, and will leave Hondurans increasingly at the mercy of the military and foreign food corporations.[54]

Militarization in Social Institutions and Religion

In addition to the military's increasing role in and control of strategic sectors of the economy and basic services, the government has developed ways to extend the influence of the military into the domestic and cultural life of the country. In March 2014, the military and the government announced a new program, Guardians of the Fatherland (*Guardianes de la Patria*), in which military instructors at military bases or in schools would provide eight hours of training on weekends to an initial group of more than one thousand middle and high school youth. The training was intended to, "help [youth] to improve in ethical, moral, spiritual, and civic principles." While the apparent purpose of this program was to counter the influence of gangs and drug trafficking among youth, it reflected the expansion of military influence into family life, education, and religious practice, since training in civic, moral, and spiritual principles was normally seen as the proper function of family, school, and church.[55] It might be noted that the program addressed the problems of gang and drug violence by focusing on youth indoctrination, while the military and the government ignored the many accusations of their own involvement in corruption, collusion with gangs and drug traffickers, and in the forceful repression of democratic civic exercises such as popular protest.

There have also been symbolic expressions of the militarization of Honduran culture. The Virgin of Suyapa, the Catholic patron saint of Honduras, was declared Captain General and Commander of the Honduran Armed Forces in the 1960s, at the time of brief war between Honduras and El Salvador. In recent years, on Armed Forces Day, the Catholic archbishop of Tegucigalpa has presided over Mass in the Cathedral of the Virgin of Suyapa. The heads of the armed forces and major government departments have been present. At this religious-civic event, the Virgin of Suyapa has been declared, once again, to be the "Captain General" and patron protector of the Honduran armed forces.[56] About half of the Honduran population is self-identified as Catholic, and the country's traditional and public culture is suffused with the symbols of Catholicism and Christianity more generally, despite the official secular stance of the Honduran state (a formal separation of church and state). There are strong criticisms of this and other examples of the identification of religion with the government, the military, and state polices.[57]

The Honduran military has had a mixed and often tense relationship with the Catholic church. The Los Horcones killings in 1975 starkly illustrated the tension between the Honduran military and the "progressive" elements of the Catholic church, even as the military enjoyed the support of the more conservative sectors of the Catholic hierarchy. It should be noted that the Catholic bishops' support has not been universal or constant. Various bishops have publicly criticized the government and the military for violations of human rights, and have stated support for the right of the people to protest peacefully.[58]

U.S. Assistance to the Honduran Military

Members of both the Honduran and the U.S. governments vigorously promote the idea that the situation of democracy and human rights can be ameliorated in Honduras by providing more aid to the security forces to combat gang and criminal violence and to the government to strengthen political institutions; and in this way, to keep Hondurans at home and lessen the flow of migration to the United States.[59]

The Honduran military has access to U.S. assistance through several channels, some direct, others mediated. Direct security aid comes through several bi-lateral and multi-lateral (regional, Central American) security assistance programs.[60] The most prominent of these is the Central American Regional Security Initiative (CARSI).[61] Various reports have been done in the past decade gauging the effectiveness of CARSI, in particular in reducing crime and violence in Central America, including Honduras.[62] It is important to note that these programs are administered in an inter-agency manner, that includes the U.S. State, Defense, and Homeland Security Departments, among others. Congress has legal oversight. For Honduras, the primary stated purposes of security aid include strengthening the ability of security forces to combat crime, providing humanitarian assistance to reduce poverty and its effects, strengthening government institutions, and ameliorating the conditions that promote migration to the United States. Thus, these security assistance programs combine military and police enforcement with social and economic programs.[63]

The hybrid nature of security assistance to Honduras (militarized and humanitarian) is reflected in the joint military operations that the U.S. military (primarily via the Southern Command) carries out with the Honduran military in mobile medical care, military engineering, and other services rendered to local communities in some areas through programs such as Beyond the Horizon.[64] The humanitarian social and economic components touch some local and immediate problems but leave intact the larger structural and systemic causes of poverty, violence, corruption, and human rights violations. In addition, some analysts and observers complain about the opaqueness or lack of transparency in public information about CARSI and other security assistance programs involving Central America regionally, and Honduras in particular.

Much of the security assistance going to Honduras provides materials, supplies, and logistical support for Honduran military and police units. This material support finds its way into situations and incidents where human rights are violated and crimes are committed. Some of this material aid may come directly, but some of it funds purchases from private corporations in the U.S. that manufacture such items as tear gas canisters, ammunition, transport vehicles, and more. Thus, some security aid ends up profiting U.S. corporations even as it enhances the ability of Honduran military units to control civilian populations. An example is the tear gas canisters, at least some of which were made in Pennsylvania, used in large numbers to control peaceful popular protests against the discredited re-election of Juan Orland Hernandez in 2017 and early 2018.[65]

Joint training exercises of Honduran and U.S. military were frequent in the 1980s. After about 2000, joint operations in anti-drug enforcement became more common. By 2012, joint operations on the Patuca River near Ahuas in the Department of Gracias a Dios reportedly involved elements of the Honduran security forces, the U.S. Drug Enforcement Agency, and the State Department. These operations were responsible for the deaths of several local people, injuries to others, and hours of sweeps through local communities that created fear, and probably made local communities even more vulnerable to the inevitable return and retaliation of drug traffickers in Gracias a Dios and Olancho.[66] Such joint, interagency and multi-agency operations are a regular feature of relations between the Honduran and the U.S. military.

The training of Honduran military officers in the United States is a much-protested component of joint training and operations with the U.S. military. The formerly named School of the Americas (SOA) located in the southern U.S. has been perhaps the most prominent component of these foreign military training programs. SOA has come under much criticism in Latin America and in the United States inasmuch as some of its graduates have been implicated in major human rights violations in their home countries, including Honduras, after returning.

Another aspect of the interagency collaboration of U.S. and Honduran security forces is reflected in the USAID-sponsored Rapid Expeditionary Development (RED) teams.[67] RED teams combine training in development project issues, cultural awareness training, and military training to be deployed in areas of a country where development projects are carried out in particularly conflictive or tense contexts. Their purpose is to provide protection for development personnel and to help smooth the way for accomplishing development projects. The RED initiative is thus interagency, involving AID, State, and the U.S. military, among others. Since a major function of the Honduran security forces in the past decade has been to control or remove local opposition to extractive development projects, often in ways that involve violence and abuse of rights in areas of high popular resistance (such as the Bajo Aguán region), the mission or mandate of RED teams seems to place them in a similar context. Whether there is close collaboration in Honduras between RED teams and the Honduran military, and with what results, is a question worthy of further investigation. The idea of combining military training with development has been criticized by a spectrum of individuals and organizations from human rights activists to cultural anthropologists who see militarization of development as certain to eliminate all local voices from development projects.

The Honduran government's national budget transfers from social services to the security forces (mentioned above) may reflect another form of security assistance. Inasmuch as U.S. humanitarian and development aid supports and subsidizes the Honduran budget in non-military areas, it may make it easier for the Honduran government to effect such transfers from its own public services budget to its military. Despite U.S. aid of all kinds, the Honduran economy has a rapidly growing debt and widespread and increasing poverty that many Honduran human rights leaders, economists, and leaders of popular organizations attribute to government corruption and such budget transfers.[68]

MILITARIZATION, SECURITY, AND RIGHTS

The militarization of Honduran society has not diminished violence, gang activity, or narcotics trafficking. There has been a quite significant reduction in the murder rate from 86 per hundred thousand to 42, a figure that the government uses to deflect international criticisms away from the rampant corruption, drug trafficking, and repression of human rights that continue unabated. Part of the reduction in the murder rate was accomplished by counting multiple and mass murder incidents as a single murder. If three or more people are killed in a violent incident, that incident may be listed as a single killing. There are many such multiple killings in Honduras—at least five in the first month of 2020 alone, in which at least thirty-five people were killed. In 2019, the murder rate rose slightly for the first time since 2012. There were almost four thousand murders in a national population of about 9.4 million, a 7 percent increase over the number of murders in 2018. Honduras remains among the most dangerous countries in the world for environmental activists, journalists, women, teenage males, and members of the LGBTQ community.[69] More military and security aid, in the absence of other major changes in Honduras and in U.S. policy, is not likely to make much progress in the protection of human rights, everyday security, and democratic participation.

The measures adopted by the Honduran government in 2020 to counter the spread of Covid-19 included mandated at-home, twenty-four-hour-per-day curfews for most of the population, with one day per week for doing errands outside of the home. People engaged in what were judged to be essential services—physicians, medical staff, public safety personnel, and others—could obtain exceptions. As food prices rose, supplies were hoarded, peasant farmers complained that military checkpoints prevented them from accessing their fields, and forced and extended unemployment deepened the country's already high rates of poverty. Food insecurity became a major concern for many people, especially the unemployed who had to decide whether to spend their money on food or on rent payments. Military and police patrolled the curfew, and several thousand people were arrested and detained for apparent violations of curfew. In what became an emblematic incident, in February 2021, a doctor and a nursing student were detained by police near the city of Esperanza, allegedly for violating the Covid curfew. The nursing student died that night while in police custody. The police first claimed she had hanged herself in her cell, but later forensic evidence indicated the likelihood that she was killed while in police custody. The incident drew national outrage and heightened the criticism that the security forces used the Covid curfews to engage in criminal activities and human rights violations.[70]

Leaders of human rights and popular organizations say that the curfew and other measures have reduced their ability to monitor human rights violations and assist victims; and that forced disappearances and other violent acts are on the rise, while the security forces either do nothing or are actively involved in these violent acts.[71] In sum, the pandemic has provided an opportunity for the government and the military to intensify repression of human rights and political opposition.

The devastation wrought by Hurricanes Eta and Iota in November 2020 greatly exacerbated the insecurity of much of the population. There were reports from local residents in the city of San Pedro Sula that neighborhood gangs had relocated along with the rest of the populations from flooded neighborhoods, and were posing a threat to neighborhoods that had not yet experienced gang activity. Victims report that government authorities and the security forces have been mostly absent during the crisis, and that the only help has come from other ordinary civilians and non-state actors.[72]

The militarization of Honduran society has raised concern among international observers. The office of the United Nations High Commissioner for Human Rights (ACNUDH, Spanish acronym) issued a report in 2017 strongly recommending that the Honduran government begin the process of de-militarizing the country, given the dangers and problems that militarization poses. In 2019, the Inter-American Commission on Human Rights (CIDH, Spanish acronym) issued a report recommending that the Honduran government implement a gradual removal of the armed forces from internal public security functions to help bring Honduras into compliance with international standards for human rights protection.[73] These recommendations have been frequently repeated, but go unheeded by both the Honduran government and its major supporter, the U.S. government.

The millions of dollars going to the Honduran military from both the Honduran and the U.S. governments often fall victim to Honduran laws that prevent or obstruct transparency in the use of much of this funding. These include the Transparency and Access to Public Information Law and the Law for the Classification of Public Documents Related to Security and National Defense. Accessing information often means running a gamut of military officials who have power to deny or impede access to information.

> To access information that falls under the purview of the law, one would have to make an appeal to the National Security and Defense Council, run by the Attorney General, the head of intelligence (active military), the head of defense and security (recently retired military) and the Chief of the Joint Staff of the Armed Forces.[74]

Honduran human rights leaders, journalists, and leaders of popular organizations criticize the lack of fiscal transparency as the gateway to impunity.[75]

MILITARIZATION AND THE WAR ON MIGRANTS

Militarization of Honduran society has been a major force in provoking emigration from the country. The use of the military and the police (security forces) to assist the forcible displacement of rural communities to make way for extractive projects, and to repress peaceful protest; the corruption that has invaded police and military making them unable and unwilling to protect innocent individuals; police-enforced criminalization of popular protest; the amplification of this repressive military force with training and material support from the United States—all of these create or contribute to conditions that eventually drive many Hondurans to emigrate or seek asylum elsewhere.

When Hondurans decide to migrate to the United States in small groups or in large caravans, they meet militarized borders and police and military intervention and harassment along the way. The Central American countries have a mutual agreement to permit citizens of their countries to pass with minimal constraint across borders. As the caravans of asylum seekers grew, however, this agreement was conveniently ignored by Honduras and Guatemala that sent their military and police to stop people at national borders. Those who managed to arrive at the U.S. southern border were met by another militarized situation, the result of years of U.S. policy and practice to turn the border into the near equivalent of a military war zone. If perchance the migrant is allowed into the United States, there is a detention facility awaiting that in many respects resembles a prison. Militarism stalks and harasses every step of the migration process for Hondurans and other Central Americans, from its root causes to its disposition in the United States. Much of this military presence is presented as protecting the immigrant. But by hindering rather than facilitating the immigrant's passage—extending or perpetuating the liminality of the immigrant experience—militarization makes migrants more vulnerable to all the dangers along the way. Militarization presents another danger to immigrants as long as some enforcement personnel are also implicated in drug or human trafficking or other criminal activities that trade on the bodies of migrants.

CONCLUSION

In Honduran society, the military has been cast as both savior and destroyer. Its mission is to save the country from evils. The evils are defined slightly differently at different times and by people in different social and economic situations. The purported evils that threaten Honduras have ranged from Nicaraguan Sandinismo and "communism" to drug trafficking, or threats to the neoliberal extractive development model. This dual function as both savior and destroyer (or disciplinarian) means that the evils from which the military saves Honduras can be both external and internal. The military retains its primary importance and power in Honduran life because anyone or anything can be defined as a threat to the state or its welfare. In the classic national security doctrine of the 1970s and 1980s South American military dictatorships, the state's welfare was seen as the highest good and the military as its protector. The welfare of the state was always the welfare of those elites who controlled the institutions of state. In Honduras, those who control the economic and political life of the country tend to see their own power and wealth as the greatest good.

In its history, the military has shown brief periods of reformism sandwiched between longer periods of authoritarian repression. If neoliberal development is characterized as both permissive and repressive, the Honduran military fulfills a primary function in enforcing this duality, creating a sense of dependency for people who have their livelihoods and rights taken by the state (the elites) and must then depend on elite controlled state institutions for survival. This helps to explain why the military is still among the more trusted national institutions. It is trust deliberately created out of dependency. The civilian political and economic elite are also dependent upon the military, and the military is dependent upon its strong connection to the U.S. military. The continued dominance of the United States in Honduras relies upon the Honduran military.

Military reform toward human rights, democracy, and civil institution building programs is hampered as long as the military is seen as a servant of U.S. and private Honduran interests—export extractive and energy industries—rather than answerable to the Honduran people. Under these conditions, investment and development aid that promotes or supports the current model of export extractive industry provides more opportunities for deployment of the Honduran military to assist in dislocation of local communities, repression of popular protest, and violation of human rights. Since the Honduran military is a key enabler in this situation and the United States is the key supporter and enabler of the Honduran military, the point of most leverage in changing the situation would seem to be a cessation of U.S. military and security aid and a thorough review and reconsideration of such aid. For decades, there have been U.S. laws calling for review and suspension of security that is used to repress human rights and democratic expression. The success or failure of these bills is likely to have a major impact on Honduran migration.

NOTES

1. Hugh Gusterson and Catherine Besteman, "Cultures of Militarism: An Introduction to Supplement 19," *Current Anthropology* 60, no. S19 (February 2019): 4.

2. Michel Foucault, *Security, Territory, Population: Lectures at the College de France 1977–1978* (New York: Palgrave Macmillan, 2007).

3. See, for example, chapter 4 of José Comblin, *The Church and the National Security State* (New York: Orbis Books, 1984).

4. Some additional readings in the history of the Honduran military: Richard Millett, *The Honduran Military: History of a Conflicted Institution* (Miami FL: Florida International University, 2016); Steve Ropp, "The Honduran Army and the Sociopolitical Evolution of the Honduran State," *The Americas* 30, no. 4 (April 1974); J. Mark Ruhl, "Honduras: Militarism and Democratization in Troubled Waters," in *Repression, Resistance, and Democratic Transition in Central America*, eds. Thomas Walker and Ariel Armony (Wilmington DE: Scholarly Resources Inc., 2000).

5. Ernesto Paz Aguilar, "Evolución reciente de la política exterior y la seguridad nacional de Honduras," in Centro de Documentación de Honduras (CEDOH), *Honduras: Realidad nacional y crisis regional* (Tegucigalpa: CEDOH, 1986), 149–150.

6. Orlando Perez and Randy Pestana, *Honduran Military Culture* (Miami FL: Florida International University, and U.S. Southern Command Academic Partnership, Military Culture Series, 2016), 6–7.

7. Longino Becerra, "The Early History of the Labor Movement," in *Honduras: Portrait of a Captive Nation*, eds. Nancy Peckenham and Annie Street (New York: Praeger, 1985), original in Longino Becerra, *Evolución Histórica de Honduras* (Tegucigalpa: Editorial Baktun, 1983).

8. Becerra, "The Early History of the Labor Movement," 95. Also Mario Posas, *Notas sobre las Sociedades Artesanales y los Origines del Movimiento Obrero Hondureño* (Tegucigalpa: Esp Editorial, 1978).

9. James Phillips, *Honduras in Dangerous Times: Resistance and Resilience* (Lanham MD: Lexington Books, 2015), 70–71.

10. Marvin Barahona, *Honduras en el siglo XX: Una síntesis histórica* (Tegucigalpa: Editorial Guaymuras, 2005), 170.

11. Stephen Schlesinger and Stephen Kinzer, *Bitter Fruit: The Untold Story of the American Coup in Guatemala* (Garden City NY: Anchor Books, 1983).

12. Barahona, *Honduras en el siglo XX*, 205–207.

13. Douglas Kincaid, "'We Are the Agrarian Reform': Rural Politics and Agrarian Reform," in *Honduras: Portrait of a Captive Nation*, eds. Nancy Peckenham and Annie Street (New York: Praeger, 1985), 135.

14. Barahona, *Honduras en el siglo XX*, 226.

15. A detailed account of this brutal incident and the involvement of the military government is found in, Penny Lernoux, *Cry of the People* (Garden City NY: Doubleday, 1980), 107–114. The massacre at Los Horcones is also discussed along with several other repressive measures of the military government against sectors of the Catholic Church from 1975 to 1980 in Equipo de Reflexión, Investigación y Comunicación, *Religión, ideología, y sociedad: Una aproximación a las iglesias en Honduras* (El Progreso: Casa Editorial San Ignacio, 2013), 107–109. See also Barahona, *Honduras en el siglo XX*, 230–232, and other sources.

16. Margarita Oseguera de Ochoa, *Honduras hoy: Sociedad y crisis política* (Tegucigalpa: Centro de Documentación de Honduras, 1987), 24; Peckenham and Street, eds., *Honduras: Portrait of a Captive Nation*, 45–49.

17. Oseguera de Ochoa, *Honduras Hoy*, 66; Mark B. Rosenberg, "Honduras: Una Introducción," in *Honduras: Realidad Nacional y Crisis Regional* (Tegucigalpa: Centro de Documentación de Honduras and Florida International University, 1986), 24–25.

18. Guillermo Molina Chocano, "Problemas de la Democracia en Honduras," in *Honduras: Realidad Nacional*, 34.

19. Tanya Kerssen, *Grabbing Power* (Oakland CA: Food First Books, 2013), 37–38; Tom Barry with Kent Norsworthy, "Honduras," in *Central America Inside Out* (New York: Grove-Weidenfeld, Press, 1991), 334.

20. Oseguera de Ochoa, *Honduras Hoy*, 67.

21. Yvonne Dilling, *In Search of Refuge* (Scottsdale PA: Herald Press, 1984).

22. Oxfam America staff in Central America at the time reported many such incidents. See Phillips, *Honduras in Dangerous Times*, 4.

23. I observed many of these practices during a three-month visit to Honduras in 1988. Other sources also detail them.

24. Leo Valladares, *The Facts Speak for Themselves: The Preliminary Report on Disappearances of the National Commissioner for the Protection of Human Rights in Honduras*, trans. Human Rights Watch/Americas and the Center for Justice and International Law (CEJIL), July 1994, http://www.hrw.org/en/reports/1994/07/01/facts-speak-themselves.

25. *The Facts Speak for Themselves* details the question of disappearances during this period.

26. In their repression of popular protests following the problematic presidential election of 2017, Honduran security forces used tear gas that injured many protesters. At least some of the tear gas canisters were labeled as made in Pennsylvania, according to members of a U.S. delegation in the country at that time.

27. Phillips, *Honduras in Dangerous Times*, 129–130; Kerssen, *Grabbing Power*, 22–23.

28. Comité para la Defensa de los Derechos Humanos en Honduras (CODEH), *Boletín* 62 (March 1990): 3.

29. Conferencia Episcopal de Honduras (Honduran Catholic Bishops' Conference), "A la opinión pública nacional," unpublished official copy, August 1992.

30. National Security Archives, George Washington University, *The Contras, Cocaine, and Covert Operations*, National Security Archive Electronic Book Briefing No. 2, https://nsarchive2.gwu.edu//NSAEBB/NSAEBB2/index.html; William Blum, "The CIA, Contras, Gangs, and Crack" (Washington DC: Institute for Policy Studies, November, 1996), https://ips-dc.org/the_cia_contras_gangs_and_crack/.

31. Marvin Barahona, *Honduras en el siglo XX*, 311–314.

32. Andres Leon, "Rebellion under the Palm Trees: Memory, Agrarian Reform, and Labor in the Aguán, Honduras" (PhD diss., Graduate School of the City University of New York, 2015), 5.

33. Rene de la Pedraja, *The United States and the Armed Forces of Mexico, Central America, and the Caribbean, 2000–2014* (Jefferson NC: McFarland, 2014), 144–165.

34. For example, Elizabeth Malkin, "Honduran President Ousted in Coup," *New York Times*, June 28, 2009, https://www.nytimes.com/2009/06/29/world/americas/29honduras.html.

35. For an example of the legality discussion, see Doug Cassel, "Honduras: Coup d'Etat in Constitutional Clothing?" *Insights*, American Society for International Law, 13, no. 9 (October 15, 2009): 1–7.

36. Tyler A. Shipley, *Ottawa and Empire: Canada and the Military Coup in Honduras* (Toronto: Between the Lines, 2017), 35–47.

37. Jake Johnston, "How Pentagon Officials May Have Encouraged a 2009 Coup in Honduras," *The Intercept*, August 29, 2017, https://theintercept.com/2017/08/29/honduras-coup-us-defense-departmetnt-center-hemispheric-defense-studies-chds/.

38. Personal communication from a colleague in Honduras during the 2009 coup.

39. Tom Kavanagh, "Honduras Is Open for Business," *New Statesman*, May 28, 2011, https://www.newstatesman.com/blogs/the-staggers/2011/05/honduras-government-zelaya.

40. Foucault, *Security, Territory, Population*, 44.

41. Honduran historian Marvin Barahona uses this term to describe this period in which the weak civilian government was controlled by the military, *Honduras en el siglo XX*, 233–269.

42. Mario Sorto, Wilfredo Serrano, and Bladimir López, *Coyuntura desda los territorios: Los bienes comunes naturales: la actual disputa socio-política en las comunidades de Honduras* (Tegucigalpa: Centro de Estudio para la Democracia CESPAD, 2019), http://cespad.org.hn/wp-content/uploads/2019/02/Bienes-Naturales-WEB.pdf.

43. Mirna Flores, "La remilitarización de la seguridad pública," Centro de Estudio para la Democracia CESPAD, August 18, 2020, http://cespad.org.hn/2020/08/18/analisis-la-remilitarizacion-de-la-seguridad-publica-signo-relevante-en-los-retrocesos-de-la-democracia-hondurena/.

44. "Contemos las balas y a quiénes las disparan: Militarización de las protestas sociales," Asociación por la Democracia y los Derechos Humanos, July 2019, 6, https://www.dropbox.com/s/uux2jzzcaij04dz/DOCUMENTO%20MILITARIZACION%20 PROTESTAS-FINAL%20PARA%20PUBLICAR.pdf?dl=0.

45. Sarah Kinosian, "Honduras' Military: On the Streets and in the Government," Latin America Working Group, 2015, https://www.lawg.org/honduras-military-on-the-streets-and-in-the-government/.

46. See, for example, "Honduran President Announces New Max Security Prison Run by Military," *Telesur*, February 27, 2019, https://www.telesurenglish.net/news/Honduran-President-Announces-New-Max-Security-Prison-Run-by-Military-20190227-0017.html.

47. David R. Dye, *Police Reform in Honduras: The Role of the Special Purge and Transformation Commission* (Washington DC: Wilson Center, 2018), https://www.wilsoncenter.org/sites/default/files/media/documents/publication/lap_dye_police-english_final.pdf; InSight Crime, "Honduras Profile," November, 2020, https://www.insightcrime.org/honduras-organized-crime-news/honduras/. Ongoing police corruption continues to be reported.

48. Flores, "La remilitarización de la seguridad pública."

49. Thelma Mejia, "Honduras, el poder y la seguridad de las botas," *Divergentes* (n.d., 2020), https://www.divergentes.com/militarismo-en-centroamerica/honduras/; Flores, "La remilitarizacion," 3.

50. Center for International Environmental Law (CIEL), "Should the Inter-American Development Bank Fund Honduras to Implement Controversial Special Economic Zones?" CIEL, December 2017, https://www.ciel.org/wp-content/uploads/2017/12/ZEDEanalysis.pdf.

51. Nina Lakhani, "Honduras deploys security forces as doctors and teachers demand president's resignation," *The Guardian*, June 5, 2019, https://www.theguardian.com/world/2019/jun/05/honduras-protests-teachers-doctors-president.

52. Zachary Goodwin, "Massively Overpriced Contracts Hamper Honduras' Pandemic Response," *InSight Crime*, July 17, 2020, https://www.insightcrime.org/news/analysis/honduras-corruption-pandemic-contracts/.

53. "Violence has pushed thousands of children in Honduras and El Salvador out of school," Norwegian Refugee Council, May 16, 2019, https://www.nrc.no/news/2019/may/violence-has-pushed-thousands-of-children-in-honduras-and-el-salvador-out-of-school/; "Time to leave Honduras? For many youths, the answer is easy," *Christian Science Monitor* (July 24, 2015), https://www.csmonitor.com/World/Americas/2015/0724/Time-to-leave-Honduras-For-many-youths-the-answer-is-easy; "Educational Challenges in Honduras and Consequences for Human Capital and Development," *The Dialogue*, February 2017, http://www.thedialogue.org/wp-content/uploads/2017/03/Educational-Challenges-in-Honduras-and-Consequences-for-Human-Capital.pdf.

54. Kelsey Jost-Creegan, "Honduras' New Militarized Agricultural Policy: A Threat to Defenders and Human Rights," *EarthRights International*, December 11, 2019, https://earthrights.org/blog/honduras-new-militarized-agricultural-policy-a-threat-to-defenders-and-human-rights/.

55. Jennifer Avila and Fernando Silva, "Guardianes de la Patria: La huella militar y religiosa en la niñez de un pais violento," *ContraCorriente,* December 4, 2019, https://contracorriente.red/2019/12/04/guardianes-de-la-patria-la-huella-militar-y-religiosa-en-la-ninez-de-un-pais-violento/; Fuerzas Armadas de Honduras, "UHR forma nuevos Guardianes de la Patria," communique, April 27, 2019, http://www.ffaa.mil.hn/?p=5935.

56. "Honduras Celebrates La Virgen de Suyapa," *Honduras News*, February 2, 2012, https://www.hondurasnews.com/virgen-de-suyapa/.

57. Leticia Salomón, "La opción religiosa es un derecho constitucional que pertenece al ámbito privado," *Radio Progreso* commentary, September 11, 2020, https://radioprogresohn.net/columnistas-categoria/la-opcion-religiosa-es-un-derecho-constitucional-que-pertenece-al-ambito-privado/. Salomón is a respected Honduran sociologist.

58. Unpublished statement of the Honduran Catholic Bishops Conference, June 6, 2019, in response to military and police repression of popular protests.

59. James D. Nealon (former U.S. Ambassador to Honduras), "The Next Immigration Time Bomb," *GoLocal Prov News*, April 9, 2020, https://www.golocalprov.com/news/the-next-immigration-time-bomb-ambassador-nealon.

60. See, for example, "Country Profile: U.S. Security Assistance to Honduras," *Security Assistance Monitor*, December 2014, https://Users/WesternDesk/DownloadsUSE_Honduras_English1%20(1).pdf, and later reports.

61. Peter J. Meyer and Clare Ribando Seelke, "Central American Regional Security Initiative: Background and Policy Issues for Congress," *Congressional Research Service*, May 2014, https://www.everycrsreport.com/files/20140506_R41731_9054cf945300a377d6ff44b4ef7f0f448c5a1b58.pdf.

62. David Rosnick, Alexander Main, and Laura Jung, *Have US-Funded CARSI Programs Reduced Crime and Violence in Central America?* Center for Economic and Policy Research (CEPR), September 2016, https://cepr.net/images/stories/reports/carsi-2016-09.pdf; Susan Berk-Seligson et al., *Impact Evaluation of USAID's Community-Based Crime and Violence Prevention Approach to Central America: Regional Report for El Salvador, Guatemala, Honduras, and Panama* (USAID and Latin American Public Opinion Project, Vanderbilt University, October 2014), https://www.vanderbilt.edu/lapop/carsi/Regional_Report_v12d_final_W_120814.pdf.

63. Congressional Research Service, "U.S. Strategy for Engagement in Central America: Policy Issues for Congress," November 12, 2019, https://crsreports.congress.gov/product/pdf/R/R44812.

64. U.S. Army SOUTHCOM, Public Affairs, "Beyond the Horizon Exercise Begins in Honduras," April 19, 2012, https://www.army.mil/article/78100/beyond_the_horizon_exercise_begins_in_honduras.

65. My interviews in Honduras with U.S. citizens observing the protests, January 2018.

66. Nina Lakhani, "US admits DEA lied about Honduras 'massacre' that killed four villagers," *The Guardian*, May 25, 2017, https://www.theguardian.com/world/2017/may/25/us-honduras-drug-enforcement-administration-shooting; Kealyn Forde, "The Ahuas Killings Five Years Later: Collateral Damage of the Drug War," *NACLA* (October 27, 2017), https://nacla.org/news/2017/10/27/ahuas-killings-five-years-later-collateral-damage-drug-war. The joint report of the Inspectors General in the Departments of State and Justice emphasized a failure of DEA and others to provide full and accurate reporting of three fatal incidents involving DEA and Honduran security forces in local communities. Inspectors General, U.S. Department of Justice and U.S. Department of State, *Special Joint Review of Post-Incident Responses by the Department of State and Drug Enforcement Administration to Three Deadly Force Incidents in Honduras* (Redacted), May, 2017, https://oig.justice.gov/reports/2017/o1702.pdf#page=1.

67. United States Agency for International Development (USAID), "Rapid Expeditionary Development (RED) Teams: Demand and Feasibility Assessment," February 28, 2018, https://pdf.usaid.gov/pdf_docs/PA00T6VQ.pdf; Michael Igoe, "USAID mulls proposal to train aid workers as special forces," *Devex World*, February 19, 2019, https://www.devex.com/news/usaid-mulls-proposal-to-train-aid-workers-as-special-forces-94321.

68. Criterio.hn, "En 2021, tres de cada cuatro hondureños serán pobres: FOSDEH," September 24, 2020, https://criterio.hn/en-2021-tres-de-cada-cuatro-hondurenos-seran-pobres-fosdeh/.

69. Tamara Tarasiuk, *After the Coup: Ongoing Violence, Intimidation, and Impunity in Honduras,* Human Rights Watch, December 2018, https://www.hrw.org/sites/default/files/reports/honduras1210webwcover_0.pdf.

70. There are various accounts of this incident, a lack of transparency, and some unanswered questions. For basic news reports, see, for example, Héctor Silva Ávalos, "Keyla Martinez and Extrajudicial Killings in Honduras," *InSight Crime*, February 15, 2021. This report draws on information from Criterio, a Honduran online news agency.

71. Comité de Familiares de Detenidos Desaparecidos en Honduras (COFADEH), *Crisis de Derechos Humanos durante la pandemia COVID-19, Defensores en Linea,* April 2020, http://defensoresenlinea.com/wp-content/uploads/2020/04/INFORME-COFADEH-DDHH-Y-COVID-19-1.pdf.

72. Personal communications from contacts in Honduras, November 8–10, 2020.

73. The Inter-American Commission for Human Rights (IACHR) has been encouraging the demilitarization of Honduran society for several years, and specifically the removal of the military from internal police functions, for example, Comisión Interamericana de Derechos Humanos (CIDH/IACHR), *Situación de derechos humanos en Honduras* (Washington, DC: Inter-American Commission for Human Rights, August 27, 2019): 39–42, https://www.oas.org/es/cidh/informes/pdfs/Honduras2019.pdf.

74. Washington Office on Latin America and National Autonomous University of Honduras, "Transparency in Honduras: Assessing Access to Public Information,"

September 2019, 6, https://www.wola.org/wp-content/uploads/2019/12/Transparencia-HN-ENG-11.27.pdf.

75. Scott Griffen, "In Honduras, government secrecy law undermines promise of greater transparency," *International Press Institute,* January 20, 2014, https://ipi.media/in-honduras-government-secrecy-law-undermines-promise-of-greater-transparency/; Sarah Kinosian, "The Law of Secrets: What the Honduran Government Doesn't Want People to Know," *Security Assistance Monitor* (February 17, 2015), https://securityassistance.org/blog/law-secrets-what-honduran-government-doesn%E2%80%99t-want-people-know. The Transparency and Access to Public Information Law can be accessed at https://ppp.worldbank.org/public-private-partnership/library/honduras-transparency-and-access-public-information-law.

Chapter 8

Migration and the Human Spirit
Keeping Body and Soul Together

People everywhere live in conditions that may try their psychological health and their human spirit. In Honduras, psychic and spiritual health must contend with the question: what is "normal"? Mental health depends in part on what is considered normal. In Honduras, the idea of normal faces the gap between what government officials say and what people actually experience. Normal is threatened by daily awareness of corruption, brutality, blaming the victim and making the perpetrator the victim, inversion of right and wrong and of legal and illegal. Hondurans also worry that people will become accustomed to the violence—both criminal and state-sponsored—that has accompanied the arrival of neoliberal extractivism and the 2009 coup; that this is the new normal.

> The western development paradigm, although at pains to promote itself as the embodiment of reason and common sense, is also a quasi-religious enterprise, although not in the way usually understood. For this system, that believes in infinite growth in a finite world and offers commercial answers to existential problems, has strayed far from anything based upon reason . . .[1]

Is this the new normal? What does this do to the psychic, affective, and spiritual life of the people and the nation? Immigrants are often people who are trying to find a normal life and are driven to seek it outside of the "new normal" in their home country. Those who do not experience this reality sometimes wonder about the mental and spiritual health of those who decide to leave everything they know to make a perilous journey to an uncertain future elsewhere. It is easy enough to blame parents who allow their children to make that journey. Are these parents uncaring, even mentally lacking? Outsiders find it easy to blame the victim and hard to imagine the experience of the victim. In reality, migration is a reasonable and calculated plan for survival, its dangers and uncertainties weighed against what "normal" life has become in the migrant's home country.

To understand something of the deeper causes and roots of emigration it is not enough to reduce causality entirely to a set of external forces such as violence, poverty, and the physical scars of extractivism and dislocation. Emigration, especially when seen as an act of resistance, is also the result of individual states of mind and spirit tempered by experiences that are both singular and shared by many others, and shaped by the constrains and expressions available in one's cultural context. Emigration and asylum seeking combine personal interior affective states with external action. The question of mental health can be engaged on individual, community, or societal levels. The role of larger economic, political, social, and cultural forces in shaping the mental health of individuals is often underestimated. It is easier and less disruptive to treat mental health as the responsibility (or the defect, illness, or sin) of the individual.[2]

One approach to the study of resistance emphasizes *affect* and *agency* or "thinking about resistance in terms of micro-scale or subjective [individual] decisions and in terms of complicated webs of actors."[3] People experience and respond to the conditions of life in different ways and engage several responses to affective states at once or sequentially over time. This approach leads to the idea that migration is multi-causal. Emigrants have different reasons for leaving, or rather, their reasons are experienced both individually and with others in differing proportions and intensities that can change over time. When I interviewed Honduran teenage males about their experiences of migrating to the United States and being deported back to Honduras, some said they would try again because they had no hope in Honduras, but hoped for better elsewhere. Others said the experience had disheartened them and they would not try again to emigrate, or that the decision depended on what they experienced next. Some of these youth saw their peers trying to survive in Honduras by gradually slipping into criminal gangs while others resisted and were killed. Some could not return to violent households. On their journey, these teens had seen violent acts and had experienced brutality and danger themselves in Guatemala and Mexico. Scarcely halfway through Mexico, they were usually caught and sent back to Honduras. Hope is fragile, yet not so fragile.[4]

We are led here to the ancient human question of body and spirit; the things humans do to keep body and soul together. The statements of asylum seekers in U.S. immigration courts are one of several sources for catching a glimpse into the art and science of keeping body and soul together. Their stories are very often chronicles of resistance to the destruction of the human spirit. So central is the spiritual to understanding resistance and its forms, including emigration, that Faubion warns that discarding the spiritual is a way of destroying social action and resistance.[5] Resistance is a physical act that purports to change the physical reality, the material context, in some way. But the power of resistance is not, or not only, in its physical manifestations but also and especially in how it manifests and nourishes the affective, inner life of individuals and groups. People may resist because they are resilient, but perhaps they are also resilient because they resist.

In this chapter we shall try to examine some of the deeper affective or "spiritual" roots of emigration and asylum seeking. We shall touch on the body-soul "problem"; the ways imperial enterprises dispose of or co-opt the "human spirit" and the spiritual; and specifically, some of the diverse affective and physical responses of people to the conditions of life in Honduras that move some to emigrate. It is impossible to know clearly and for certain what is in the minds and hearts of humans in any situation, and exactly how and why internal states change over time. I rely here on an approach, an approximation that draws on reports, ethnographic materials (including my own observations), the statements of asylum seekers in U.S. immigration hearings, and interviews with many people in Honduras.

KEEPING BODY AND SOUL TOGETHER

A Honduran Catholic priest and human rights leader once told me that the struggle in Honduras was fundamentally a spiritual struggle. But this idea of "spiritual struggle" was a problem to understand and explain because Western social science has tended to relegate "the spiritual" to a category beyond social scientific analysis, or has reduced the spiritual to what is categorized as religion, ritual, or myth. The spiritual also suffers from the fact that individual attitudes are affected by negative experiences of what society has called religion.[6] Yet, in anthropology and cross-cultural studies there is recognition that, for many people, these terms—spiritual and religion—have little distinct meaning apart from all other experiences of daily life. "Spiritual" is a slippery concept, but for some people it suffuses every aspect of life. It must also be said that spiritual struggle is not the same as "spiritual warfare" that conjures images of angels and demons, and emphasizes an individual's internal conflicts. Spiritual struggle as this Honduran priest meant it, refers to a communitarian endeavor to promote a society of peace, justice, respect, and love.

The tendency to separate the spiritual as a different and somewhat mysterious (or superstitious) plane of reality is a reflection of the larger tendency to separate human experience into "the physical" and " the spiritual," to separate the physical from the mental (the so-called Cartesian bifurcation), and to divide Western philosophical thought between idealism (ideas shape behavior and physical reality) and materialism (physical reality and the conditions of life shape ideas). Marx argued, more or less, that capitalism's tendency to turn everything, including human labor, into an economic commodity stripped human work of its humanity—a sense of satisfaction, creativity, joy, fulfillment, empowerment, and community—and that the result was alienation, fragmentation, individual isolation, and vulnerability to manipulation, as if the human were a machine. Imperial enterprises such as those extant in Honduras also demand this fragmentation of the human experience. Dualism is a religious theology that preaches separation of body and soul, and even conflict between these. Dualism can deaden the conscience of people in a way that, according to one Honduran religious observer, has been present in the political life of the country, especially the events around the 2009 coup.[7]

A related critique pertains to psychological analysis and psychotherapy which, according to some of its critics, can act to reduce human affective experience to categories such as anger, envy, and fear, and to pronounce these as mostly undesirable in any large or sustained quantity; controlling human affective response in ways that generally suppress rebellion or resistance (labeled as antisocial behavior), and instead favor acquiescence to the "normal." Such power to label and condemn is a form of controlling human bodies, a necessary condition for the imperial enterprise that must individualize responsibility and misery or blame targeted groups. In reality, human misery is both individual and social, both physical and spiritual. As this chapter is being written at the end of the year 2020, the COVID-19 pandemic is raging through much of the world. People everywhere experience both the physical pains of the disease and the emotional and spiritual pains of loss, of watching loved ones or even strangers suffer in their bodies, and of social distancing for extended periods. The spiritual and psychological cannot be divorced from the physical without inviting serious consequences that some might term sociopathic.

The conceptual attempt to divorce body from soul (the physical from the spiritual) can have dire consequences. The Spanish colonial version of triumphal Christianity that was a vehicle for spreading empire and genocide in Indigenous America had to separate and prioritize the salvation of the Indigenous soul above and against the welfare of the Indigenous body in order to justify the genocidal misery of the conquest. Disciplining, enslaving, and killing Indigenous bodies was justified in order to save Indigenous souls.[8] But the Mayan prophecy of Chilam Balam of Chumayel in the *Libro de Los Linajes* describes starkly how the physical destruction wrought by the Spanish conquest was also and especially a spiritual disaster.

> It was only because of the mad time, the mad priests, that sadness came among us, that Christianity came among us; for the great Christians came here with the true God; but that was the beginning of our distress, the beginning of the tribute,

the beginning of the alms, what made the hidden discord appear, the beginning of the fighting with firearms, the beginning of the outrages, the beginning of being stripped of everything, the beginning of slavery for debts, the beginning of the debts bound to the shoulders, the beginning of the constant quarreling, the beginning of the suffering. It was the beginning of the Spaniards and the priests.[9]

There is a sense in which this physical and spiritual disaster is not past but remains today. The Guatemalan military's destruction of four hundred Mayan villages and the massacre of thousands of Mayans in the early 1980s is a stark reminder.[10] What was in the hearts and minds of the Guatemalan soldiers who perpetrated this genocide? It is as if spiritual misery and the loss of soul still ravage the land, almost five hundred years later. Yet, the Mayan people survive today.   Some traditional and tribal societies seem to understand the danger, and they tend to express this violent bifurcation of human experience and its consequences by imagining the spiritual as a physical reality (soul, perhaps) that inhabits the physical body and may leave it, causing physical and mental suffering, wasting away, suicide, or alienation of the person from the community. The cultural concept of demonic or spirit possession is a related experience, but in reverse—the evil spirit enters the physical body and torments the person physically and mentally. The spirit is evil because or when it is considered alien to the human body. These "folk beliefs" may be seen as expressions or cautionary tales of the danger of separating body from spirit.[11]

In the anti-colonial literature of the mid-twentieth century, there is an evolving narrative of rising self-awareness and social identity emerging with much struggle from the sense of personal worthlessness, and non-identity imposed on subject people by colonial rule. But it arises out of misery among what Fanon called "the wretched of the earth" and it is heard in the subaltern voices that modern imperial enterprises try to co-opt or stifle.[12] This narrative continues today in narratives of resistance. Resistance may be many things with various manifestations, but it is an act of self-awareness and identity.[13] Whether resistance is the product or the catalyst of awareness and identity is not always easy to discern. Resilience is a sense of purpose, identity, self-awareness, and hope—things that imperial or colonial regimes steal, along with land and resources, from their subject peoples.

In the context of imperial relationships such as that between the Mayan people and the conquering Spaniards, or the modern relationship between Honduras and the United States, Ann Laura Stoler's discussion of *duress* is relevant to our inquiry. For Stoler, *duress* captures a colonial relationship that strains both body and spirit.

Duress figures . . . to capture three principal features of colonial histories of the present: the hardened, tenacious qualities of colonial effects; their extended, protracted temporalities; and their durable, if sometimes intangible, constraints and confinements. . . . But endurance figures here too, in the capacity to "hold out" and "last," especially in its active verb form, "to endure," as a countermand to "duress" and its damaging and disabling qualities. . . . Duress, then, is neither a thing nor an organizing principle so much as a relation to a condition, a pressure exerted, a troubling condition borne in the body, a force exercised on muscle and mind. . . . But it is productive, too, of a diminished, burned-out will not to succumb, when one is stripped of the wherewithal to have acted differently or better.[14]

Duress in this characterization also affects and shapes its perpetrators—those who create its conditions—as well as its victims. Imperial enterprises become hothouses for the production of insecurities that demand security states. "Duress as I conceive it is a relationship of actualized and anticipated violence. It bears on those who are its perpetrators, produces anxieties and expanding definitions of insecurities that are its effect, a demolition project that is eminently modern . . ."[15] If "development" is a new guise of imperial reach, then we are confronted here with the contradiction of development as demolition project.

The structured division of chapters in this book is itself a reflection of the problem of trying to keep body and soul together. Previous chapters were devoted to the physical realities of neoliberal extractive development in Honduras—what is happening outside of people and to their bodies. This chapter focuses specifically on what is happening inside, the psychological, affective life of the human spirit. Emigration is in large part a product of how the human spirit engages and is shaped by the physical realities in which people live. Saying that people emigrate because of gangs, political oppression, violence, or dire poverty and insecurity is only part of the picture, the part that seems to interest policy-makers. Thus, their proposed solutions to ending emigration are often partial and less than fully human. The "misery financing the model of development" is an integral human experience, both physical and spiritual.[16]

How people experience and respond to the miseries of development that are extant in Honduras, or anywhere else, is in some sense an unanswerable question. But there are signs, clues, glimpses, and much to explore that provide an approach to such knowing. The question is worth turning around, as well. How are citizens of the United States affected—in mind, emotion, spirit and morally—by the realization of immigrant children taken forcefully from their parents at the U.S. southern border or locked in cages in U.S. detention centers? Or the shooting of a Central American teenager whose only offense is crossing the border without papers in the gunsights of the U.S. Border Patrol? Or the sight of Border Patrol officers pouring out water intended for migrants crossing the Arizona desert? Or perhaps the knowledge that one's neighbor has been taken from his family and deported? What do such realizations do to the human spirit of the perpetrators and the by-standers?

HONDURAS: PRIVATIZED BLAME AND
THE PSYCHIC COST OF DEPENDENCY

In a previous book, I tried to show how an ideology of domination perpetrated by those who control the economy and politics of Honduras reduces the reality of life for most Hondurans to three lessons. The first is that things are bad and getting worse. The second lesson is that this state of affairs is the new normal. The third is that this is the fault not of the government or the economic model or those who rule the country, but rather of individual ordinary Hondurans, since Honduras are a violent people.[17] This perspective is reinforced by politicians, police and military officials, news media, legal institutions, and some religious leaders. Such a view of reality invites individual depression and despair. Social critique, popular protest, and acts of resistance become symptoms of the evil and disordered emotions and personal failings of individuals who refuse to see themselves as the source of their own miseries. Popular protest and resistance can then be characterized as evil. Popular resistance to mining and dam building projects is characterized as a selfish attempt to deprive Honduras of new sources of income and "clean" energy, or as actions that will impoverish the nation.[18] What better way to repress opposition than to individualize misery and responsibility? In addition to planting the seeds of personal guilt and blame, this view of reality invites people to fear and distrust each other, since humans, including one's fellow Hondurans, are prone to evil. It becomes easier to sow distrust and division within protest movements and popular organizations.

In this privatization of misery, the country's soaring poverty rate is not the fault of the predations of extractive corporations, corrupt politicians, or failed and compromised institutions, but rather of the personal character failures or inferior cultural practices of the poor. Poverty becomes a sign of moral weakness and personal guilt. Youth who drop out of school and are not working have themselves to blame for their poverty and their vulnerability to youth gangs. Poor youth are assumed to be morally suspect, prone to criminal behavior. The inferior education system, lack of opportunity, pervasive violence, and the government and police that are patently corrupt are not considered as things that might dissuade young people. This criminalization of poverty is a version of the *culture of poverty* argument familiar to, and roundly criticized by anthropologists: poor people are poor because of their inferior cultural practices that hinder their "progress."[19] It is here combined with a version of the Gospel of Prosperity: wealth is a sign of God's blessing, while poverty is a sign of personal moral failing and God's punishment. Blame is privatized. It is turned into a psychological and moral, not a social, economic, or political matter. The privatization of blame is achieved in part through the public statements of government officials, religious leaders, and mainstream media that reinforce the image of a violent people with daily images of killings and violence divorced from any analysis of government policy or corporate practice. In this narrative, assassinations are never political events; they are always common crimes.

The creation of dependency is a powerful related way of reducing both blame and responsibility to a personal level and deflecting criticism from those who control the political economy. In a neoliberal economy such as that of Honduras, people are rendered dependent in a three-step process: (1) removing anything that allows people self-reliance—land, decent jobs, a good education, access to adequate health care; (2) providing people instead with a small amount of largess from the state or the political party that allows people to survive, barely; (3) threatening withdrawal of that lifeline of largess for any reason. People are reduced from citizens to clients of the state or the party.[20] In Honduras, we have already seen examples of the creation of dependency, most notably in the forcible displacement of self-reliant local villages, turning people into job seekers or actors in an informal economy or a limited job market that will not provide a living wage. Since the 2009 coup, the Honduran government and the ruling National Party have initiated a series of programs to provide assistance to the poor—but only to the worthy poor, those who support the government or at least do not criticize, protest, or resist. (It is worth noting that many of these programs have been criticized for corruption, enriching their administrators rather than their intended recipients.) People who are known to engage in popular protest may be shut out of these programs, or their children may be denied access to school aid programs.

Elsewhere, I have described how in Honduras situations of dependency have been created in areas such as food security, health care, education, environmental protection, public order and safety, and even highway usage and transportation.[21] The intentional creation of dependencies is another form of control that relies on "expanding definitions of insecurities." The created dependencies into which many Hondurans are forced breeds a pervasive sense of insecurity and a disorienting loss of social identity. Is one a productive citizen or a needy client, reduced from self-reliant contributor to "just surviving"? All of these affective states can be experienced, along with the capacity and the need to "hold out," to endure.

How individuals experience the affective and psychic states that such hardships engender, and the ways in which individuals express or counter these externally in action, are at least in part structured by social and cultural forms, traditions, expectations—habitus. One can "deal with" and try to ameliorate duress through adherence to accepted practices such as religion, or through a conscious rejection of social and cultural norms by adherence to, for example, gang life; but gang life entails its own set of accepted norms and practices. Both acceptance and rejection of norms still allows the norms to shape the reaction. But in a society where violence and corruption seem to be widespread and unpunished—even, and perhaps especially, among political leaders—what are the "acceptable" and "unacceptable" norms and practices? Living in a society where the "official" version of reality differs starkly from the lived daily experience, where what is legal and illegal are reversed, where corruption blurs morality, and where good is punished and violence is rewarded, an Orwellian 1984 world—this can disorient and destabilize identity and spirit. In many ways, such is the Honduras created by neoliberal extractivism and its elites.

Social class, race, and gender also shape the identities and experiences of individuals. Resources such as education, a steady job, living in a "good" neighborhood, having "connections" provide options for dealing with duress that poverty does not permit. Poverty and its cultural stereotypes provide a different set of options for survival. Identification as male or female, gay or transgender also shapes how duress is experienced, and it narrows or expands the social and cultural options available to deal with duress. Duress is experienced in some forms by all, but in different ways, and in a context of differing options for survival.

It is not difficult to imagine that a variety of affective responses might take form—anxiety and insecurity, depression, powerlessness, cynicism, rage, or determination, or all of these at once or in sequence. What are some of the external manifestations of this dynamic in daily life? How do these shape the narrative of emigration? These questions are examined next.

AUXILIARIES TO SURVIVAL

A Word about Suicide

Historically, suicide as a response to extreme duress has not been widespread in Honduras—that is an impressionistic and anecdotal perspective since accurate statistics are not often available, especially in a country where authorities sometimes declare a death to be suicide when it may well be murder.[22] There is concern in Honduras about an apparently rising level of suicide, especially among Honduran youth ten to sixteen years of age. In 2020, more than three hundred deaths in Honduras were reported as suicides, the majority of them young people.[23] Suicide may be an answer to duress and depression, a form of escape, or something else. Suicide precludes emigration or ends it, but its relation to migration does not stop with that. Do brutal immigration policies in the United and other host countries discourage people, and lead them to abandon hope in emigration as a last resort?

Drinking

Drinking is always shaped by social and cultural expectations, including gender, social class, and age, but also by how one is expected to react to alcohol. Society defines the range of accepted, expected effects of drink upon the drinker, "whether the contents of the cup will cheer or stupefy, induce affection or aggression, guilt or pleasure."[24] Adrienne Pine adds, "Drunken comportment is not an aberration from normal social behavior; it is culturally prescribed behavior that is acceptable in part because of its circumscribed nature."[25] Drinking is a culturally defining behavior; in Honduran society it is often associated with two groups in particular: men and the poor, and especially poor and working-class men. That drinking and drunkenness are markers of manhood in Latin America is often repeated.[26] For young gang members in Honduras, drinking is part of gang membership and is a marker of manhood achieved. Heavy drinking and drunkenness are part of the complex of cultural behaviors that define *machismo* and is often ascribed to the poor and the working class.

The assumption that all or most poor Hondurans drink, get drunk at least occasionally, is another side of the message that Hondurans are a violent people. Drinking is assumed to engender violent behavior, and this drunken violence is sometimes assumed to be a trait of the poor. Drinking, drunkenness are not confined to the poor, of course, since middle-class and wealthy people also drink, but they have the luxury of doing so in relative privacy, whereas the working class and the poor tend to drink in public bars or pool halls. The realty demonstrated by statistics and ethnography shows that in Honduras drinking and drunkenness are not nearly as widespread as the myth assumes.[27] Among other restraints, drinking costs money, something many Hondurans, especially in rural areas, have in short supply; and the influence of the Evangelical churches, to which many Hondurans adhere, also discourages drinking.

Drink tends to be part of larger socially constructed cultural definitions, in particular that of the "violent poor" and that of the "real man," *machismo*. Both of these are contested cultural identities that are not appropriate to the large majority, and they do not lead people to flee; but they exacerbate conditions that do, if not for the drinker, then for those close to the drinker.

Drugs

In Honduras, drug trafficking is widespread, controlled by a few powerful families and individuals who often enjoy the protection of state security forces and immunity from prosecution.[28] Illegal drug trafficking affects almost everyone and every aspect of life in Honduras, not because many Hondurans use drugs but because trafficking generates violence and corruption, with negative effects that filter into daily life. The illegal status of drug possession and consumption, the cost, and the association of drugs with violent traffickers and gangs may discourage more widespread use. Regular use of illegal drugs seems to be most apparent among two groups: hired enforcers or killers (*sicarios*), and gang members. S*icarios* are sometimes plied with drugs before committing their violent acts. Use of marijuana, cocaine, and other drugs is also a part of "gang culture," according to gang members and researchers.[29]

For some, drug consumption alone may be a way of dealing with the "duress" of life in Honduras; but it is for others an auxiliary to different ways of seeking survival, including hiring oneself as a *sicario* or becoming a gang member. Assassins and gangs are two of the larger forces of violence that become a major part of the reasons for some Hondurans to emigrate. Gendered and domestic violence is another.

FAMILY, GENDER, AND DOMESTIC VIOLENCE

In Honduras, family life is a crucial locus for understanding the psychological, social, and spiritual roots of emigration. In countries where people experience high levels of insecurity coupled with very low or no confidence in major social institutions, the family is most likely to emerge as the only important group that seems to provide a measure of safety and security for its members. Blood and marriage relationships become strongly recognized and defined. This includes the so-called nuclear family unit, but also almost always involves the "extended family," comprising several generations, as well as siblings and their spouses and children.

The Importance of Family

According to a U.S. Government Honduras Country Study, "The family is the fundamental social unit in Honduras, providing a bulwark in the midst of political upheavals and economic reversals. . . . In all areas of life and at every level of society, a person looks to family and kin for both social identity and assistance."[30] Family serves also as a metaphor for relations of trust, mutual help, and security beyond the family. Decisions about where to live or where to move are very often made with the idea of remaining geographically close to other family members, especially parents, grandparents, and siblings. People often make it a point to visit older parents on weekends and bring the grandchildren. On weekend evenings, one can find entire groups of parents, grandparents, siblings, and their children frequenting restaurants and social or cultural events together. In dealing with bureaucratic agencies of government or in business, people very often prefer to seek out family members or close relatives who work in or are associated with the agency or business in question. A family member or close relative is bound by kinship and custom to assist and facilitate, if possible. This often extends to close friends. In Latin America, this practice is sometimes known as *personalismo.*

Differential social and economic status does shape the structure of Honduran families. Middle-class Hondurans are more likely to be in officially registered marriages. Many poor and rural Hondurans often live for many years in stable common law marriages that are socially recognized in Honduran society. Religious authorities may also recognize these stable unions as legitimate, even if they lack formal legal status.

The Honduran Family Code, Decree 76–84 (1984), defines and describes in detail issues related to marriage, paternity, and more. Title 9, "On Relations," of the Family Code, specifically defines the family as composed of both consaguineal (blood) and affinal (marriage or union) relationships, and stipulates that family groups include ancestry that ascends for generations. It is important to add that although the family as a distinct social group is protected in Honduran law, the law is very often ignored, and the state engages policies and practices that often undermine the integrity or functionality of the family.

Catholic and Evangelical churches preach the centrality and importance of the family in daily life. Religious leaders exhort men to remain faithful to their spouses and to be "good" fathers. The union between a married couple or faithful partners is likened to the union of Jesus to the church. In both Catholic and Evangelical theology and in churches, the family is sometimes described as an earthly expression of the "heavenly kingdom."

Destabilizing the Family

Despite the widespread norms of family importance and the experience of stable family relations among Hondurans, there are real threats to family security and stability. Such threats combine the power of the political economy and certain traditional cultural norms or identities—including especially patriarchy and machismo—that may be widespread but are by no means universal. The Honduran political economy results in the violent or forced displacement of communities and families and a growing number of families living in poverty and insecurity, whose members may find the family unit increasingly incapable of providing identity, security, and physical survival. Family fracture and gradual disintegration is one result. The government, a zealous and often ruthless proponent and guardian of the neoliberal extractive economy and the power of the few, makes a show of providing support for these victims of its own policies through special programs to dispense aid to the needy. Instead, administrative corruption helps itself to the funds.[31] There are reports of families whose children are refused government sponsored scholarships because the parents are not members or supporters of the ruling party.[32] The "punishment" extends to the children of such families as well as the parents. In other examples of political patronage, the pattern tends to be the same. If one member, perhaps an older son or daughter, is known to oppose or criticize the ruling party, the entire family may be deprived of the benefits of government programs. The neoliberal extractive political economy extends supports that are really controls and punishments.

For some Hondurans caught in the misery of (often multiple) displacement, poverty, insecurity, and vulnerability, cultural patterns of patriarchy and machismo can take on a meaning as potential instruments of survival or of danger. Honduran police generally do not respond to problems of domestic violence in which men beat or threaten their spouses, partners, and/or children. These incidents are generally regarded as "domestic" disputes within the family in which the state should not intervene. This idea is based in part on the cultural practice of patriarchy: the male partner in a family unit is considered the authority within the family unit. A woman who reports incidents of abuse by her husband or partner may be told that she herself is probably to blame for not being a "good" wife or partner—that is, not submissive enough, or perhaps too "promiscuous." In its extreme form, this mentality regards women as the property of men. The result is a high degree of impunity for men who are violent toward their female partners or their children. In the statements of asylum seekers, one finds descriptions of women and children forced to witness violence within the family unit, or children who themselves have been victims of violence, including rape and threats of death. Asylum seekers also describe situations in which family members behave aggressively or violently toward other family members—older male cousins who rape younger cousins; children beaten, called names, and treated as if they were slaves by their aunts and cousins in whose household they may be living.

What prompts people to act so violently toward family members? It is risky to generalize. People under the same sorts of external duress often behave quite differently. Asylum seekers' declarations are also full of stories about grandmothers, older siblings, and other family members who took them in, protected and cared for them when the asylum seeker's own nuclear family disintegrated. Does violence become internalized as a way of survival that must also be taught to family members if they are to survive? Is violence for some (men) a way of asserting control over a small part of an insecure and unstable world? Or is it simply that people are overwhelmed and unable to protect others?

Patriarchy and Machismo

There are several strong forces pulling some Honduran men in the direction of committing acts of "domestic" violence. The complex of poverty, dependency, and insecurity can produce a sense of powerlessness and reduced self-worth that the cultural tropes of patriarchy and machismo may seem to address, especially when one sees a larger societal context in which violent and corrupt men—from the neighborhood to the national level—seem to be in control without suffering any consequences for their violence. Even the police may seem to acquiesce in the "normalcy" of macho violence. Thus, getting drunk or taking drugs and acting aggressively—supposedly salient aspects of machismo or "real" manhood—become "normal" for the man seeking both to escape his own miseries and to feel empowered as a real man.[33] Compounding this set of conditions is the fact that alcohol and especially drug consumption are exactly what local gangs and drug traffickers purvey, so that the man seeking machismo and empowerment is likely also to become engaged (entangled) with gangs and drug trafficking. In the stories of asylum seekers, the increasingly erratic and violent behavior of the fathers, husbands, partners, or brothers who are the perpetrators of family violence is often attributed, at least in part, to involvement with gangs or drug traffickers.

This situation of intertwined forces becomes a perfect storm for violence, and it usually develops gradually. The macho man is supposed to control his family, and family members are easy targets of control compared with the forces of the larger society. Men who are attracted to this violence are sometimes survivors themselves of violence perpetrated against them in their childhood or youth, or in the wider society. They are both victims and learners of violence. It bears repeating that patriarchy is a trope that can apply at both the domestic and the national level. The patriarch is the dictator who monopolizes state power, the large landowner who controls the lives of many people, the head of a drug trafficking family, the gang leader, or the man who dominates his family.[34] These become images of manhood for those who are vulnerable.

One of the more insidious aspects of this cycle of male violence is that it may seem to offer a form of physical and psychological survival, an identity of power in a context of insecurity. The cultural tropes of patriarchy and machismo (exaggerated or deformed manhood) become cultural resources for male survival. The tragedy is that the promised survival leads only to destruction of women, the family, and the men themselves. The destruction also bears on the next generations.

Family as the Future

A final word must be added about the large sector of Honduran society in which young people do stay in Honduras, get married or find a partner, perhaps raise or adopt children, and live a life that is rewarding and joyful. It is like planting trees in in the middle of a war—a consummate act of hope. External conditions such as middle-class resources and access to education or the example of a strong and loving childhood family experience may help, but living for the future in a precarious present is itself a means of psychic and spiritual survival, an exercise of the human spirit. It deserves more study and reflection. How people perceive the situation, and how perceptions change with time, external conditions, and experience have much to do with this.

GANGS IN HONDURAS

In the statements of asylum seekers in U.S. immigration proceedings, domestic and family violence is one of the most cited causes for leaving Honduras. A close second is gang violence. These two proximate causes are closely related. The family disintegration that is described in the previous section shapes young people who are vulnerable to the allure of gang membership.

Honduran gangs (whose origin story lies in the United States) invite different characterizations—as criminal enterprises or as brotherhoods. They can also be seen as forms of survival or as forms of resistance, or both at once. So Honduran gangs are criminal enterprises that are also brotherhoods, forms of survival, and forms of resistance. But here again, the survival offered by gang membership is very likely to create the opposite for the gang member and others touched by him. The resistance that gang membership seems to embody against a corrupt, hypocritical, and non-functional polity can also be harnessed (co-opted) by that polity for its own corrupt purposes as another form of population control, using gangs to control areas of the Honduran population. With these inherent contradictions, gangs may be clear expressions of the desperation of some young Hondurans, a desperation that drives some to adhere to gangs and others to flee them.

Criminal Enterprises

Central American gangs recruit largely from among poor youth. "Recruit" is not exactly correct. Some youth become increasingly attracted and integrated into gang life over time, while others resist and become the targets of increasing gang pressure and threats to force the resister to join or to work for the gang. Threats come in the form of beating the recalcitrant youth and threatening to kill him "next time," or threatening violence against family members or people important to the youth—raping a sister, beating or killing a beloved grandmother. The impossible dilemma this presents exacerbates the desperation of many poor youth. Escaping to another part of a country like Honduras does not solve this dilemma, since gangs are composed of networks of informers and enforcers that may be nationwide. Far from being a source of protection, police in Honduras are very often in some form of collusion with gangs. Often, a Honduran teen who is being pressured by a gang also becomes the target of local police.[35]

Some youth try to walk a precarious line, agreeing to work for the gang—delivering or selling drugs, passing messages, being a lookout, robbing from other gangs—but trying to stop short of killing or violence. Inevitably, gang demands increase until the youth is required to commit acts from which there seems to be no turning back; refusal or hesitation can mean more severe beatings and torture or death. When a young Honduran seeks asylum in the United States to escape this nightmare, his attempts to walk the thin line may be interpreted as voluntary gang membership, weakening or negating his case for asylum. The question of coercion must be argued forcefully to explain the dilemma adequately to skeptical immigration officials.

Honduran gangs stake out areas of control (neighborhoods in cities) which they defend against rival gangs. Within these areas of control, gang members monitor the movement of the local population and the transit of outsiders into the area. Members may extort local businesses and households, demanding regular payments for "protecting" people from other gangs. Tellingly, Hondurans call this a war tax (*impuesto de guerra*). Gang life is warfare, and gangs are occupying armies.[36] Failure to pay the war tax is likely to result in damage to one's business or house, beatings or torture, or a swift death. Some of the gang's enforcers are young. In one incident, a sixteen-year-old gang member shot and killed a minibus driver in a busy Tegucigalpa street in midday. The driver was head of a local minibus collective that had failed to pay the monthly extortion.[37] Gangs also make money by selling drugs. This can lead to collusion between gangs and drug trafficking rings, or to competition as gangs try to establish their own trafficking. Gangs sometimes expand into production of drugs, taking land from rural families by force, threat, and murder, in order to use the land for drug production.[38]

Control

Gangs operate their own tax system of extortion. They make the rules and enforce them brutally in many poor neighborhoods. They carve out their own territories and protect them. They threaten or bribe police who become accomplices or gang members. They recruit youth and replenish their numbers. In effect, gangs become the de facto law and order in some areas, with the passive acquiescence or absence of state security forces. Honduran governments since the 2009 coup have used this situation to their advantage in several ways. Describing gangs and drug trafficking enterprises as domestic terrorist threats to national sovereignty provides a rationale for militarizing Honduran society.[39] Promising to reduce gang violence and put a policeman or soldier on every street corner becomes an attractive presidential campaign slogan, used to effect by the current Honduran president in his 2013 and 2017 election campaigns. But gangs also provide a mechanism for "privatizing" citizen security, allowing gangs to take the place of police and state security forces in some areas.[40] The goal here is not the safety of citizens but rather control over them. Control is achieved using both a militarized state and gangs. One might ask if such a system leads ultimately to a sense of chaos. A sense of chaos is simply another form of control.

Survival and Resistance

Interpreting gangs as criminal enterprises and as a mechanism of population control presents a view from the outside, accurate but incomplete. How do young Hondurans see their own lives in this situation? How do they become gang members? The statements of youthful asylum seekers mostly represent those who experience coercion and threat. But not all gang members are coerced into the gang. What about those who seem to be attracted to gang life? Is there a more empathetic or affective reality? There are a number of ethnographic studies of gangs in the United States, gangs that are historically linked to the origins of Honduran gangs.[41] The link has taken on the characteristics of an origin myth for some Honduran gangs. There are also several ethnographic and sociological studies of Honduran gangs by both U.S. and Honduran researchers.[42] Most of these studies attempt to catch a glimpse into the mind and affective life of youth who join gangs, and they tend to present a somewhat more empathetic, or at least complex, picture of youthful gang members.

Family destabilization and disintegration is seen as a major force in moving Honduran youth to gang life.[43] The process is gradual. Domestic violence and especially parental abandonment of the family, or even prolonged absences of parental figures are seen as triggers. In the insecure context of Honduras, many family units lack permanent adult male presence. Violence in the household shows a Honduran boy that he cannot rely on the family for security and affective support. In this situation, there is also likely to be some form of abandonment. Men and older sons are sometimes absent for a variety of reasons. Some are killed or have been kidnapped and "disappeared" by gangs/or the police. Others travel in Honduras to seek employment. Some have been abandoned by female partners and children because of ongoing domestic abuse in the context of a culture where machismo (male dominance) is demonstrated often by violence toward spouses and partners. Often, it is the mother who flees, perhaps taking one child but unable to care for older children as she migrates in search of asylum. Aunts and grandmothers become surrogate parents, but they may be unable or unwilling to care effectively for the added burden. The youth learns that he is powerless and not important; he cannot rely on the family for physical or emotional security.

All of this devolves in a context where a Honduran boy sees models of manhood and power shaped by patriarchy and machismo. Some of the very characteristics that may have contributed to the disintegration of his family now become gradually attractive to him. Increasingly, he may seek escape from the disfunction or violence of his family life, by spending more time in the streets and pool halls. He is alone, increasingly facing life on his own. He notices and is noticed by gang members. They see him as a potential recruit. He may begin to see them as examples of powerful manhood, and the gang as a place or group that offers security, and a new and more powerful identity of manhood. Gradually, the gang may also become for him a brotherhood of mutual care. Eventually, the gang becomes home for the youth. It becomes the locus of his emotional and affective life. The transition is not without danger, mishap, and new starts. It demands much but seems to give much. The demands, brutal as they may be, also test his "manhood." Drinking, drug use, violence, and sexual exploitation may be some of the components of this new shared brotherhood. The transition from family to gang resembles a classic rite of passage—disintegration of the old identity; stripped of identity, alone, and liminal; the performance of various dangerous acts that leads to acceptance into a new identity and community. Gang membership is a strategy for survival for this Honduran youth whose spirit, identity, self-worth, and affective life must seem to have been brutalized or stripped from him.

Anthropologist Jon Wolseth who studied gangs in El Progreso, Honduras, describes the personal histories of young men whom he met in the gangs. While not all of them had experienced family disintegration, most had experienced abandonment in some form:

> Sergio's biography of personal loss, unaccountable anger springing from abandonment and grief, and the tragedy of seeing over half of his family die is, unfortunately, typical of many of the gang members I met. I had heard others in the neighborhood talk of how Sergio and his brother, Julio, had been left orphaned in their early teens. The two brothers took divergent paths after that defining moment. Julio joined a Pentecostal church, and Sergio became a central figure in the local clique of the 18th Street Gang.[44]

Wolseth describes the sense of brotherhood, identity, and belonging that the gang offered youth like Sergio; how for gang members this brotherhood ran deep and was both physical and affective, even affectionate. Gang members like Sergio wear tattoos with the same emblem the gang displays on wall graffiti. "The iconic similarity between the name sprayed on the wall and that same name etched on the skin is the immediate visceral recognition that you belong."[45] Members are also bound to other members who become closer than biological siblings. In gang parlance, the Spanish term *carnal* (bodily, in the flesh) designated such a close bonding; carnal because the two were bound to protect and care for each other as if they were one body. "Because it is worked into the flesh, symbolized through the term carnal, these new relationships are difficult to sever and come with a blood price."[46]

This empathetic glimpse of gang life runs counter to the dominant view of gang members as violent criminals, but in reality gangs and their members seem to partake of a fractured reality, violent and affectionate, alienated and intimate. Gang life is dangerous in many ways even as it offers a kind of security. In some sense, gang security is tested and secured through violence, a "blood price." The day comes gradually for some gang members when they begin to question whether the price—physical and emotional—is too high. The inherent contradiction of gang life, offering security and brotherhood through danger and violence, must begin to trouble a youthful member. The murder of many gang members by a rival gang or the police can be a trigger for such reflection. But exiting a gang is fraught with danger.

There is yet another facet of gang life that bears recognition. Gangs can be seen as forms and expressions of resistance. It is resistance to everything that seems to be hypocritical—demanding polite observance, even acquiescence as social authority itself is corrupt and violent; presenting a view of reality that is far from the miserable reality of many Honduran youth. Gang membership provides a form of survival that is also a form of resistance, a sort of truth. Honduran gangs provide a type of sovereignty, "Gothic sovereignty" as anthropologist Jon Carter describes it.[47] But this form of resistance and survival contains inherent contradictions. Gangs offer security through danger, healing from violence through the performance of violence, truth that can be co-opted by untruthful governments as an excuse for measures to control resistance.

While the deeper origins of Honduran gang life lie in large part in the violence of the neoliberal economic development model, the immediate dynamics of the human spirit and the attempt to keep body and soul together are laid bare in the choices and coercions of gang life experienced by many Honduran youth. Experiencing this or fearing it, some Honduran teens decide to flee Honduras.

RELIGION, SURVIVAL, AND RESISTANCE

In Wolseth's ethnographic study, religion is seen as another alternative to gang life that some Honduran youth can access as a form of survival. Wolseth describes the different ways in which neighborhood Catholic and Protestant churches attract Honduran youth who are flirting with gang membership in the city of El Progreso. The local Protestant church makes itself a sanctuary of sorts for youth. The church becomes a substitute for the family and the home, providing a fellowship that tries to keep its members away from gang members and activities. The path to salvation from gang life here lies in removal and dedication to the church and its youth group. In contrast, the Catholic church encourages its youth to go out to gang members and engage them, hoping to influence by association, empathy, and example. The one approach moves inward, the other outward. Both are effective in helping some youth to find an alternative to survival and empowerment without the gangs.[48]

On almost any night of the week in almost any Honduran city or town one can hear the guitars, the singing, and the preacher's voice rising above it. The music and the singing, usually begin early and gently, becoming increasingly louder and more intense as the evening grows late. The experience provides some neighborhood people with a few hours of release, expression, palpable communion with others and with a powerful God. One cannot venture to assume what this does for the souls and spirits of the participants—or for the other neighborhood residents who hear this from afar several evenings each week. Many of these church worship sessions are small, Pentecostal or Evangelical, and not connected formally to any mainline Protestant denomination. The local Catholic churches tend to hold fewer services, and these are usually more subdued in tone. Instead, the priest and members of the congregation engage in a variety of activities in the local community, supporting people in various crises and needs, both temporal and spiritual. In small remote villages in the countryside, Catholic priests and Protestant ministers are in short supply. If there are religious services, they are conducted by local people acting as deacons or Delegates of the Word.

There is a tendency to make religious services and expressions less formal and more accessible to everyday neighborhood life—a process one may observe throughout Latin America. Again, the underlying question often seems to be whether religion should provide a haven or sanctuary from everyday life or an impetus to engage everyday life and transform it. Or both. These are strategies for survival, both for individuals and for religious institutions. The engagement of religion in everyday life can also encourage critical action to change everyday life, thereby provoking reaction and repression from those who benefit from the status quo.

The Duality and Variety of Religion

The history of major world religions is often paradoxical. The appeal to religion accompanies the best of human endeavors and the worst. It was the stuff of Martin Luther King's speeches for equality and justice, but it also inflamed the antisemitism that haunted much of European history. In Latin America, Catholicism arrived as an integral component of empire. The patron of Spain, Santiago (Saint James) was transformed in iconography from the humble fisherman and disciple of Jesus to the conquering warrior on a white horse. But in Latin American Catholicism there were always a few dissident voices to point out the contradiction between the teachings of the humble and loving Jesus and the haughty violence of imperial rule. When in the early 1960s the Second Vatican Council moved the Catholic Church toward a "preferential option for the poor," and a "theology of liberation," the divisions within the church widened, following the fault lines that divided society. In part, perhaps, these divisions illustrate the difference between religion and spirituality, as some have argued. Religion is the formal structure, the body of doctrines, hierarchy, and disciplines. Spirituality is what informs and moves the human spirit. Religion is a human enterprise prone to human error; spirituality transcends that to appeal to people's better angels. In practice, however, things are not so clear cut.

The Honduran Constitution mandates separation of church and state; the state cannot openly support any particular religion or religious institution. In practice, Honduran governments after the 2009 coup have relied on religion to bolster their legitimacy. In return, religious institutions or their leaders have received special considerations from the government. The President is pictured beside the leaders of the Evangelical churches who are endorsing and blessing the President and his policies.[49] Evangelical leaders are given a place at the table for important social policies. The Virgin of Suyapa, Catholic patron saint of Honduras, is declared Captain General of the Honduran army (principal enforcer of the government's policies) each year on Armed Forces Day at a Mass offered by the Cardinal Archbishop of Tegucigalpa. The Catholic Archbishop receives funds from the government for Catholic institutions.[50]

Statistically, the Catholic and Evangelical churches each claim about half of the Honduran population, although some of this adherence may be nominal only. Some Indigenous peoples integrate orthodox Catholic beliefs with traditional beliefs. In a sense, there are as many variants of Catholic and Evangelical belief as there are adherents. Within Honduran Catholicism, one might discern at least three different interpretations of faith and its meaning. In one, faith becomes nearly synonymous with adherence to patriarchal hierarchy, obedience to the bishops and traditional teaching, or to the pastor and the more-or-less literal interpretation of Scriptures. In another, faith is only real if it is made physical in deeds, in adherence to social justice and the liberation of the human spirit—the core of "liberation theology." In a third, faith is expressed in the humble practices of "folk" Catholicism, reverence for the Virgin Mary, the Way of the Cross, and other traditional pious beliefs and practices that support and give meaning to people's lives in the midst of suffering, misery, or struggle. Contrary to some dismissive evaluations of them as religious opiates, these "folk" beliefs have quite powerful *potential* in support of political expression and even resistance inasmuch as they buoy the human spirit and keep human affect alive.[51]

Thus, religious faith has many forms and expressions and is a source of support for the human spirit in a time of violence and death, even as it can also be used to legitimate and support a government of violent and repressive practice. These ways of interpreting faith are not entirely mutually exclusive, and one's sense of faith can be dynamic and changing. For many people, religion provides a powerful tool for interpreting the reality in which they live, supporting hope, survival, resistance both in Honduras and on the journey to asylum. It permits an interpretation that helps many people maintain a middle road between false trust in external authorities (whether the Honduran government or the U.S. immigration system) and cynical despair. But it matters whether this interpretation portrays a world that is individualistic or communitarian.

Religion, Empire, and Migration

In Honduras, one observes signs on outside walls and billboards that carry ostensibly religious messages. Many are financed or placed by Evangelical churches and U.S.-based groups. Some are posted or painted by individuals.

One of the messages, "Jesus is my President," appears, not as a critique or rejection of the current Honduran President, but as a more subtle invitation to disregard or "transcend" mere human politics in favor of individual adherence to and hope in Jesus alone. There are also signs, some placed by Catholic groups, that exhort Hondurans to return to a strong family life, on the model of the Holy Family, in order to create a better country; no mention of the crushing external forces operating against family life. The pronouncements of some religious leaders exhort to love rather than resistance, for resistance is an act of division and hatred. Here we see examples of a de-politicization campaign in the guise of religious faith. The effect of de-politicizing is not only to undermine political critique and protest but also to narrow the ground for hope and survival to a strictly narrow focus that is not political or even truly social; or that reduces political reality to a symbol of individualized religious belief. There is also an imperial subtext operating. At least some of this messaging is funded by U.S.-based church groups, some with U.S. political ties, that tend to equate U.S. influence over Honduras with spreading the faith—and both with capitalist expansion.

The Protestant Latin American theologian Elsa Tamez believes that the Bible is really a book written by migrant and exiled people, and can be deeply understood only by migrant and displaced people—a people driven out of Eden, led out of slavery in Egypt into the desert toward a promised land, freed from years of captivity in Babylon, the infant Jesus and his family fleeing from King Herod to Egypt to escape death, and the itinerant preacher Jesus who told his followers to take nothing with them on their journey.[52] Other Latin American Christian theologians since the 1970s have written books with titles like *Theology for a Nomad Church.*[53] There is a restless spirit about all of this that is always fleeing the enslavement of empire—Egyptian, Babylonian, Roman. These migrant people are seeking liberation and a new earth. Their leaders protest and resist the domination of empire. One of the interpretations to come from this perspective might be that God does not want people to be enslaved under imperial duress. Religion may be a tool for empire, but it is also a critique of empire and a support for the migrant and the wayfarer. It may be enlightening that the beliefs and customs of other religious traditions, including those of many Indigenous people, feature something like a journey, a pilgrimage, a vision quest, and emphasize hospitality to the stranger and the traveler. In this subaltern perspective, migration is physical but it is also spiritual in the sense that it envisions liberation of the human spirit.

The image of the two paths, one of life and one of death, is an ancient expression of this liberation, appearing in both Judaic and early Christian imagery.[54] In several places, the Judeo-Christian scriptures exhort people to choose the path of life, the projects of life, not the path of death, the projects of death. For some, this might read as an apt expression of what emigrants from Central America are doing, the dilemma they are facing, in the present day. Together with this assertion is a transformation in the understanding of God and Jesus that has come out of the so-called theology of liberation, especially in Central America. The god who resides high in the heavens and rules with power and might is instead the god who, as Jesus, "checks the tires of a truck" or toils and "sweats in the street."[55] God is no longer an emperor above all, but rather has become a laborer, co-worker, neighbor. The strand of liberation theology that has grown in Central America is a conscious response to the physical and spiritual misery of people under imperial duress. The message is "spiritual" but also political: there is nothing godly about imperial rule, or for that matter patriarchy; people are liberated by the collective action of the people themselves and the god who lives among and with them. In Honduras, religion is for many a support for the survival of the human spirit and resistance to empire, and they may or may not express it in these terms. It may even exhort some to work for social, political, and economic change, the liberation of the body as well as the spirit from the duress of empire. This work itself is for some a means of survival.

Many Hondurans claim no religious affiliation and do not attend church; many do not rely on religion for salvation or survival. Religion in Honduras is complex, supporting both imperial hierarchies and liberating action. It may be part of what keeps hope alive among some Hondurans to remain in their country, and what gives courage and hope to others to leave. Migration and asylum seeking are not simple acts of desperation, but also acts of hope, spirit, and resistance.

WALKING ON SHIFTING GROUND

This chapter has reviewed some of the ways in which Hondurans may try to keep body and soul together in response to the conditions of life imposed upon many of them by an extractive and corrupt political economy. This "spiritual struggle" involves preserving self-identity, hope, empowerment, and even joy. It also shows that means of survival are often complex, contradictory, fluid, and sometimes destructive. The various means of survival described in this chapter are not mutually exclusive, but rather fluid. The teenager who becomes a gang member to survive the disintegration of his family may also decide to survive gang life by fleeing the country. From one perspective, some of these practices are confining; from another perspective, they are liberating. People are aware of the dangers and the contradictions. They see and live the consequences daily.

There is much danger in emphasizing the trauma of life in Honduras. Pretending to understand how people think and feel can be both arrogant and badly mistaken. No one really knows how or where another's mind and spirit will lead. It is easy to describe conditions in Honduras in ways that lend credence to negative stereotypes of Honduras and its people, failing to discern differences and nuances. Descriptions can be (mis)used to support anti-immigrant tropes in which the duress that moves people to migrate is conflated or equated with mental instability, reckless behavior, even propensity to commit desperate criminal acts—classic anti-immigrant discourse. The dangers of essentializing, stereotyping, and reductionism are also dangers that confront anthropologists and others who provide expert witness in asylum hearings in U.S. immigration courts.[56] Dangerous conditions must be described in ways that do not incriminate an entire people and their society. This chapter may seem to describe vulnerability. Rather, it tries to describe the counter pole of vulnerability: the strength and empowerment of people finding ways to live in difficult conditions not of their making.

The question is not how much trauma is enough to push people to emigrate—something that concerns asylum hearings. Rather, the question is how much strength, hope, and clarity are required for people to decide to emigrate—something that should commend people seeking asylum. From this perspective, immigrants and asylum seekers are not simply vulnerable victims but people who contribute much, if given the chance. How would an immigration and asylum system based on this positive perspective actually function?

The whole meaning of "spirituality" might thus be summed up in the words attributed to an early Christian writer: "The glory of God is the human being fully alive." There is hardly a more damning critique of empire or a more telling description of the migrant's search.

A final but critical question concerns the psychic and spiritual effects of these imperial structures on the people of the United States. How to come to terms with the duress caused to other people by one's own country? This is a large question addressed in different ways by various scholars, writers, and others. It deserves more attention, since the answers must enlighten immigration policy, but also the future or the dismantling of imperial enterprise and reach.

NOTES

1. Jeremy Seabrook, "The Mental Health of Societies," *Race and Class* 59, no. 4 (2018): 61–62.
2. Seabrook, 56.

3. Othon Alexandrakis, "Introduction: Resistance Reconsidered," in *Impulse to Act: A New Anthropology of Resistance and Social Justice*, ed. Othon Alexandrakis (Bloomington IN: Indiana University Press, 2016), 6.

4. From my field notes in Honduras, August 2019.

5. James Faubion, "Cosmologicopolitics: Vitalistic Cosmology Meets Biopower," in *Impulse to Act: A New Anthropology of Resistance and Social Justice*, ed. Othon Alexandrakis (Bloomington IN: Indiana University Press, 2016), 89–111.

6. James Phillips, *Honduras in Dangerous Times: Resistance and Resilience* (Lanham MD: Lexington Books, 2015), 193.

7. Carmen Manuela Delcid, "Espiritualidad y derechos humanos en el contexto actual," *Envío Honduras* 8, no. 4 (April 2010): 46–48.

8. James Phillips, "Body and Soul: Faith, Development, Community, and Social Science in Nicaragua," *NAPA Bulletin* 33 (2010): 12–30, esp. 13–15 (NAPA is the National Association for the Practice of Anthropology); Leonardo Boff and Virgil Elizondo, eds., *1492–1992: The Voices of the Victims* (Philadelphia: Trinity Press International, 1990), a collection of articles on the Spanish conquest of America from a theological and sociological perspective.

9. Enrique Dussel, "The Real Motives for the Conquest," in *1492–1992: The Voices of the Victims*, 30–46, quoted on page 42, from Miguel Leon-Portilla, *El reverso de la conquista: relaciones aztecas, mayas, e incas* (México: Mortiz, 1964), 86.

10. Sheldon H. Davis and Julie Hodson, *Witnesses to Political Violence in Guatemala: The Suppression of a Rural Development Movement* (Boston: Oxfam America, 1982); Ricardo Falla, *Masacres de la selva: Ixcán, Guatemala, 1975–1982* (Guatemala: Editorial Universitaria, 1992).

11. For an anthropological perspective on some of the questions involved in the body-soul discussion, see Charles Whitehead, "The Anthropology of Consciousness: Keeping Body and Soul Together?" *Anthropology Today* 16, no. 4 (August 2000): 20–22.

12. Frantz Fanon, *The Wretched of the Earth*, trans. Richard Philcox (New York: Grove Press, 1961).

13. Many of the chapters in Alexandrakis's *Impulse to Act* highlight the self-awareness that acts of resistance engage.

14. Ann Laura Stoler, *Duress: Imperial Durabilities in Our Times* (Durham NC: Duke University Press, 2016), 7.

15. Stoler, *Duress*, 8.

16. "La miseria financiando el modelo de desarrollo," was the headline summarizing an interview with Honduran Central Bank economist Edmundo Valladares in the Honduran daily *El Tiempo* on January 5, 1980. The neoliberal development model was introduced in Honduras by the U.S. Embassy and the Honduran Association for the Progress of Honduras (APROH) and adopted by the government in 1980.

17. Phillips, *Honduras in Dangerous Times*, 29–32; Adrienne Pine, *Working Hard, Drinking Hard: On Violence and Survival in Honduras* (Berkeley: University of California Press, 2008).

18. Danielle Mackey and Chiara Eisner, "Inside the Plot to Murder Honduran Activist Berta Cáceres," *The Intercept*, Dec. 21, 2019, theintercept.com/2019/12/21/berta-caceres-murder-plot-honduras/.

19. Oscar Lewis, "The Culture of Poverty," *Scientific American* 215, no. 4 (October 1966): 19–25, https://www.ssc.wisc.edu/~gwallace/Papers/Lewis%20(1966).pdf; Patricia Cohen, "'Culture of Poverty' Makes a Comeback," *New York Times,* October 17, 2010, https://www.nytimes.com/2010/10/18/us/18poverty.html.

20. Marvin Barahona, "Auge de decadencia de la ideología de desigualdad: Un cuestionamiento necesario a la hegemonía neoliberal," *Envío* 15, no. 2 (May 2017): 27–32.

21. James Phillips, "The Misery Financing Development: Subsidized Neoliberalism and Privatized Dependency in Honduras," *Urban Anthropology* 46, nos. 1–2 (Spring–Summer 2017): 1–60.

22. A recent example is Héctor Silva Ávalos, "Keyla Martinez and Extrajudicial Killings in Honduras," *InSight Crime*, February 15, 2021, https://insightcrime.org/news/keyla-martinez-extrajudicial-killings-honduras/. Martinez died in police custody. The police claim suicide, but others claim it was murder.

23. Proceso Digital, "Suicidios en Honduras siguen al alza en 2020," January 2, 2020, https://proceso.hn/suicidios-en-honduras-siguen-al-alza-en-2020/.

24. David G. Mandelbaum, "Alcohol and Culture," *Current Anthropology* 6, no. 3 (June 1965): 284–293; Dwight B. Heath, *Drinking Occasions: Comparative Perspectives on Alcohol and Culture* (Milton UK: Taylor and Francis, 2015).

25. Pine, *Working Hard*, 92.

26. Matthew C. Gutmann, "Abstinence, Antibiotics, and *Estar Jurado:* The Manners of Drinking in Working-Class Mexico City," in *Contemporary Cultures and Societies of Latin America*, third edition, ed. Dwight B. Heath (Prospect Heights IL: Waveland Press, 2002), 294–302; an article adapted from chapter 7 of Gutmann, *The Meanings of Macho: Being a Man in Mexico City* (Berkeley: University of California Press, 1996).

27. Pine, *Working Hard*, 87–90.

28. The control of drug trafficking in Honduras by a few powerful individuals and groups was dramatically demonstrated by the conviction in New York state in 2020 of Antonio (Tony) Hernandez, brother to President Juan Orland Hernandez for trafficking large quantities of illegal drugs into the United States, allegedly with the help of his brother and other top government and police officials.

29. Testimonies of Honduran asylum seekers in U.S. immigration courts frequently describe drug use and trafficking by local gang members. See also Equipo de Reflexión, Investigación y Comunicación (ERIC), *Maras y Pandillas en Honduras* (Tegucigalpa: Editorial Guaymuras, 2005).

30. Tim Merrill, ed., *Honduras: A Country Study* (Washington DC: GPO for the Library of Congress, 1995), http://countrystudies.us/honduras/51.htm.

31. One of many articles in Honduran and international news on various Honduran government scandals is Jeff Ernst, "Exclusive: A Pandora's Box of Corruption in Honduras," *Univision News*, August 26, 2019, Pulitzer Center, https://pulitzercenter.org/stories/exclusive-pandoras-box-corruption-honduras.

32. My interview in Honduras, September, 2019.

33. Pine, *Working Hard*, 85–134; Gutmann, "Abstinence," 294–302.

34. Elizabeth Dore, *Myths of Modernity: Peonage and Patriarchy in Nicaragua* (Durham NC: Duke University Press, 2006), 15, 151–155.

35. Statements of young asylum seekers in U.S. immigration proceedings often describe harassment and violence from police as well as local gang members.

36. Max Manwaring, *State and Nonstate Associated Gangs: Credible "Midwives of New Social Orders"?* (Carlisle PA: U.S. Army War College Strategic Studies Institute, 2009); ERIC, *Maras y Pandillas*.

37. My field notes in Honduras, August, 2016.

38. Eduin Fuñes, "Familia Amador aclara que no participó en masacre suscitada en Olancho," *Tiempo Digita*l, February 1, 2020, https://tiempo.hn/familia-amador-aclara-no-participo-masacre-olancho-1/. Testimony of asylum seekers also describes incidents of being forced off land by gangs and drug traffickers.

39. Ross Everton, *Justifying militarization: Counter-narcotics and Counter-narcoterrorism*, Policy Report 3 (Swansea UK: Global Drug Policy Observatory, Swansea University, 2015).

40. Phillips, "The Misery Financing Development," 38–42.

41. Susan Phillips, *Wallbangin': Graffiti and Gangs in L.A.* (Chicago: University of Chicago Press, 1999); James Diego Vigil, "Group Processes and Street Identity: Adolescent Chicano Gang Members," *Ethos* 16:4 (1988): 421–445.

42. Jon Wolseth, *Jesus and the Gang: Youth Violence and Christianity in Urban Honduras* (Tucson: University of Arizona Press, 2011); Jon Horne Carter, "Gothic Sovereignty: Gangs and Criminal Community in a Honduran Prison," *The South Atlantic Quarterly* 113, no. 3 (2014): 475–502.

43. This description of transition to gang membership is based on research by Honduran sociologists Leticia Salomón and Julietta Castellannos and detailed in, Equipo de Reflexión, (ERIC), *Maras y Pandillas, 70–113*.

44. Wolseth, *Jesus and the Gang*, 52.

45. Wolseth, *Jesus and the Gang*, 70.

46. Ibid.

47. Jon Horne Carter, "Gothic Sovereignty."

48. Wolseth's *Jesus and the Gang* is entirely devoted to describing these processes of integration.

49. Evangelical Focus, "Honduran President thanks evangelicals for their support during the pandemic," *Evangélico Digital*, July 21, 2020, https://evangelicalfocus.com/world/7169/honduran-president-thanks-evangelicals-for-their-support-during-the-pandemic; David Agren, "In Latin American politics, public piety can gain allies," *Catholic Courier*, February 7, 2014, https://catholiccourier.com/articles/in-latin-american-politics-public-piety-can-gain-allies. For a critical perspective, see "U.S. Funded Evangelicals and Coup Supporters Behind the New Commission to Purge the Honduran Police," *Aquí Abajo*, June 8, 2016, https://www.aquiabajo.com/blog/2016/6/8/evangelicalism-us-financing-and-coup-supporters-behind-the-new-commission-to-purge-the-honduran-police.

50. Andrea Gagliarducci, "Cardinal Maradiaga responds to allegations of corruption," *Catholic News Agency,* December 22, 2017, https://www.catholicnewsagency.com/news/37418/cardinal-maradiaga-responds-to-allegations-of-corruption.

51. Eric Canin, "Minguito, Managua's Little Saint: Christian Base Communities and Popular Religion in Nicaragua," in *Contemporary Cultures and Societies of Latin America*, third edition, ed. Dwight B. Heath (Prospect Heights IL: Waveland Press, 2002), 467–479. During the Contra war in Nicaragua in the 1980s, Nicaraguans participated in events such as the *Via Crucis* (Way of the Cross). Hundreds of people walked from the northern war zones to Managua, the capital as both a religious procession and a political protest. They identified the suffering of their people in the war with the suffering of the crucified Jesus; they invoked the authority of God in demanding that the Contra war end.

52. Elsa Tamez, *Bible of the Oppressed*, trans. Matthew J. O'Connell (Maryknoll NY: Orbis Books, 1983). This publication examines the Bible from the perspective of the oppressed: "There is an almost complete absence of the theme of oppression in European and North American biblical theology. But the absence is not surprising, since it is possible to tackle this theme only within an existential situation of oppression. As a result, the theology of liberation, which came into existence in Latin America, regards this historical experience of oppression and liberation as the root of all its theological work" (4). Also see Elsa Tamez, "The Refugee Crisis, Sanctuary, and the Bible," in *Sanctuary: A Resource Guide for Understanding and Participating in the Central American Refugees' Struggle*, ed. Gary MacEoin (San Francisco: Harper and Row, 1985), 39–48.

53. Hugo Assmann, *Theology for a Nomad Church* (Maryknoll NY: Orbis Books, 1976).

54. *Deuteronomy* 30: 19–20.

55. From a hymn in the Nicaraguan Mass (*Misa Campesina Nicaragüense*).

56. James Phillips, "Expert Witnessing in Honduran Asylum Cases: What Difference Can Twenty Years Make?" in *Cultural Expert Witnessing*, ed. Leila Rodriguez, *Studies in Law, Politics, and Society 74* (Bingley UK: Emerald Publishing Ltd., 2018), 38–41.

Chapter 9

Reflecting on the Journey

This journey began with a question: How has it become a crime to give water? How has an act of mercy become a crime? Along the way, we met some of those who try to protect their rivers from dams and mines; those who criminalize the water defenders; those who know that the spirits of their children and ancestors live in the rivers; those who pass laws to privatize and to colonize the waters and the land; those who cross many rivers and deserts to find survival, safety, and dignity; those who leave water for others in the desert; and those who pour out the waters of life to prevent the thirsty from drinking. All are related in a larger reality, but that reality is inhabited also by many chimeric realities, falsehoods, and illusions.

In this book I have tried to construct a holistic response to the question of why there is large-scale emigration from Central America, specifically from the perspective of Honduras. Such a larger contextual approach is essential for at least five reasons. First, the deeper roots and causes of emigration have become complex, generational, and not easily summed up in news bites. Second, emigration from Honduras is very likely to be one side of immigration to the United States. Honduran migration occurs within the structures of modern imperial reach—or neocolonialism, if you prefer—and cannot be understood without that larger relational framework. Emigration and immigration together form an integral aspect of this imperial relationship between the United States and Honduras, benefiting but also threatening the basic premises of imperial control.

Third, the people who migrate or flee from Honduras are each complex human beings of body-spirit. The physical, economic, and political forces that shape lives are crucial to understanding their actions, but the forces that try the human spirit are equally crucial to our understanding of why people feel compelled to leave their homeland. Fourth, the search for "solutions" to the "immigration crisis" is an exercise in futility—or rather, in perpetuity—unless the "crisis" is grasped in its fullness. At best, the daily lives of some Hondurans may be eased by some of the proposed policies for keeping

221

Hondurans from having to emigrate. At worst, some of the proposed solutions help to maintain or worsen the conditions that drive people to emigrate. Fifth, it is not enough to focus on trying to solve the "immigration problem" at the border or in Central America. The problem involves the conflict between different understandings of human beings and the natural world. It is, in part, a conflict between a purely commercialized transactional understanding of the value of human beings and our environment—an understanding shaped by the demands of neoliberal capitalism—and a definitional, communitarian, and inclusive understanding.

COMPONENTS OF A HOLISTIC PERSPECTIVE

In previous chapters, I laid out the skeletal structure of the contemporary "immigration crisis," as I understand it. The resulting picture is not pretty. It is quite literally grounded in the fetishistic global grab for resources, especially strategic resources. Corporations based in the United States, Canada, Europe, and the Far East invest in extractive projects in Central America, funded in large part by an international financial network, sometimes in lopsided partnership, in Honduras at least, with government agencies. The mentality and urgency of this resource grab is such that it tends to obscure or take priority over everything else. Corporate and individual wealth and power are the actual objects of fetish, and people's development becomes an illusion. The imperial debris that this produces includes widespread and violent displacement of communities by legal maneuvers, pollution that makes local lifeways unsustainable, and/or direct force supplied by military, police, and private company guards, or sometimes also by criminal gangs. People and communities who resist this theft are eliminated by physical violence or legal criminalization. The Honduran state controlled by a small elite, the state's security forces, private parties, and gangs all have a hand in this.

In Honduras, this process has gone on apace since at least the 1990s, and in some form long before, but it intensified after the 2009 coup. It results in a large and growing population of displaced and landless people whose way of life has been exploded, whose community has been shattered and fragmented, and whose self-identity and subjectivity have been reduced from self-reliance and interdependency to dependency as job-seekers and clients of the state. The resultant displaced population of people seeking jobs is not simply an unfortunate side effect but an integral part of the plan, creating a large pool of desperate—therefore presumably docile—workers and clients. This neo-extractive model does not generate enough paying jobs, and poverty spreads quickly. Indeed, inequality is a specific characteristic of this extractivism. The children of the displaced, growing up in (largely urban) poverty, must find ways to survive and create a measure of self-respect. Here, another bit of imperial debris provides both opportunity and terror in the way of the rising generation. Gangs and drug trafficking as specific consequences of U.S. policies in the 1980s and since offer a kind of survival for youth in poverty, but also a mortal threat for the same youth and for others.

The corrosive effects of this neoliberal extractive model are deeply felt in the country's political economy. The state's abandonment of the people's wellbeing in favor of a rush to individual enrichment results in a society (or at least a political economy) in which corruption is the operating system. Privatization is a mechanism for the massive transfer of wealth from the nation to those who control the economy and the state. In this situation, privatization has two meanings; the country's wealth is privatized in the hands of the few, while the basic functions of social welfare—health care, education, public infrastructure, security—become the private responsibility of the rest of the population who must fend for themselves as the state withdraws from public service. With corruption comes a culture of impunity. Laws are bent, broken, and ignored. Violence goes unpunished. The powerful are immune while the powerless are defenseless before the law.

Such a system forces people to seek ways to survive. Some paths to survival turn out to be contradictory and destructive—machismo, gangs. Political participation is rigged or foreclosed. Popular protest and resistance, especially organized resistance, invites criminalization and is strongly repressed by the state's security forces. Still, people find resilience in resistance, as a physical placement of the body and the exercise of the human spirit. Resistance humanizes the inhumanity of this political economy and its imperial grasp. Emigration is another road to survival and, simultaneously or from another perspective, also a form of resistance.

This sort of neoextractive regime contains the seeds of its own demise, but that does not mean that it will go quietly or quickly. It destroys its natural resource base through extraction, its human resources through poverty, violence, criminalization, and emigration. It provokes popular resistance and emigration, both of which lay bare the contradictions in both the extractive model and the imperial relationship that sustains it. It requires constant financial input from foreign investment, corporations, financial institutions, and foreign aid; constant militarization and "security" assistance from the United States and elsewhere; and constant political support in the form of expressions and certifications of "progress" in human rights and democracy building that are belied by the daily reality of life for many Hondurans and other Central Americans. These forms of financial, military, and political subsidizing help to keep this imperial system functioning. Finally, a pliant population at both ends of the immigration trail is required. The Honduran people must be kept from disrupting the extractive process; murder, criminalization, repression of protest, and spiritual depression are employed to this end. U.S. citizens cannot be allowed to change current policies toward Honduras and the rest of Central America; historical currents of racism, nativism, and fear are at work in the United States to blunt any such initiatives. But these currents are monsters whose power cannot be easily controlled from tearing at American society itself. If immigration is a threat to the United States, it is not the immigrants that are the threat; rather, it is these historic currents of exclusion, hate, and fear that serve the interests of the imperial relationship. They are part of the "blowback," the domestic cost of imperial reach. This raises another question: When does this domestic cost—in the United States and in Honduras—outweigh the benefits to the few of maintaining such a repressive system? Honduras is the focus here, but the same elements are at work in other countries.

SOLUTIONS: MYTHIC, DECEPTIVE, AND POSSIBLE

The final pages of this book beg the logical follow-up query: Is the migration of Hondurans and other Central Americans a "crisis" that requires a solution? What is the crisis? What is the solution? How one answers these questions will shape both the responses proposed and the efficacy of those responses. The question is complex, but the situation that has been presented in previous chapters provides some perspective for evaluating some of the measures that are advocated. What follows is a brief and simplified review of some of the prevailing proposals for "solving" the "crisis."

The Border

The militarization of the U.S. southern border—increased surveillance, detention, deportation—has grown apace with the increasing criminalization of "illegal" immigrants and the imposition of draconian measure such as family separation that are meant to "send a message" to desperate Central Americans that they are not welcome. This approach has transcended the border region and now pervades the United States. It depends on immigration raids and stigmatization, creating a climate of fear for those who have come seeking escape from fear. Aside from the morality of this approach, it is problematic. Its deterrent effect is limited as long as conditions in Central America, and specifically in Honduras, do not change. It also supports some of the more destructive forces of exclusion, racism, and militarism in the United States. Morally, it represents abrogation of responsibility for the imperial debris that makes life unbearable for many Hondurans and other Central Americans. The opposite proposal—an open border—is also problematic, as long as conditions do not change in Central America and the entire Unites States beyond the border areas is not committed to providing effective support for immigrants. Open borders would seem to require nationwide acceptance of the responsibilities for immigrant integration and radical acceptance of the identity of a truly immigrant nation.

Foreign Aid

The foreign aid approach tends to argue that providing more assistance to Central American countries aimed at improving economy and security will create more livable conditions that keep people from needing to emigrate. We have seen that security assistance to Honduran and other military and police forces may be as likely to increase repression and insecurity. This has prompted calls, both in Honduras and in the United States, for stopping foreign security assistance, or for a re-evaluation of how such aid is used.

Humanitarian assistance that should improve aspects of daily life for Central Americans is also frequently proposed. Some aid does improve aspects of daily life. The problems, however, are several. In a context of widespread official corruption, aid is as likely to be diverted from its intended purposes. Aid that fills the vacuum created by the Honduran government's abandonment and privatization of public services raises questions about the proper responsibilities of government in relation to its citizens. NGOs that provide humanitarian aid are not always free from government pressure, and may struggle to avoid becoming simply an agency of government policy and practice—an especially troubling problem in a context of widespread corruption.

Creative ways to provide aid, including nonmaterial aid, accompaniment, and "solidarity," can take many forms. The crucial issue is the extent that such solidarity follows the lead and needs determined by Central Americans rather than the providers of solidarity or their governments. Solidarity that supports Hondurans in their efforts for change rather than reinforcing the status quo would seem more effective in resolving the conditions that encourage migration. This is a difficult political path.

Human Rights and the Environment

Since the introduction of neoliberal extractivism in Honduras in the 1980s, two forms of discourse have been increasingly employed to express the need for change and livability in Honduras: human rights and environmental rights. These are used to address the violence and theft wrought by neoliberal extractivism and its environmental consequences that make life unlivable for many. The discourse of human rights is powerful, but in Honduras it is also deployed by those who demand their rights to dam rivers and mine the land, or to run for re-election in violation of the law. Human rights rhetoric is a two-edged sword wielded by both its defenders and its most egregious violators. As Hondurans have learned, human rights are only as good as the struggle to protect what is most valuable and important. "We are the agrarian reform." The strength of human rights and environmental discourse is that they attract the attention and support of a global community that has in recent decades become increasingly aware of the cost of ignoring the rights of people and the environment. This concern extends now to the rights of migrants and asylum seekers as they travel and when they reach their new destination; and in the emerging discourse that identifies environmental refugees as those uprooted not only by climate change but also by the environmental wreckage of neoextractivism.

Corporate and Government Accountability

The foreign and Honduran corporations that extract resources, the investors and financial institutions that fund extractive projects, and the agencies of Honduran and foreign governments that promote and support extractivism are subject to little or no accountability in Honduras or the United States. There are several international organizations that monitor mining, for example, and provide guidelines for fair and sustainable practices. But when corporations and governments violate the rights of Honduran communities or contribute to the corruption of officials and state institutions, there is little to stop them except popular resistance in Honduras and public pressure in corporate home countries. These have succeeded in slowing or stopping some extractive projects. But the legal accountability that is required and the political will to enforce it at both ends of the immigrant trail are hard to attain. The products that neoextractivism promises and produces are items in daily demand and use in the centers of empire. Is there a moral, economic, political, and legal equivalent of "fair trade" for the production and distribution of the products of extractive industries? The international community can fashion new laws and restrictions but along with that, consumer decisions and actions may provide further impetus in calling corporate capital to account.

Changing the Dominant Paradigm

The massive increases in both the rate and extent of extractivism and resource grabbing and the numbers of immigrants and asylum seekers going north in recent years have become for many a moment of reflection and accountability. Critiques of empire, development, neoextractivism, progress, and growth are also, in a profound sense, critiques of immigration—not of the immigrants, but of the system that produces and processes immigrants and asylum seekers as commodities. This system is fraught with contradictions, both practical and moral. Perhaps the moment is akin to the historic moment in modern imperialism in which chattel slavery became the crisis for a new way of perceiving. If what has been described in these pages is essentially accurate, what can be learned from it to imagine and promote a new paradigm? What will be the place and meaning, if any, of migration and asylum in the new paradigm?

THE MEANINGS OF MIGRATION

I must leave it to the reader to decide what migration—emigration, immigration—really means, for it has many meanings. Migration, at least in and from Honduras, is burdened with the meanings of everything described in these pages, and more. I am grateful to the reader for accompanying this journey and engaging these many and complex meanings. The reflexivity this implies for the citizens at the heart of empire is difficult but necessary.

Bibliography

Acker, Alison. *Honduras: The Making of a Banana Republic.* Boston: South End Press, 1988.

Agren, David. "In Latin American Politics, Public Piety Can Gain Allies." *Catholic Courier*, February 7, 2014. https://catholiccourier.com/articles/in-latin-american-politics-public-piety-can-gain-allies.

Ainsley, Julia, and Daniella Silva. "Five Myths about the Honduran Caravan Debunked." *NBC News. October 22, 2018. https://www.nbcnews.com/news/latino/five-myths-about-honduran-caravan-debunked-n922806.*

Alemán, Joel. "Fiscalidad y desarrollo: Los privilegios fiscales no son desarrollo." Tegucigalpa: Honduran Social Forum on the External Debt and Development (FOSDEH), October 10, 2019. https://fosdeh.com/editoriales/fiscalidad-y-desarrollo-los-privilegios-fiscales-no-son-desarrollo/.

Alexandrakis, Othon. "Introduction: Resistance Reconsidered." In *Impulse to Act: A New Anthropology of Resistance and Social Justice,* edited by Othon Alexandrakis, 1–15. Bloomington, IN: Indiana University Press, 2016.

Ali, Raiesa. "Income Inequality and Poverty: A Comparison of Brazil and Honduras." Council on Hemispheric Affairs, July 1, 2015. https://www.coha.org/income-inequality-and-poverty-a-comparison-of-brazil-and-honduras/.

Alvarez, Priscilla. "What Happened to the Migrant Caravans?" *CNN,* March 4, 2019. https://www.cnn.com/2019/03/04/politics/migrant-caravans-trump-immigration/index.html.

American Immigration Lawyers Association. "U.S. and Guatemala Enter into Agreement Designating Guatemala as a 'Safe Third Country.'" Text of agreement, July 26, 2019. https://www.aila.org/infonet/us-guatemala-agreement-safe-third-country.

Americas Watch. *Honduras Without the Will.* Washington, DC: Americas Watch, 1989.

Amnesty International. "Key Facts about the Migrant and Refugee Caravans Making Their Way to the USA." November 16, 2018. https://www.amnesty.org/en/latest/

news/2018/11/key-facts-about-the-migrant-and-refugee-caravans-making-their-way-to-the-usa/.

Appadurai, Arjun. "Disjuncture and Difference in the Global Cultural Economy. *Theory, Culture, and Society* 7 (June 1990): 295–310.

Aquí Abajo. "U.S. Funded Evangelicals and Coup Supporters Behind the New Commission to Purge the Honduran Police." *Aquí Abajo*, June 8, 2016. https://www.aquiabajo.com/blog/2016/6/8/evangelicalism-us-financing-and-coup-supporters-behind-the-new-commission-to-purge-the-honduran-police.

Arriagada, Genaro. "National Security Doctrine in Latin America." *Peace and Change*, January, 1980. https://onlinelibrary.wiley.com/doi/abs/10.1111/j.1468-0130.1980.tb00404.x.

Asociación para la Democracia y los Derechos Humanos. "Contemos las balas y a quiénes las disparan: Militarización de las protestas sociales." *Pasos de Animal Grande*, July, 2019? https://www.dropbox.com/s/uux2jzzcaij04dz/DOCUMENTO%20MILITARIZACION%20PROTESTAS-FINAL%20PARA%20PUBLICAR.pdf?dl=0.

Assmann, Hugo. *Theology for a Nomad Church*. Maryknoll, NY: Orbis Books, 1976.

Ávila, Jennifer. "The Difficulties of Reporting in Honduras." *El Faro*, January 7, 2020. elfaro.net/en/201912/internacionales/23899/Seen-as-Either-a-Sell-Out-or-a-Rebel-On-the-Difficulties-of-Reporting-in-Honduras.htm.

Ávila, Jennifer, and Fernando Silva. "Guardianes de la Patria: La huella militar y religiosa en la niñez de un pais violento." *ContraCorriente*, December 4, 2019. https://contracorriente.red/2019/12/04/guardianes-de-la-patria-la-huella-militar-y-religiosa-en-la-ninez-de-un-pais-violento/.

Banktrack. "Dinant, Honduras." March 27, 2016. https://www.banktrack.org/company/dinant.

Barahona, Marvin. *Honduras en el siglo XX: Una síntesis histórica*. Tegucigalpa: Editorial Guaymuras, 2005.

———. *Pueblos indígenas, Estado y memoria colectiva en Honduras*. Tegucigalpa: Editorial Guaymuras, 2009.

———. "Auge de decadencia de la ideología de desigualdad: Un cuestionamiento necesario a la hegemonía neoliberal." *Envío* 15, no. 2 (May 2017): 27–32.

Barry, Tom with Kent Norsworthy. "Honduras." In *Central America Inside Out*, edited by Tom Barry. New York: Grove-Weidenfeld Press, 1991.

Bauman, Zigmunt. *Wasted Lives: Modernity and Its Outcasts*. Cambridge UK: Polity, 2003.

BBC News. "Migrant Caravan: What Is It and Why Does It Matter?" November 26, 2018. https://www.pewresearch.org/hispanic/wp-content/uploads/sites/5/2017/12/Pew-Research-Center_Central_American-migration-to-U.S._12.7.17.pdf

Becerra, Longino. *Evolución histórica de Honduras*. Tegucigalpa: Editorial Baktun, 1983.

———. "The Early History of the Labor Movement." In *Honduras: Portrait of a Captive Nation*, edited by Nancy Peckenham and Annie Street, 95–101. New York: Praeger, 1985.

Beckford, George L. *Persistent Poverty: Underdevelopment in Plantation Economies of the Third World.* New York: Oxford University Press, 1972.

Benedict, Ruth. *Patterns of Culture.* London: Routledge and Kegan Paul Ltd., 1935.

Bennett, Louise. *Jamaica Labrish.* Kingston: Sangster Books, 1966.

Berk-Seligson, Susan, et al. *Impact Evaluation of USAID's Community-Based Crime and Violence Prevention Approach to Central America: Regional Report for El Salvador, Guatemala, Honduras, and Panama.* Nashville TN: US Agency for International Development and Latin American Public Opinion Project, October, 2014. https://www.vanderbilt.edu/lapop/carsi/Regional_Report_v12d_final_W_120814.pdf.

Bhatt, Wasydha. "The Crisis of Development: A Historical Critique from the Focal Point of Human Wellbeing." *Indian Journal of Political Science* 68, no. 1 (January–March, 2007): 41–55.

Bird, Annie, and Alexander Main with Karen Spring. *Collateral Damage of a Drug War: The May 11 Killings in Ahuas and the Impact of the U.S. War on Drugs in Honduras.* Washington, DC: Rights Action and the Center for Economic and Policy Research, August, 2012.

Bishop, Marlon. "Central American Gangs, Made in L.A." Latino USA, January 22, 2016. https://www.latinousa.org/2016/01/22/central-american-gangs-made-in-la/.

Bloom, Deborah. "In Portland, some Black activists frustrated with white protesters." *Reuters* online, July 31, 2020. https://www.reuters.com/article/us-global-race-protests-portland-activis/in-portland-some-black-activists-frustrated-with-white-protesters-idUSKCN24W2QD

Blum, William. "The CIA, Contras, and Crack." Institute for Policy Studies, November 1, 1996. https://ips-dc.org/the_cia_contras_gangs_and_crack/.

Bodley, John. *Victims of Progress,* Sixth Edition. Lanham, MD: AltaMira Press, 2015.

———. *Anthropology and Contemporary Human Problems*, Sixth Edition. Lanham, MD: Rowman & Littlefield, 2012.

Boff, Leonardo, and Virgil Elizondo, eds. *1492–1992: The Voices of the Victims.* Philadelphia: Trinity Press International, 1990.

Bozmoski, Maria Fernanda. "The Northern Triangle: The World's Epicenter for Gender-based Violence." *New Atlanticist,* March 3, 2021. https://www.atlanticcouncil.org/blogs/new-atlanticist/the-northern-triangle-the-worlds-epicenter-for-gender-based-violence/.

Breman, Jan. "Work and Life of the Rural Proletariat in Java's Coastal Plain." *Modern East Asian Studies* 29, no. 1 (1995): 1–44.

Brondo, Keri Vacanti. *Land Grab: Green Neoliberalism, Gender, and Garifuna Resistance in Honduras.* Tucson: University of Arizona Press, 2013.

Bryceson, Deborah. "Peasant Theories and Smallholder Policies: Past and Present." In *Disappearing Peasantries? Rural Labour in Africa, Asia, and Latin America,* edited by Deborah Bryceson, Cristóbal Kay, and Jos Mooij, 1–36. London: Intermediate Technology Publications, 2000.

Buijtenhuijs, Robert. "Peasant Wars in Africa: Gone with the Wind?" In *Disappearing Peasantries: Rural Labour in Africa, Asia, and Latin America,* edited by

Deborah Bruceson, Cristóbal Kay, and Jos Mooij, 112–122. London: Intermediate Technology Publications, 2000.

Canin, Eric. "Mingüito, Managua's Little Saint: Christian Base Communities and Popular Religion in Nicaragua." In *Contemporary Cultures and Societies of Latin America*, edited by Dwight B. Heath, 467–479. Prospect Heights, IL: Waveland Press, 2002.

Cardoso, Lawrence A. *Mexican Emigration to the United States, 1897–1931*. Tucson: University of Arizona Press, 1980.

Carter, Jon Horne. "Gothic Sovereignty: Gangs and Criminal Community in a Honduran Prison." *South Atlantic Quarterly* 113, no. 3 (Summer 2014): 475–502.

Cassel, Doug. "Coup d'Etat in Constitutional Clothing?" *American Society for International Law* 13, no. 9 (October 15, 2009): 1–7. https://www.asil.org/insights/volume/13/issue/9/honduras-coup-d%E2%80%99etat-constitutional-clothing-revision.

Castellanos, Julieta. *Honduras: Armamentismo y violencia.* Tegucigalpa: Fundación Arias para la Paz y el Progreso Humano, 2000.

Center for International Environmental Law (CEIL). "Should the Inter-American Development Bank Fund Honduras to Implement Controversial Special Economic Zones?" CEIL, December, 2017. https://www.ciel.org/wp-content/uploads/2017/12/ZEDEanalysis.pdf.

Center for Latin American and Caribbean Studies, University of London. "1998–2013 Honduran Mining Laws." 2020, https://ilas.sas.ac.uk/research-projects/legal-cultures-subsoil/1998-2013-honduran-mining-laws.

Centro de Documentación de Honduras (CEDOH). *25 Años de Reforma Agraria.* Tegucigalpa: Centro de Documentación de Honduras, 1988.

Centro de Estudios para la Democracia (CESPAD). "Azacualpa, MINOSA, Copán." August 18, 2020. http://cespad.org.hn/2020/08/18/alerta-minosa-comienza-de-nuevo-a-dinamitar-cementerio-de-azacualpa-y-pone-en-riesgo-decenas-de-familias/.

Chayes, Sarah. *When Corruption Is the Operating System: The Case of Honduras*. Washington, DC: Carnegie Endowment for International Peace, 2017.

Chishti, Muzaffar, Sarah Pierce, and Jessica Bolter. "The Obama Record on Deportations: Deporter in Chief or Not?" *Migration Policy Institute*, January 26, 2017. https://www.migrationpolicy.org/article/obama-record-deportations-deporter-chief-or-not.

Chomsky, Aviva. *Central America's Forgotten History: Revolution, Violence, and the Roots of Migration.* Boston: Beacon Press, 2021.

Christian Science Monitor. "Time to Leave Honduras? For Many Youths, the Answer Is Yes." July 24, 2015. https://www.csmonitor.com/World/Americas/2015/0724/Time-to-leave-Honduras-For-many-youths-the-answer-is-easy.

Cockcroft, James D., André Gunder Frank, and Dale L. Johnson, eds. *Dependence and Underdevelopment: Latin America's Political Economy*. New York: Anchor Books, 1972.

Cohen, D'Vera, Jeffrey Passel, and Ana Gonzalez-Barrera. "Rise in U.S. Immigrants from El Salvador. Guatemala, and Honduras Outpaces Growth from Elsewhere." Pew Research Center Hispanic Trends, December 7, 2017. https://www.

pewresearch.org/hispanic/wp-content/uploads/sites/5/2017/12/Pew-Research-Center_Central_American-migration-to-U.S._12.7.17.pdf.

Cohen, Gary, and Ginger Thompson. "When a wave of torture staggered a small U.S. ally, truth was a casualty." *Baltimore Sun*, June 11, 1995. https://www.baltimore-sun.com/maryland/bal-negroponte1a-story.html.

Cohen, Patricia. "'Culture of Poverty' Makes a Comeback." *New York Times*, October 17, 2010. https://www.nytimes.com/2010/10/18/us/18poverty.html.

Comblin, José. *The Church and the National Security State.* Maryknoll, NY: Orbis Books, 1979.

Comisión Interamericana de Derechos Humanos (CIDH/IACHR). *Situación de derechos humanos en Honduras.* Washington DC: Inter-American Commission for Human Rights, August 27, 2019. https://www.oas.org/es/cidh/informes/pdfs/Honduras2019.pdf.

Comité para la Defensa de los Derechos Humanos en Honduras (CODEH). *Boletín* 62, March, 1990.

———. *Boletín* 80, September, 1991.

———. *Boletín* 85, February, 1992.

Comité de Familiares de Detenidos/Desaparecidos en Honduras (COFADEH). *Crisis de Derechos Humanos durante la pandemia COVID-19*. Tegucigalpa: Defensores en Linea, April, 2020. http://defensoresenlinea.com/wp-content/uploads/2020/04/INFORME-COFADEH-DDHH-Y-COVID-19-1.pdf.

ConexiHon. "Privilegios fiscales en energía y minería agudizan desigualdades en Honduras." July 2, 2019. http://www.conexihon.hn/index.php/transparencia/1140-privilegios-fiscales-en-energia-y-mineria-agudizan-desigualdades-en-honduras.

Congressional Research Service. "U.S. Strategy for Engagement in Central America: Policy Issues for Congress." November 12, 2019. https://crsreports.congress.gov/product/pdf/R/R44812.

Contreras Natera, Miguel Angel. "Insurgent Imaginaries and Postneoliberalism in Latin America." In *Neoliberalism Interrupted: Social Change and Contested Governance in Contemporary Latin America,* edited by Mark Goodale and Nancy Postero, 250–258. Palo Alto: Stanford University Press, 2013.

Cotler, Julio. "Traditional Haciendas and Communities in a Context of Political Mobilization in Peru." In *Agrarian Problems and Peasant Movements in Latin America,* edited by Rodolfo Stavenhagen, 533–558. Garden City, NY: Anchor Books, 1970.

Coutin, S.B. *The Culture of Protest: Religious Activism and the U.S. Sanctuary Movement.* Boulder, CO: Westview Press, 2000.

Criterio.hn. "En 2021, tres de cada cuatro hondureños serán pobres: FOSDEH." September 24, 2020. https://criterio.hn/en-2021-tres-de-cada-cuatro-hondurenos-seran-pobres-fosdeh/.

Davis, Shelton, and Julie Hodson. *Witnesses to Political Violence in Guatemala.* Boston: Oxfam America, 1982.

Deal, Michael. "United States Dependence on Caribbean Bauxite and the Formation of the International Bauxite Association." *Maryland Journal of International Law* 4, no. 1 (1978): 68–76.

Delcid, Carmen Manuela. "Espiritualidad y derechos humanos en el contexto actual." *Envío Honduras* 8, no. 4 (April 2010): 46–48.

Detention Watch Network. "Financial Incentives" (n.d., 2019 or later). https://archive.nytimes.com/www.nytimes.com/library/world/americas/110598honduras-destruction.html.

———. "Immigration Detention 101" (n.d., 2019 or later). https://archive.nytimes.com/www.nytimes.com/library/world/americas/110598honduras-destruction.html.

Dialogue. "Educational Challenges in Honduras and Consequences for Human Capital and Development." February 2017. http://www.thedialogue.org/wp-content/uploads/2017/03/Educational-Challenges-in-Honduras-and-Consequences-for-Human-Capital.pdf.

Diaz, Elizabeth. "Honduras: Criminalization of the Garifuna People Defending Their Territory from the Advance of the African Palm." *World Rainforest Movement Bulletin* 206 (September 26, 2014). https://wrm.org.uy/articles-from-the-wrm-bulletin/section1/honduras-criminalization-of-the-garifuna-people-defending-their-territory-from-the-advance-of-the-african-palm/.

Dichter, Thomas. "When Criticism Falls on Deaf Ears: The Case of U.S. Foreign Aid." *Foreign Service Journal* (November 2017). https://www.afsa.org/when-criticism-falls-deaf-ears-case-us-foreign-aid.

Dilling, Yvonne. *In Search of Refuge.* Scottsdale, PA: Herald Press, 1984.

Dinkel, Jurgen. *The Non-Aligned Movement: Genesis, Organization and Politics (1927–1992).* Leiden: Brill Publishers, 2018.

Dore, Elizabeth. *Myths of Modernity: Peonage and Patriarchy in Nicaragua.* Durham, NC: Duke University Press, 2006.

Doughty, Paul. "Ending Serfdom in Peru: The Struggle for Land and Freedom in Vicos." In *Contemporary Cultures and Societies of Latin America*, Third Edition, edited by Dwight B. Heath, 225–243. Prospect Heights, IL: Waveland Press, 2002.

Duffield, Mark, and Vernon Hewitt. *Development and Colonialism: The Past in the Present.* Rochester, NY: Boydell and Brewer, 2009.

Dunbar-Ortiz, Roxanne. *An Indigenous People's History of the United States.* Boston: Beacon Press, 2014.

Dussel, Enrique. "The Real Motives for the Conquest." In *1492–1992: The Voices of the Victims*, edited by Leonardo Boff and Virgil Elizondo, 30–46. Philadelphia: Trinity Press International, 1990.

Dye, David R. *Police Reform in Honduras: The Role of the Special Purge and Transformation Commission.* Washington, DC: Wilson Center, 2018. https://www.wilsoncenter.org/sites/default/files/media/documents/publication/lap_dye_police-english_final.pdf.

Earth Rights International. "Criminalized Earth Rights Defenders Should Be Immediately Released." February 27, 2020. https://earthrights.org/blog/criminalized-guapinol-earth-rights-defenders-should-be-immediately-released/.

El Pais (Mexico). "Viacrucis migrante llama a las puertas de Estados Unidos." April 3, 2018. https://elpais.com/elpais/2018/04/03/album/1522754657_996005.html.

Environmental Investigation Agency and Center for International Policy. *The Illegal Logging Crisis in Honduras.* Washington, DC: Environmental Investigation

Agency, 2005. https://eia-international.org/wp-content/uploads/Honduras-Report-English-low-res1.pdf.

Environmental Law Alliance Worldwide (ELAW). "Honduras: Holding the Mining Industry Accountable." Winter 2008. https://elaw.org/es/node/5169.

Equipo de Reflexión, Investigación y Comunicación (ERIC). *Maras y Pandillas en Honduras.* Tegucigalpa: Editorial Guaymuras, 2005.

———. *Religión, ideología, y sociedad: Una aproximación a las iglesias en Honduras.* El Progreso: Casa Editorial San Ignacio, 2013.

———. *Impacto socioambiental de la mineria en la region noroccidental de Honduras en la luz de tres estudios de casos.* El Progreso: ERIC, 2016.

Equipo de Reflexión, Investigación y Comunicación (ERIC) and Universidad Centroamericana José Simeón Cañas. *Sondeo de opinion pública: Percepciones sobre la situación hondureña.* 2017, but published annually.

Ernst, Jeff. "Exclusive: A Pandora's Box of Corruption in Honduras." *Univision News*, August 26, 2019 (from Pulitzer Center). https://pulitzercenter.org/stories/exclusive-pandoras-box-corruption-honduras.

———. "'Everything Buried in Mud': Hurricane Eta's Devastating Blow to Honduras." *The Guardian*, November 11, 2020. https://www.theguardian.com/global-development/2020/nov/11/everything-buried-in-mud-hurricane-etas-devastating-blow-to-honduras.

Escobar, Arturo. *Encountering Development: The Making and Unmaking of the Third World.* Princeton, NJ: Princeton University Press, 1995.

Ettinger, Aaron. "Neoliberalism and the Rise of the Private Military Industry." *International Journal* 66, no. 3 (2011): 731–752.

Euraque, Darío. *Reinterpreting the Banana Republic: Region and State in Honduras, 1870–1972.* Chapel Hill, NC: University of North Carolina Press, 1996.

Evangelical Focus. "Honduran President thanks Evangelicals for their support during the pandemic." *Evangélico Digital*, July 21, 2020. https://evangelicalfocus.com/world/7169/honduran-president-thanks-evangelicals-for-their-support-during-the-pandemic.

Everton, Ross. *Justifying Militarization: Counter-Narcotics and Counter-Terrorism.* Policy Report 3. Swansea, UK: Global Drug Policy Observatory, Swansea University, 2015.

Extractive Industries Transparency Initiative (EITI). "Honduras." February 4, 2021. https://eiti.org/honduras.

Faber, D. "Imperialism, Revolution, and Ecological Crisis in Central America." *Latin American Perspectives* 19, no. 1 (1992): 1–32.

Falla. Ricardo. *Masacres en la selva: Ixcán (1975–1982).* Guatemala: Editorial Universitaria, 2007.

Fals-Borda, Orlando. *Peasant Society in the Colombian Andes.* Gainesville: University of Florida Press, 1955.

Fanon, Frantz. *The Wretched of the Earth.* Translated by Richard Philcox. New York: Grove Press, 1961.

Faubion, James. "Cosmologicopolitics: Vitalistic Cosmology Meets Biopower." In *Impulse to Act: A New Anthropology of Resistance and Social Justice*, edited by Othon Alexandrakis, 89–111. Bloomington, IN: Indiana University Press, 2016.

Feder, Ernest. *The Rape of the Peasantry: Latin America's Landholding System.* Garden City, NY: Doubleday Anchor, 1971.

Ferguson, James. *The Anti-Politics Machine: Development, Depoliticization, and Bureaucratic Power in Lesotho* Cambridge: Cambridge University Press, 1990.

Ferris, Elizabeth. *The Central American Refugee.* New York: Praeger, 1987.

Fiallos, Maria. "Honduran Indigenous Community in Standing Forest Area." *Honduras This Week*, June 9, 2003.

FIAN International. "Agrarian Reform in Honduras" (2015). https://www.fian.org/fileadmin/media/publications_2015/Agrarian-Reform-in-Honduras-2000.pdf.

Flores, Mirna. "Le remilitarización de la seguridad pública. Centro de Estudios para la Democracia (CESPAD)," August 18, 2020. http://cespad.org.hn/2020/08/18/analisis-la-remilitarizacion-de-la-seguridad-publica-signo-relevante-en-los-retro-cesos-de-la-democracia-hondurena/.

Forde, Kealyn. "The Ahuas Killings Five Years Later: Collateral Damage of the Drug War." *NACLA Report*, October 27, 2014. https://nacla.org/news/2017/10/27/ahuas-killings-five-years-later-collateral-damage-drug-war.

Foster, George M. "What Is a Peasant?" In *Peasant Society: A Reader*, edited by Jack M. Potter, May N. Diaz, and George M. Foster, 2–14. Boston: Little Brown and Company, 1967.

Foucault, Michel. *Security, Territory, Population: Lectures at the College de France, 1977–1978.* New York: Palgrave Macmillan, 2007.

Frank, Dana. *The Long Honduran Night: Resistance, Terror, and the United States in the Aftermath of the Coup.* Chicago, IL: Haymarket Books, 2018.

Fuerzas Armadas de Honduras. "UHR forma nuevos Guardianes de la Patria." Communiqué, April 27, 2019. http://www.ffaa.mil.hn/?p=5935.

Fuñez, Eduin. "Familia Amador aclara que no participó en masacre susci-tada en Olancho." *Tiempo Digital*, February 1, 2020. https://tiempo.hn/familia-amador-aclara-no-participo-masacre-olancho-1/.

Fuñez Martinez, Mayra Lisset. *Problemática ambiental en Honduras.* Tegucigalpa: Asociación de Ecología, 1989.

Gagliarducci, Andrea. "Cardinal Maradiaga Responds to Allegations of Corruption." *Catholic News Agency*, December 22, 2017. https://www.catholicnewsagency.com/news/37418/cardinal-maradiaga-responds-to-allegations-of-corruption.

Gane-McCalla, Casey. *Inside the CIA's Secret War on Jamaica.* Los Angeles: Over the Edge Books, 2016.

Gannon, J. D. "Living with the Contra War's Legacy." *Christian Science Monitor*, July 19, 1989. https://www.csmonitor.com/1989/0719/ocont.html.

Gilder Lehrman Institute of American History. "The Doctrine of Discovery, 1493" (n.d.). https://www.gilderlehrman.org/history-resources/spotlight-primary-source/doctrine-discovery-1493.

Girvan, Norman. *Corporate Imperialism: Conflict and Expropriation.* New York: Monthly Review Press, 1976.

Gleijeses, Piero. *Shattered Hope: The Guatemalan Revolution and the United States, 1944–1954.* Princeton, NJ: Princeton University Press, 1991.

Global Americans. "Femicide and International Women's Rights: An Epidemic of Violence in Latin America." *Global Americans Report* (2021). https://theglobalamericans.org/reports/femicide-international-womens-rights/.

Global Witness. *Illegal Logging in the Rio Plátano Biosphere: A Farce in Tree Acts.* Washington, DC: Global Witness, 2009.

———. "Honduras: The Deadliest Country in the World for Environmental Activism." January 31, 2017. https://www.globalwitness.org/en/campaigns/environmental-activists/honduras-deadliest-country-world-environmental-activism/.

Gonzalez, Juan. *Harvest of Empire: A History of Latinos in America.* New York: Penguin Books, 2011.

Gonzalez, Marlon. "Honduras' New Penal Code Lightens Sentences for Corruption." *Associated Press* (AP), June 25, 2020. https://apnews.com/article/1efbd7e8a44f6c2458fb6a15c2950642.

Goodale, Mark, and Nancy Postero. "Revolution and Retrenchment: Illuminating the Present in Latin America." In *Neoliberalism Interrupted: Social Change and Contested Governance in Contemporary Latin America*, edited by Mark Goodale and Nancy Posero, 1–24. Palo Alto: Stanford University Press, 2013.

Goodenough, Patrick. "U.S. Diplomat in Honduras Tells 'Caravan' Migrants to Return Home, But Still They Come." *CNS News*, October 18, 2018. https://www.cnsnews.com/news/article/patrick-goodenough/us-diplomat-honduras-tells-caravan-migrants-return-home-still-they.

Goodwin, Zachary. "Massively Overpriced Contracts Hamper Honduras' Pandemic Response." *InSight Crime*, July 17, 2020. https://www.insightcrime.org/news/analysis/honduras-corruption-pandemic-contracts/.

Gould, Jeffrey L. *To Die in This Way: Nicaraguan Indians and the Myth of Mestizaje, 1880–1965.* Durham, NC: Duke University Press, 1998.

Goulet, Denis. *A New Moral Order: Development Ethics and Liberation Theology.* Maryknoll, NY: Orbis Books, 1974.

Grandin, Greg. *Empire's Workshop: Latin America, the United States, and the Rise of the New Imperialism.* New York: Holt, 2007.

Griffen, Scott. "In Honduras, Government Secrecy Law Undermines Promise of Greater Transparency." International Press Institute, January 20, 2014. https://ipi.media/in-honduras-government-secrecy-law-undermines-promise-of-greater-transparency/.

Guardiola-Rivera, Oscar. *Story of a Death Foretold: The Coup Against Salvador Allende, September 11, 1973.* London: Bloomsbury Publishing, 2013.

Gusterson, Hugh, and Catherine Besteman. "Cultures of Militarism: An Introduction to Supplement 19." *Current Anthropology* 60, no. S19 (February 2019): 2–15.

Gutmann, Matthew C. "Abstinence, Antibiotics, and Estar Jurado: The Manners of Drinking in Working-Class Mexico City." In *Contemporary Cultures and Societies of Latin America*, edited by Dwight B. Heath, 294–302. Prospect Heights, IL: Waveland Press, 2002.

Haenn, Nora, et al. "Trump's First World Revivalism Pits Globalization Against Development." *Anthropology News*, March 20, 2020. https://www.anthropology-news.org/index.php/2020/03/20/trumps-first-world-revivalism-pits-globalization-against-development/.

Haines, David W. *Immigration Structures and Immigrant Lives: An Introduction to the U.S. Experience.* Lanham, MD: Rowman & Littlefield, 2017.

Hall, Catherine. "White Visions, Black Lives: The Free Villages of Jamaica." *History Workshop* 36 (Autumn 1993): 100–132.

Hanke, Lewis. *The Spanish Struggle for Justice in the Conquest of America.* Boston: Little Brown, 1965.

Harrison, Faye, ed. *Decolonizing Anthropology: Moving Further Toward an Anthropology of Liberation.* Washington, DC: American Anthropological Association, 1997.

Heath, Dwight B. *Drinking Occasions: Comparative Perspectives on Alcohol and Culture.* Milton, UK: Taylor and Francis, 2015.

Hernandez, Alcides. *El Neoliberalismo en Honduras.* Tegucigalpa: Editorial Guaymuras, 1987.

Hogenboom, Barbara. "Latin America's Transformative New Extraction and Local Conflict." *European Review of Latin American and Caribbean Studies* 99 (October 2015): 143–151.

Holland, Lynn. "The Dangerous Path Toward Mining Law Reform in Honduras." Council on Hemispheric Affairs, December 18, 2015. https://www.coha.org/the-dangerous-path-toward-mining-law-reform-in-honduras/.

Honduran Social Forum on the External Debt (FOSDEH). "Pobreza sigue en aumento a pesar de milionario gasto estatal." *Dinero Honduras*, March 8, 2019. http://dinero.hn/pobreza-sigue-en-aumento-a-pesar-de-millonario-gasto-estatal-fosdeh-ine/.

———. "El presupuesto público: Danza milionaria que bailan los pobres." *Realidad Nacional*, February 2020. https://fosdeh.com/tag/honduras/.

Honduras News. "Honduras Celebrates La Virgen de Soyapa." February 2, 2012. https://www.hondurasnews.com/virgen-de-suyapa/.

Hymes, Dell, ed. *Reinventing Anthropology.* New York: Pantheon, 1972.

Igoe, Michael. "USAID Mulls a Proposal to Train Aid Workers as Special Forces." *Devex World*, February 19, 2019. https://www.devex.com/news/usaid-mulls-proposal-to-train-aid-workers-as-special-forces-94321.

InSight Crime. "Los Cachiros: Honduras." October 23, 2019. http://www.defensoresenlinea.com/sobreseimiento-definitivo-para-ambientalistas-querellados-por-defender-el-bosque/.

———. "Honduras Profile." November, 2020. https://www.insightcrime.org/honduras-organized-crime-news/honduras/.

Inspectors General, U.S. Department of Justice and U.S. Department of State. *Special Joint Review of Post-Incident Responses by the Department of State and Drug Enforcement Administration to Three Deadly Force Incidents in Honduras* (redacted). May 2017. https://oig.justice.gov/reports/2017/o1702.pdf#page=1.

Instituto de Derechos Ambientales de Honduras. *La Mina San Martin en el Valle de Siria, exploración, explotación y cherries: Impactos y consecuencias.* Tegucigalpa: Instituto de Derechos Ambientales, 2013.

Inter-American Commission on Human Rights. *Honduras: Human Rights and the Coup D'etat.* Washington, DC: Inter-American Commission on Human Rights, 2009.

International Business Standards Organization. "Facts and Stats about NGOs Worldwide." October 6, 2015. https://www.standardizations.org/bulletin/?p=841.

International Organization for Migration. "Northern Triangle of Central America Regional Integration." n.d. https://triangulonorteca.iom.int/regional-integration.

Jagan, Cheddi. *The West on Trial: The Fight for Guyana's Freedom.* London: Michael Joseph, Ltd., 1966.

Jansen, Kees. "Structural Adjustment, Peasant Differentiation, and the Environment in Central America." In *Disappearing Peasantries? Rural Labour in Africa, Asia, and Latin America,* edited by Deborah Bryceson, Cristóbal Kay, and Jos Mooij, 192–212. London: Intermediate Technology Publications, 2000.

Johnson, Chalmers. *Blowback: The Cost and Consequences of American Empire.* New York: Henry Holt, 2000.

Johnson, Tim. "U.S. Export: Central American Gangs Began in Los Angeles." *MacLatchy News,* August 5, 2014. https://www.mcclatchydc.com/news/nation-world/world/article24771469.html.

Johnston, Barbara Rose. "Dam Legacies: Guatemala's Chixoy Dam-Affected Communities." In *Life and Death Matters: Human Rights, Environment, and Social Justice,* Second Edition, edited by Barbara Rose Johnston, 460–465. Walnut Creek, CA: Left Coast Press, 2011.

———. "Water and Human Rights." In *Life and Death Matters: Human Rights, Environment, and Social Justice,* Second Edition, edited by Barbara Rose Johnston, 443–453. Walnut Creek, CA: Left Coast Press, 2011.

Johnston, Jake. "How Pentagon Officials May Have Encouraged a 2009 Coup in Honduras." *The Intercept,* August 29, 2017. https://theintercept.com/2017/08/29/honduras-coup-us-defense-departmetnt-center-hemispheric-defense-studies-chds/.

Jost-Creegan, Kelsey. "Honduras' New Militarized Agricultural Policy: A Threat to Defenders and Human Rights." EarthRights International, December 11, 2019. https://earthrights.org/blog/honduras-new-militarized-agricultural-policy-a-threat-to-defenders-and-human-rights/.

Kaplan, Amy, and Donald E. Pease. *Cultures of United States Imperialism.* Durham, NC: Duke University Press, 1993.

Kaplan, Robert D. "In Defense of Empire." *The Atlantic,* April 2014. https://www.theatlantic.com/magazine/archive/2014/04/in-defense-of-empire/358645/.

Kavanagh, Tom. "Honduras Is Open for Business." *New Statesman,* May 28, 2011. https://www.newstatesman.com/blogs/the-staggers/2011/05/honduras-government-zelaya.

Kay, Cristóbal. "Latin America's Agrarian Transformation: Peasantization and Proletarianization." In *Disappearing Peasantries? Rural Labour in Africa, Asia, and Latin America*, edited by Deborah Bruceson, Cristóbal Kay, and Jos Mooij, 123–138. London: Intermediate Technology Publications, 2000.

Kearney, Michael. *The Winds of Ixtepeji: World View and Society in a Zapotec Town.* New York: Holt, Rinehart, Winston, 1972.

Kempner, Charles D., and Jay H. Soothill. *The Banana Empire: A Case Study of Economic Imperialism.* New York: Russell and Russell, 1967.

Kerssen, Tanya. *Grabbing Power: The New Struggle for Land, Food, and Democracy in Northern Honduras.* Oakland, CA: Food First Books, 2013.

Kincaid, Douglas. "We Are the Agrarian Reform: Rural Politics and Agrarian Reform." In *Honduras: Portrait of a Captive Nation*, edited by Nancy Peckenham and Annie Street, 135–142. New York: Praeger, 1985.

Kinosian, Sarah. "Honduras' Military: On the Streets and in the Government." *Latin American Working Group*, 2015. https://www.lawg.org/honduras-military-on-the-streets-and-in-the-government/.

———. "The Law of Secrets: What the Honduran Government Doesn't Want People to Know." *Security Assistance Monitor*, February 17, 2015. https://securityassistance.org/blog/law-secrets-what-honduran-government-doesn%E2%80%99t-want-people-know.

———. "Call for Fresh Honduras Election after President Juan Orlando Hernandez Wins." *The Guardian*, December 18, 2017.

Krausch, Meghan. "Fighting to Protect the Forest in Honduras." *The Progressive*, May 15, 2019. https://progressive.org/dispatches/forest-protection-under-dictatorship-honduras-krausch-190515/.

———. "Honduran Indigenous Protesting Logging Killed." *The Progressive*, October 3, 2019. https://progressive.org/dispatches/Honduran-indigenous-protesting-logging-killed-Krausch-191002/.

Kumarappa, Bharatan. *Capitalism, Socialism or Villagism?* Madras: Shakti Karalayam, 1946.

Lakhani, Nina. "Did Hilary Clinton Stand By as Honduras Coup Ushered in an Era of Violence?" *The Guardian*, August 31, 2016. https://www.theguardian.com/world/2016/aug/31/hillary-clinton-honduras-violence-manuel-zelaya-berta-caceres.

———. "U.S. Admits DEA Lied About Honduras Massacre That Killed Four Villagers." *The Guardian*, May 25, 2017. https://www.theguardian.com/world/2017/may/25/us-honduras-drug-enforcement-administration-shooting.

———. "Honduras Deploys Security Forces as Doctors and Teachers Demand President's Resignation." *The Guardian*, June 5, 2019. https://www.theguardian.com/world/2019/jun/05/honduras-protests-teachers-doctors-president.

———. *Who Killed Berta Cáceres? Dams, Death Squads, and an Indigenous Defender's Battle for the Planet.* London: Verso, 2020.

———. "Indigenous Environmental Defender Killed in Latest Honduras Attack." *The Guardian*, December 29, 2020. https://www.theguardian.com/environment/2020/dec/29/indigenous-environmental-defender-killed-felix-vasquez.

Langlois, Joseph E. "The 2014 Humanitarian Crisis at the Border: A Review of the Government's Response to Unaccompanied Minors One Year Later." Testimony Before the Senate Committee on Homeland Security. U.S. Citizenship and Immigration Service, July 16, 2015. https://www.uscis.gov/archive/the-2014-humanitarian-crisis-at-our-border-a-review-of-the-governments-response-to-unaccompanied.

La Prensa, "Iniciativa de gestión de la información en el Triángulo Norte." August 20, 2018, 4.

Latin America Working Group. "Negative Consequences of Ending Temporary Protective Status (TPS) for U.S. Investment in El Salvador and Honduras" (March 2019). https://www.congress.gov/116/meeting/house/109000/documents/HHRG-116-JU00-20190306-SD021.pdf.

Leon, Andres. "Rebellion under the Palm Trees: Memory, Agrarian Reform, and Labor in the Aguán, Honduras." PhD diss., City University of New York, 2015.

Lernoux, Penny. *Cry of the People*. Garden City, NY: Doubleday, 1980.

Letelier, Orlando. "Chile: Economic Freedom and Political Repression." Transnational Institute Pamphlet Series 1. Washington, DC: Transnational Institute, 1976.

Leverty, Sally. "NGOs, the UN, and APA." American Psychological Association, 2008. https://www.apa.org/international/united-nations/publications.

Levinson, Jerome. *The Alliance That Lost Its Way: A Critical Report on the Alliance for Progress.* New York: Quadrangle Books, 1972.

Levitz, Eric. "American Exceptionalism Is a Dangerous Myth." *New Yorker* (January 2, 2019). https://nymag.com/intelligencer/2019/01/american-exceptionalism-is-a-dangerous-myth.html.

Levy, Jordan. "The Politics of Honduran School Teachers: State Agents Challenge the State." PhD diss., Western Ontario University, 2014. https://ir.lib.uwo.ca/cgi/viewcontent.cgi?article=3603&context=etd.

———. "Schoolteachers and National 'Public' Education in Honduras: Navigating the Reforms and Refounding the State." *Journal of Latin American and Caribbean Anthropology 22*, no. 1 (2017): 137–156.

Lewis, Gordon K. *The Growth of the Modern West Indies*. New York: Modern Reader Paperback, 1968.

Lewis, Oscar. "The Culture of Poverty." *Scientific American* 215 no. 4 (October 1966): 19–25. https://www.ssc.wisc.edu/~gwallace/Papers/Lewis%20(1966).pdf.

Li, Fabiana. *Unearthing Conflict: Corporate Mining, Activism, and Expertise in Peru.* Durham, NC: Duke University Press, 2015.

Lumpe. Lora. "The U.S. Arms Central America—Past and Present." Norwegian Initiative on Small Arms Trade, May 1999. http://nisat.prio.org/Publications/The-US-Arms-Central-AmericaPast-and-Present/.

MacEoin, Gary. "A Brief History of the Sanctuary Movement." In *Sanctuary: A Resource Guide*, edited by Gary MacEoin, 14–29. San Francisco: Harper and Row, 1985.

———. "The Constitutional and Legal Aspects of the Refugee Crisis." In *Sanctuary: A Resource Guide*, edited by Gary MacEoin, 118–129. San Francisco: Harper and Row, 1985.

MacEoin, Gary, and Nivita Riley. *No Promised Land: American Refugee Policies and the Rule of Law.* Boston: Oxfam America, 1982.

MacKay, John, ed. *Four Russian Serf Narratives.* Translated by John MacKay. Madison: University of Wisconsin Press, 2009.

Mackey, Danielle. "I've Seen All Sorts of Horrific Things in My Time, but None as Detrimental to the Country as This." *The New Republic,* December 14, 2014. https://newrepublic.com/article/120559/ive-seen-sorts-horrific-things-time-none-detrimental-country-this.

Mackey, Danielle, and Chiara Eisner. "Inside the Plot to Murder Honduran Activist Berta Cáceres." *The Intercept,* December 21, 2019, https://theintercept.com/2019/12/21/berta-caceres-murder-plot-honduras/.

Malkin, Elizabeth. "Honduran President Ousted in Coup." *New York Times,* June 28, 2009. https://www.nytimes.com/2009/06/29/world/americas/29honduras.html.

Mandelbaum, David G. "Alcohol and Culture." *Current Anthropology* 6, no. 3 (June 1965): 281–293.

Manley, Michael. *A Voice at the Workplace: Reflections on Colonialism and the Jamaican Worker.* Washington, DC: Howard University Press, 1975.

Manwaring, Max. *State and Nonstate Associated Gangs: Credible "Midwives of New Social Orders?"* Carlisle, PA: Army War College Strategic Studies Institute, 2009. https://apps.dtic.mil/sti/pdfs/ADA499689.pdf.

Marti y Puig, Salvador, and David Close. *Nicaragua y el FSLN, 1979–2009.* Barcelona: Editions Bellaterra, 2009.

Martin, Michael J. "Agrarian Reform Cooperatives in Honduras." PhD diss., University of Florida, 1996. https://ufdc.ufl.edu/AA00029921/00001.

McKinley, James C, Jr. "Honduras' Capital: City of the Dead and the Dazed." *New York Times,* November 5, 1998. https://archive.nytimes.com/www.nytimes.com/library/world/americas/110598honduras-destruction.html.

Mcdonnell, Patrick. "Return to Morazan: Despite the Still-Raging Civil War, a Brave Band of Salvadoran Refugees Goes Home." *Los Angeles Times,* July 29, 1990. https://www.latimes.com/archives/la-xpm-1990-07-29-tm-1517-story.html.

Mejia, Thelma. "Honduras, el poder y la seguridad de las botas." *Divergentes* n.n., 2020. https://www.divergentes.com/militarismo-en-centroamerica/honduras/.

Mendoza, Claudia. "El sol, el agua, un fusil en la frente." Centro de Estudios para la Democracia (CESPAD), September 29, 2020. http://cespad.org.hn/2020/09/29/el-sol-el-aguao-un-fusil-en-la-frente/.

Merrill, Tim, ed. *Honduras: A Country Study.* Washington, DC: GPO for the Library of Congress, 1995. http://countrystudies.us/honduras/51.htm.

Meyer, Peter J., and Clare Ribando Seelke. "Central American Regional Security Initiative: Background and Policy Issues for Congress." *Congressional Research Service,* May 2014. https://www.everycrsreport.com/files/20140506_R41731_905 4cf945300a377d6ff44b4ef7f0f448c5a1b58.pdf.

Mignolo, Walter D. *Local Histories/Global Designs: Coloniality, Subaltern Knowledges, and Border Thinking.* Princeton, NJ: Princeton University Press, 2000.

Migration Policy Institute. "Refugee and Asylum Seeker Populations by Country of Origin and Destination, 2000–2019." 2020. https://www.migrationpolicy.org/

programs/data-hub/charts/refugee-and-asylum-seeker-populations-country-origin-and-destination.

Millett, Richard. *The Honduran Military: History of a Conflicted Institution.* Miami, FL: Florida International University, 2016.

Mintz, Sidney. "Historical Sociology of the Jamaican Church-founded Free Village System." *New West Indian Guide 38*, no. 1 (January 1958): 46–70.

———. "The Rural Proletariat and the Problem of Rural Proletarian Consciousness." *Journal of Peasant Studies 1*, no. 3 (1974): 291–325.

Molina Chocano, Guillermo. *Estado Liberal y desarrollo capitalista en Honduras.* Tegucigalpa: Universidad Nacional Autonoma de Honduras, Editorial Universitaria, 1982.

———. "Problemas de la democracia en Honduras." In *Honduras: Realidad Nacional y Crisis Regional,* edited by Mark Rosenberg and Philip Shepherd, 27–44. Tergucigalpa: Centro de Documentación de Honduras, 1986.

Moreno Coto, Ismael. "Dimensión social de la misión de la iglesia Católica: Una mirada nacional desde la región noroccidental de Honduras." In *Religión, ideología y sociedad: Una aproximación a las iglesias en Honduras,* 102–152. El Progreso: Editorial Casa San Ignacio, 2013.

Morison, Samuel Eliot. *The Oxford History of the American People.* New York: Oxford University Press, 1965.

Morris, James A. *Honduras: Caudillo Politics and Military Rulers.* New York and London: Routledge, Taylor and Francis, 1984.

Muñoz, Echart, and Maria del Carmen Villareal. "Women's Struggles Against Extractivism in Latin America and the Caribbean." *Contexto Internacional 41*, no. 2 (May–August 2019): 303–325.

Murphy, Francis X. "A Historical View of Sanctuary." In *Sanctuary: A Resource Guide,* edited by Gary MacEoin, 75–84. San Francisco: Harper and Row, 1985.

Narayan, John, and Leon Sealy-Huggins. "What Has Become of Imperialism?" *Third World Quarterly 38*, no. 11 (2017): 2376–2395.

National Security Archive. National Security Archive Electronic Briefing Book 2, *The Contras, Cocaine, and Covert Operations.* Washington, DC: George Washington University, n.d. https://nsarchive2.gwu.edu//NSAEBB/NSAEBB2/index.html.

Nazario, Sonia. *Enrique's Journey.* New York: Random House, 2007.

Nealon, James D. "The Next Immigration Time Bomb." *GoLocal Prov News* (Providence, RI), April 9, 2020. https://www.golocalprov.com/news/the-next-immigration-time-bomb-ambassador-nealon.

Negroponte, Diana Villers. "The Surge in Unaccompanied Children from Central America: A Humanitarian Crisis at Our Border." Brookings Institution, July 2, 2014. https://www.brookings.edu/blog/up-front/2014/07/02/the-surge-in-unaccompanied-children-from-central-america-a-humanitarian-crisis-at-our-border/.

Newcomb, Stephen T. "The Evidence of Christian Nationalism in Federal Indian Law: The Doctrine of Discovery, Johnson v. McIntosh, and Plenary Power." *New York University Review of Law and Social Change* (1993): 303–343. https://social-changenyu.com/wp-content/uploads/2017/12/Steven-Newcomb_RLSC_20.2.pdf.

Newman, Elizabeth Teresa. *Biography of a Hacienda: Work and Revolution in Rural Mexico.* Tucson: University of Arizona Press, 2014.

Newsome, Linda A. *The Cost of Conquest: Indian Decline in Honduras Under Spanish Rule.* Boulder CO: Westview Press, 1986.

New York Times archives. "The Contra War, 1981-1990." *New York Times*, June 29, 1990. https://www.nytimes.com/1990/06/29/opinion/the-contra-war-1981-1990. html.

New York Times. "Honduran President Declared Winner, but O.A.S. Calls for New Election," December 17, 2017. https://www.nytimes.com/2017/12/17/world/americas/honduran-presidential-election.html.

Norwegian Refugee Council. "Violence Has Pushed Thousands of Children in El Salvador and Honduras Out of School," May 16, 2019. https://www.nrc.no/news/2019/may/violence-has-pushed-thousands-of-children-in-honduras-and-el-salvador-out-of-school/.

Nyerere, Julius. *Ujamaa: Essays on Socialism.* New York: Oxford University Press, 1971.

Olivier, Sydney. *The Myth of Governor Eyre.* London: L and Virginia Woolf, 1933.

———. *Jamaica, the Blessed Island.* London: Faber and Faber, 1936.

Olson, Eric L., and John Wachter. *What If They Return? How El Salvador, Honduras, and the United States Could Prepare for an Effective Reintegration of TPS Beneficiaries.* Washington, DC: Wilson Center, n.d. (but 2019 or later).

Ortiz, Victor M. "The Unbearable Ambiguity of the Border." *Social Justice* 28, no. 2 (Summer 2001): 96–112.

Oseguera de Ochoa, Margarita. *Honduras hoy: Sociedad y crisis política.* Tegucigalpa: Centro de Documentación de Honduras, 1987.

Overseas Development Institute UK. *Governance and Poverty Impacts of the Illegal Timber Trade in Central America.* London: Overseas Development Institute, 2002. https://www.odi.org/projects/1187-governance-and-poverty-impacts-illegal-timber-trade-central-america.

Paget, Hugh. "The Growth of Villages in Jamaica and British Guiana." *Caribbean Quarterly* 10, no. 1 (1964): 38–51.

Palencia, Gustavo, and Anahi Rama. "Left Behind by the U.S., Honduras Turns to Chavez." *Reuters*, August 26, 2008.

Pan American Health Organization. "Impact of Hurricane Mitch in Central America." *Epidemiological Bulletin* 19, no. 4 (December 1998). https://www.paho.org/english/sha/epibul_95-98/be984mitch.htm.

Patterson, Orlando. *The Confounding Island: Jamaica and the Postcolonial Predicament.* Cambridge, MA: Belknap/Harvard University Press, 2019.

Payer, Cheryl. *The Debt Trap: The International Monetary Fund and the Third World.* New York: Monthly Review Press, 1974.

Paz Aguilar, Ernesto. "Evolución reciente de la política exterior y la seguridad nacional de Honduras." In *Honduras: Realidad nacional y crisis regional*, edited by Mark Rosenberg and Philip Shepherd, 341–392. Tegucigalpa: Centro de Documentación de Honduras (CEDOH), 1986.

Peckenham, Nancy and Annie Street, eds. *Honduras: Portrait of a Captive Nation.* New York: Praeger, 1985.

Pedraja, Rene de la. *The United States and the Armed Forces of Mexico, Central America, and the Caribbean, 2000–2014.* Jefferson, NC: McFarland, 2014.

Perez, Orlando, and Randy Pestana. *Honduran Military Culture.* Miami, FL: Florida International University and U.S. Southern Command Academic Partnership, Military Culture Series, 2016.

Pérez-Melgosa, Adrián. "Low-Intensity Necropolitics: Slow Violence and Migrant Bodies in Latin American Films." *Arizona Journal of Hispanic Cultural Studies* 20 (2016): 217–236.

Phillips, Arthur. "Charter Cities in Honduras." Open Democracy, January 7, 2014. https://www.opendemocracy.net/en/opensecurity/charter-cities-in-honduras/.

Phillips, James. "Renovation of the International Economic Order: Trilateralism, the IMF, and Jamaica." In *Trilateralism: The Trilateral Commission and Elite Planning for World Management*, edited by Holly Sklar, 468–491. Boston: South End Press, 1980.

———. "Who Is a Refugee?" *Global Justice* 1, no. 2 (Summer 1995): 10–20.

———. "Body and Soul: Faith, Development, Community, and Social Science in Nicaragua." *NAPA (National Association of Practicing Anthropologists) Bulletin* 33 (2010): 12–30.

———. "Democratic Socialism, the New International Economic Order, and Globalization: Jamaica's Sugar Cooperatives in the Post-Colonial Transition." *The Global South* 4, no. 2 (Fall 2010): 178–196.

———. "Resource Access, Environmental Struggles, and Human Rights in Honduras." In *Life and Death Matters: Human Rights, Environment, and Social Justice*, edited by Barbara Rose Johnston, 209–232. Walnut Creek, CA: Left Coast Press, 2011.

———. *Honduras in Dangerous Times: Resistance and Resilience.* Lanham, MD: Lexington Books, 2015.

———. "Tolupanes Put Their Lives on the Line Defending All Hondurans." *Cultural Survival Quarterly* (July 12, 2015). https://www.culturalsurvival.org/news/tolupanes-put-their-lives-line-defending-all-hondurans.

———. "The Misery Financing Development: Subsidized Neoliberalism and Privatized Dependency in Honduras." *Urban Anthropology and Studies in Cultural Systems and World Economic Development* 46, nos. 1–2 (Spring–Summer 2017): 1–59.

———. "Expert Witnessing in Honduran Asylum Cases: What Difference Can Twenty Years Make?" In *Special Issue: Cultural Expert Witnessing*, Studies in Law, Politics, and Society, volume 74, edited by Leila Rodriguez, 11–48. Bingley, UK: Emerald Publishing, 2018.

Phillips, Susan. *Wallbangin': Graffiti and Gangs in L.A.* Chicago: University of Chicago Press, 1999.

Pine, Adrienne. *Working Hard, Drinking Hard: On Violence and Survival in Honduras.* Berkeley: University of California Press, 2008.

Ponce, Riccy. "Sobreseimiento definitivo para ambientalistas querellados por defender el bosque." Defensores en Linea, February 10, 2020. http://www.

defensoresenlinea.com/sobreseimiento-definitivo-para-ambientalistas-querellados-por-defender-el-bosque/.

Pope Paul VI. *Populorum Progressio* (1967). http://www.vatican.va/content/paul-vi/en/encyclicals/documents/hf_p-vi_enc_26031967_populorum.html.

Portes, Alejandro, and Rubén Rumbaut. *Immigrant America: A Portrait,* Fourth Edition. Oakland, CA: University of California Press, 2014.

Posas, Mario. *Notas sobre las Sociedades Artesanales y los Origines del Movimiento Obrero Hondureño.* Tegucigalpa: Esp Editorial, 1978.

Power, Margaret. "The U.S. Movement in Solidarity with Chile in the 1970s." *Latin American Perspectives* 36, no. 6 (November 2009): 46–66.

Power, Thomas M. *Metals Mining and Sustainable Development in Central America.* Boston: Oxfam America, 2008. https://s3.amazonaws.com/oxfam-us/www/static/media/files/metals-mining-and-sustainable-development-in-central-america.pdf.

Proceso Digital. "Suicidios en Honduras siguen al alza en 2020." January 2, 2020. https://proceso.hn/suicidios-en-honduras-siguen-al-alza-en-2020/.

Purlevski, Savva. *A Life under Russian Serfdom: The Memoirs of Savva Dimitrievich Purlevski, 1800–1868.* Translated by Boris B. Gorshkov. Budapest: Central European University, 2005. Open End Edition Books, 2013, https://books.openedition.org/ceup/488.

Quijano, Anibal, and Michael Ennis. "Coloniality of Power and Eurocentrism in Latin America." *Nepantla: Views from South* 1, no. 3 (2000): 533–580. https://edisciplinas.usp.br/pluginfile.php/347342/mod_resource/content/1/Quijano%20(2000)%20Colinality%20of%20power.pdf.

Rabben, Linda. *Give Refuge to the Stranger: The Past, Present, and Future of Sanctuary.* Walnut Creek, CA: Left Coast Press, 2011.

Radio Progreso. "Proyecto minero desplaza familias enteras en Colon" (2020). https://wp.radioprogresohn.net/proyecto-minero-desplaza-familias-enteras-en-colon/.

Radwin, Max. "It's Getting Worse: National Parks in Honduras Hit Hard by Palm Oil." *Mongabay Series Forest Trackers*, April 11, 2019. https://news.mongabay.com/2019/04/its-getting-worse-national-parks-in-honduras-hit-hard-by-palm-oil/.

Richard, Analiese. "Taken into Account: Democratic Change and Contradiction in Mexico's Third Sector." In *Neoliberalism Interrupted: Social Change and Contemporary Governance in Contemporary Latin America*, edited by Mark Goodale and Nancy Postero, 137–166. Palo Alto: Stanford University Press, 2013.

Ricker, Tom. "Manufacturing Dissent: The N.E.D., Opposition Media, and the Political Crisis in Nicaragua." *Quixote Center News from Nicaragua*, May 11, 2018. https://www.quixote.org/manufacturing-dissent-the-n-e-d-opposition-media-and-the-political-crisis-in-nicaragua/.

Riding, Alan. "In Honduras Refugee Tangle, UN Takes Charge." *New York Times*, April 27, 1982. https://www.nytimes.com/1982/04/27/world/in-honduras-refugee-tangle-un-takes-charge.html.

Riley, Hannah C., and James Sebenius. "Stakeholder Negotiations over Third World Resource Projects." *Cultural Survival* 19, no. 3 (1993): 39–43.

Rivera Hernandez, Raúl Diego. "Making Absence Visible: The Caravan of Central American Mothers in Search of Central American Migrants," trans. Mariana Ortega Breña. *Latin American Perspectives* 44, no. 5 (September 2017): 108–126.

Rocha, José Luis. *Expulsados de la globalización: Politicas migratorias y deportados centramericanos.* Managua: Instituto de Historia de Nicaragua y Centroamérica, 2010.

———. "La exitosa desobediencia civil de ligrantes indocumentados, informales y cuentapropistas." *Envío Honduras* 17, no. 59 (September 2019): 42–51.

Rodas, Karla. "Yorito: el pueblo hondureño que expulso una minería." *Revista Gato Encerrado*, January 9, 2020, https://gatoencerrado.news/2020/01/10/yorito-el-pueblo-hondureno-que-expulso-a-una-minera-de-su-territorio/.

Rodney, Walter. *How Europe Underdeveloped Africa.* London: Bogle-L'Ouverture Publications, 1972.

Ropp, Steve. "The Honduran Army and the Sociopolitical Evolution of the Honduran State." *The Americas* 30, no. 4 (April 1974): 504–528. https://doi.org/10.2307/980035.

Rosenberg, Mark B. "Honduras: Una Introducción." In *Honduras: Realidad Nacional y Crisis Regional*, edited by Mark Rosenberg and Philip Shepherd, 3–26. Tegucigalpa: Centro de Documentación de Honduras and Florida International University, 1986.

Rosnick, David, Alexander Main, and Laura Jung. *Have US-Funded CARSI Programs Reduced Crime and Violence in Central America?* Center for Economic and Policy Research, September, 2016. https://cepr.net/images/stories/reports/carsi-2016-09.pdf.

Rostow, W. W. *The Stages of Economic Growth: A Non-Communist Manifesto.* Cambridge: Cambridge University Press, 1960.

Ruhl, J. Mark. "Honduras: Militarism and Democratization in Troubled Waters." In *Repression, Resistance, and Democratic Transition in Central America*, edited by Thomas Walker and Ariel Armony. Wilmington, DE: SR Books, 2000.

Ruiz, Elías. *El Astillero: masacre y justicia.* Tegucigalpa: Editorial Guaymuras, 1992.

Saalfeld, Lawrence J. *Forces of Prejudice in Oregon, 1920–1925.* Portland: University of Portland Press, 1984.

Salomón, Leticia. "La opción religiosa es un derecho constitucional que pertenece al ámbito privado." *Radio Progreso,* commentary, September 11, 2020. https://radioprogresohn.net/columnistas-categoria/la-opcion-religiosa-es-un-derecho-constitucional-que-pertenece-al-ambito-privado/.

Sanchez, Alex. "Honduras Becomes U.S. Military Foothold for Central America." *NACLA* (September 4, 2007). https://nacla.org/news/honduras-becomes-us-military-foothold-central-america.

Schlesinger, Stephen, and Stephen Kinzer. *Bitter Fruit: The Untold Story of the American Coup in Guatemala.* Garden City, NY: Anchor Books, 1983.

Schuller, Mark. *Killing with Kindness: Haiti, International Aid, and NGOs.* New Brunswick, NJ: Rutgers University Press, 2012.

Scott, James C. *Seeing Like a State: How Certain Schemes to Improve the Human Condition Have Failed.* New Haven, CT: Yale University Press, 1982.

———. *Weapons of the Weak: Everyday Forms of Peasant Resistance.* New Haven: Yale University Press, 1985.

Seabrook, Jeremy. "The Mental Health of Societies." *Race and Class* 59, no. 4 (2018): 54–64.

Security Assistance Monitor. "Country Profile: U.S. Security Assistance to Honduras." December 2014. https://Users/WesternDesk/DownloadsUSE_Honduras_English1%20(1).pdf.

Senate Select Committee on Intelligence, Activities Staff Report. "Covert Action in Chile, 1963–1973." Declassified ISCAP 2010-09, Document 17. https://www.archives.gov/files/declassification/iscap/pdf/2010-009-doc17.pdf.

Shaw, Terri, and Herbert H. Denton. "Honduran Death Squad Alleged." *New York Times*, May 2, 1987. https://www.washingtonpost.com/archive/politics/1987/05/02/honduran-death-squad-alleged/b5ed4183-626d-4183-8b78-592631b2b330/.

Shipley, Tyler. *Ottawa and Empire: Canada and the Military Coup in Honduras.* Toronto: Between the Lines Press, 2015.

Shiva, Vandana. *Monocultures of the Mind: Perspectives on Biodiversity and Biotechnology.* New York: Palgrave Macmillan, 1993.

———. *Water Wars: Privatization, Pollution, and Profit.* Boston: South End Press, 2002.

Silva Ávalos, Hector. "Honduras' New Criminal Code Will Help Impunity Prosper." *InSight Crime*, June 29, 2020. https://insightcrime.org/news/analysis/honduras-new-criminal-code/.

———. "The Logging Barons of Catacamas, Honduras." *InSight Crime*, September 18, 2020. https://insightcrime.org/investigations/logging-barons-catacamas-honduras/.

———."Keyla Martinez and Extrajudicial Killings in Honduras." *InSight Crime*, February 15, 2021. https://insightcrime.org/news/keyla-martinez-extrajudicial-killings-honduras/.

Singham, A. W., ed. *The Nonaligned Movement in World Politics.* Westport, CT: Lawrence Hill and Company, 1977.

Sklar, Holly, ed. *Trilateralism: The Trilateral Commission and Elite Planning for World Management.* Boston: South End Press, 1980.

———. "Trilateralism: Managing Dependence and Democracy—An Overview." In *Trilateralism: The Trilateral Commission and Elite Planning for World Management*, edited by Holly Sklar, 1–57. Boston: South End Press, 1980.

Sorto, Mario, Wilfredo Serrano, and Bladimir Lopez. *Coyuntura desde los territorios: Los bienes comunes naturales: La actual disputa socio-politica en las comunidades de Honduras.* Tegucigalpa: Centro de Estudio para la Democracia (CESPAD), 2019.

Stavenhagen, Rodolfo, ed. *Agrarian Problems and Peasant Movements in Latin America.* Garden City, NY: Doubleday Anchor, 1970.

Steward, Julian. *Theory of Culture Change: The Methodology of Multilinear Evolution.* Chicago: University of Illinois Press, 1955.

Stock, Anthony. "Land War." *Cultural Survival Quarterly* 16, no. 4 (1992): 16–19.

Stoler, Ann Laura. *Duress: Imperial Durabilities in Our Times.* Durham, NC: Duke University Press, 2016.

Stonich, Susan, and Billie R. DeWalt. "The Political Ecology of Deforestation in Honduras." In *Tropical Deforestation: The Human Dimension*, edited by Leslie E. Sponsel, Thomas N. Headland, and Robert C. Bailey, 187–215. New York: Columbia University Press, 1996.

Suazo, Javier. "Coalianza: Negocio de pocos." *America Latina*, December 5, 2019. https://www.alainet.org/es/articulo/203673.

Svampa, Maristella. "Commodities Consensus: Neoextractivism and Enclosure of the Commons in Latin America." *South Atlantic Quarterly* 114, no. 1 (2015): 65–82. https://read.dukeupress.edu/south-atlantic-quarterly/article-abstract/114/1/65/3719/Commodities-Consensus-Neoextractivism-and?redirected From=fulltext.

———. *Las fronteras del neoextractivismo en América Latina: Conflictos socioambientales, giro ecoterritorial y nuevas dependencias.* Guadalajara: Universidad de Guadalajara, 2019.

Taffet, Jeffrey. *Foreign Aid as Foreign Policy: The Alliance for Progress in Latin America.* London: Routledge, 2007.

Tamez. Elsa. *Bible of the Oppressed.* Translated by Matthew J. O'Connell. Maryknoll, NY: Orbis Books, 1983.

———. "The Refugee Crisis, Sanctuary, and the Bible." In *Sanctuary: A Resource Guide for Understanding and Participating in the Central American Refugees' Struggle*, edited by Gary MacEoin, 39–48. San Francisco: Harper and Row, 1985.

Tarasiuk, Tamara. *After the Coup: Ongoing Violence, Intimidation, and Impunity in Honduras.* Human Rights Watch, December 2018. https://www.hrw.org/sites/default/files/reports/honduras1210webwcover_0.pdf.

Taussig, Michael. *The Devil and Commodity Fetishism in South America*, Thirtieth Edition. Chapel Hill, NC: University of North Carolina Press, 2010.

Telesur. "Honduran Police Fire Tear Gas, Water Cannon at Student Protest." July 25, 2017. https://www.telesurenglish.net/news/Honduran-Police-Fire-Tear-Gas-Water-Cannon-at-Student-Protest-20170725-0029.html.

———. "Honduran President Announces New Max Security Prison Run by Military." February 27, 2019. https://www.telesurenglish.net/news/Honduran-President-Announces-New-Max-Security-Prison-Run-by-Military-20190227-0017.html.

———. "Chile Marks Anniversary of Coup Against President Allende, September 11, 2019." https://www.telesurenglish.net/news/Chile-The-Coup-Against-President-Allende-Was-The-First-911--20190911-0002.html.

Trucchi, Giorgio. "Zacate Grande: Nos Desalojan en Nombre de Desarrollo." *AlbaSud,* December 31, 2018. http://www.albasud.org/noticia/es/1080/zacate-grande-honduras-nos-desalojan-en-nombre-del-desarrollo.

Uenuma, Francine. "During the Mexican-American War Irish-Americans Fought for Mexico in the 'Saint Patrick's Battalion.'" *Smithsonian Magazine* (March 15, 2019). https://www.smithsonianmag.com/history/mexican-american-war-irish-immigrants-deserted-us-army-fight-against-america-180971713/.

United Nations Human Rights Council. *Report of the Spacial Rapporteur on Extrajudicial, Summary, or Arbitrary Executions.* New York: United Nations, April 2017.

United Nations Refugee Agency. "With Love from Central America." New York: United Nations Refugee Agency, September 11, 2019. https://www.unrefugees.org/news/with-love-from-central-america-four-stories-of-central-american-refugees/.

United States Agency for International Development (USAID). "Rapid Expeditionary Development (RED) Teams: Demand and Feasibility Assessment," February 28, 2018. https://pdf.usaid.gov/pdf_docs/PA00T6VQ.pdf.

United States Army, SOUTHCOM Public Affairs. "Beyond the Horizon Exercise Begins in Honduras." April 19, 2012. https://www.army.mil/article/78100/beyond_the_horizon_exercise_begins_in_honduras.

United States Department of State, Office of the Historian. "Chinese Immigration and the Chinese Exclusion Act." Washington, DC: Department of State, n.d. https://history.state.gov/milestones/1866-1898/chinese-immigration.

United States Department of State Overseas Security Advisory Council. "Honduras 2020: Crime and Safety Report." Washington, DC: U.S. Department of State, March 31, 2020. https://www.osac.gov/Country/Honduras/Content/Detail/Report/14441101-11fd-487c-9d15-18553e50609c.

Valencia, Jorge. "Why people are migrating from Honduras—and why many want them to stay." *Arizona Public Media* (September 11, 2019), https://news.azpm.org/p/news-splash/2019/9/11/157941-why-people-are-migrating-from-honduras-and-why-many-want-them-to-stay/.

Valladares, Leo. *The Facts Speak for Themselves: The Preliminary Report on Disappearances of the National Commissioner for the Protection of Human Rights in Honduras.* Translated by Human Rights Watch and Center for Justice and International Law. Tegucigalpa: Honduran National Commission for Human Rights, July 1984.

Vigil, James Diego. "Group Processes and Street Identity: Adolescent Chicano Gang Members." *Ethos* 16, no. 4 (1988): 421–445.

Waddell, Benjamin. "Laying the Groundwork for Insurrection: A Closer Look at the U.S. Role in Nicaragua's Social Unrest." *Global Americans*, May 1, 2018. https://theglobalamericans.org/2018/05/laying-groundwork-insurrection-closer-look-u-s-role-nicaraguas-social-unrest/.

Walsh, Lawrence E., et al. *Final Report of the Independent Counsel for Iran/Contra Matters, Volume 1.* Washington, DC: United States Court of Appeals for the District of Columbia, 1993. https://fas.org/irp/offdocs/walsh/index.html.

Walt, Stephen M. "The Myth of American Exceptionalism." *Foreign Policy* online (October 11, 2011). https://foreignpolicy.com/2011/10/11/the-myth-of-american-exceptionalism/.

Warner, Faith. "Refugee Reparation and Ethnic Revitalization: Q'eqchi' in Maya Tecun, Mexico." In *Selected Papers on Refugee Issues* 4, edited by Ann Rynearson, 45–72. Washington, DC: American Anthropological Association, 1996.

Washington Office on Latin America (WOLA) and National Autonomous University of Honduras. "Transparency in Honduras: Assessing Access to Public Information." Washington, DC: WOLA, September, 2019. https://www.wola.org/wp-content/uploads/2019/12/Transparencia-HN-ENG-11.27.pdf.

Washington Post archives online. "Pinochet's Chile." (2020). https://www.washingtonpost.com/wp-srv/inatl/longterm/pinochet/overview.htm.

Waxenecker, Harald. *Redes de poder político-económico en Honduras: Un análisis post-golpe.* San Salvador: Fundación Heinrich Boll, Stiftung y Equipo Maíz, 2019. https://sv.boell.org/sites/default/files/2020-03/Redes%20en%20Honduras%20HW%202019.pdf.

Webb, Gary. *Dark Alliance: The CIA, the Contras, and the Crack Cocaine Explosion.* New York: Seven Stories Press, 1998.

Weismantel, Mary J. *Food, Gender, and Poverty in the Ecuadorian Andes.* Philadelphia: University of Pennsylvania Press, 1989.

Whitehead, Charles. "The Anthropology of Consciousness: Keeping Body and Soul Together." *Anthropology Today* 16, no. 4 (August 2000): 20–22.

Wiles, Tay. "Malheur occupation explained." *High Country News*, January 4, 2016. https://www.hcn.org/articles/oregon-occupation-at-wildlife-refuge.

Williams, Eric. *Capitalism and Slavery.* Chapel Hill, NC: University of North Carolina Press, 1944.

———. *From Columbus to Castro: The History of the Caribbean, 1492–1969.* London: André Deutsch, 1970.

Williams, Kareen Felicia. "The Evolution of Political Violence in Jamaica, 1940–1980." PhD diss., Columbia University, 2011.

Williamson, John. *Latin American Adjustment: How Much Has Happened.* Washington, DC: Institute for International Economics, 1990.

Wolf, Eric R. *Peasants.* Englewood Cliffs, NJ: Prentice-Hall, 1966.

———. *Peasant Wars of the Twentieth Century.* New York: Harper and Row, 1969.

———. *Europe and the People Without History.* Berkeley: University of California Press, 1982.

Wolfe, Patrick. *Settler Colonialism and the Transformation of Anthropology: The Politics and Poetics of an Ethnographic Event.* London and New York: Cassell, 1999.

Wolseth, Jon. *Jesus and the Gang: Youth Violence and Christianity in Urban Honduras.* Tucson: University of Arizona Press, 2011.

Woodward, Ralph Lee, Jr. "Review: William Walker and the History of Nicaragua in the Nineteenth Century." *Latin American Research Review* 15, no. 1 (1980): 237–270.

World Bank. "International Homicides (per 100,000 people)—Honduras (2010–2019)," 2021. https://data.worldbank.org/indicator/VC.IHR.PSRC.P5?locations=HN.

———. "Personal Remittances, Received (% of GDP), Honduras (1974–2019)." https://data.worldbank.org/indicator/BX.TRF.PWKR.DT.GD.ZS?locations=HN

———. "Poverty and Equity Brief: Honduras." April 2020. https://databank.worldbank.org/data/download/poverty/33EF03BB-9722-4AE2-ABC7-AA2972D68AFE/Global_POVEQ_HND.pdf.

World Politics Review. "Why Honduras Remains Latin America's Most Unequal Country. *World Politics Review*, editorial, January 6, 2017. https://www.worldpoliticsreview.com/insights/20856/why-honduras-remains-latin-america-s-most-unequal-country.

Worsley, Peter. *Two Blades of Grass: Rural Cooperatives in Agricultural Modernization.* Manchester, UK: Manchester University, 1971.

Zilberg, Elana. "Yes We Did It! Si se pudo! Regime Change and the Transnational Politics of Hope Between the United States and El Salvador." In *Neoliberalism Interrupted: Social Change and Contested Governance in Contemporary Latin America*, edited by Mark Goodale and Nancy Postero, 230–246. Palo Alto: Stanford University Press, 2013.

Index

Agency for International Development
(U.S.), 179
agrarian conflict, 11. *See also*
Indigenous communities; peasants
agrarian (land) reform, different
meanings of, 93. *See also* Agrarian
Reform Law of 1974
Agrarian Reform Law of 1974
(Honduras), 65, 92, 120, 167
agribusiness (industrial export
agriculture), 149–50; in Aguán
Valley, 120–21; and palm oil, 149–
50; and peasant communities, 93;
and peasant cooperatives, 120; and
political control, 86
Aguán Valley. *See* agribusiness
Ahuas incident, 145–46; and Operation
Anvil, 145. *See also* Drug
Enforcement Agency (DEA)
Alliance for Progress, 65
American Institute of Free Labor
Development, 63
anthropology: and decolonization, 17;
and militarization, 163; and the
spiritual, 7
arms trafficking and regional conflicts
in Central America, 39–40

Association for the Progress of
Honduras (APROH) and neoliberal
development, 168, 170
asylum, 37–38

banana (fruit) companies in Honduras,
92; banana workers' strike of 1954,
92. *See also* agribusiness
Battalion 316, 34, 169
Berta Cáceres Human Rights in
Honduras Act (U.S. House), 165
border: different meanings of (physical,
legal, social, cultural), 26; as shifting
reality within U.S., 25, 48
Border Patrol, U.S., 30
Bracero Program, 45

Cáceres, Berta, emblematic case of, 5–6
Callejas, Rafael, government of and
neoliberal development, 121, 130
Canadian mining in Honduras,
127, 129–30
caravans (of immigrants), 44–48
Carías Andino, Tiburcio, dictatorship
of, 63, 118
Caribbean coast: and green
neoliberalism, 70; and palm oil,
149–150; and tourism, 150. *See also*
Garifuna; model cities

About the Author

James Phillips is a retired professor of anthropology and international studies at Southern Oregon University. He first visited Honduras in 1974 and has been a student of Central America for almost four decades. His major research concerns have been social change, popular movements, human rights, refugee populations, and immigration. He has conducted extensive fieldwork in Honduras, Nicaragua, and Jamaica, and has published many articles and book chapters about change in peasant and plantation societies, Central American refugee populations, and the role of human rights and religion in social change. After receiving a PhD in anthropology from Brown University, he joined the staff of the American Friends Service Committee as a writer and speaker on the international political economy. He also served as a policy analyst on the staff of Oxfam America, and has taught at several universities. Of Phillips's book *Honduras in Dangerous Times: Resistance and Resilience* (Lexington, 2015), one reviewer wrote: "This book is essential reading for understanding contemporary Central America."

Ingram Content Group UK Ltd.
Milton Keynes UK
UKHW041331140523
421709UK00003B/28